WIRED TO RESIST

The Brain Science of Why Change Fails and a New Model for Driving Success

Second Edition
Revised and Expanded

Britt Andreatta, PhD

7th Mind Publishing

Copyright © 2025 by Britt Andreatta
All Rights Reserved.

No part of this publication may be reproduced, stored in a retrieval system, or transmitted, in any form or by any means, electronic, mechanical, photocopying, recording, or otherwise, without the written permission of the author.

Revised edition originally published 2017.
This second edition May 2025.
7th Mind Publishing
Santa Barbara, California

The following are all registered trademarks of 7th Mind, Inc.: Brain Aware®, Change Quest®, Four Gates to Peak Team Performance®, Three Phase Model of Learning™, Growth Culture®, Learn Remember Do™, and Survive Belong Become®.

For orders or bulk purchases of this book, please write Orders@7thMindPublishing.com.

For training materials affiliated with this book, visit BrittAndreatta.com/Training.

For speaking engagements, please contact Speaking@BrittAndreatta.com, or visit BrittAndreatta.com/Speaking.

ISBN: 978-1-963703-00-9 (paper)
ISBN: 978-1-963703-01-6 (ebook)

This book is printed on acid-free paper in the United States of America.

For my daughter, Kiana.
You are the source of so much love, learning, and growth in our lives.
It has been an honor to be your mom. I can't wait to watch the rest
of your life unfold and all the wonderful adventures you'll have.

CONTENTS

Introduction vi

Take a Learning Journey ix

I: Understanding Change

1. The Costs of Change Gone Wrong 3
2. Change in the Modern World 8
3. Change vs. Transition 12
4. The Change Curve 17
5. The Rise of Change Fatigue and Burnout 23

Your Learning Journey 28

II: The Brain Science of Change + Resistance

6. The Brain on Change 31
7. Amygdala: Our Voice of Fear 33
8. Entorhinal Cortex: Our Personal GPS 37
9. Basal Ganglia: Our Habit Factory 41
10. Habenula: Our Failure-Avoidance Center 45
11. The Dangerous Biological Cocktail 49

Your Learning Journey 51

III: A New Model for Change + Transition

12. The Change Quest® Model: Mountains Instead of Valleys 55
13. The Travelers of Change 59
14. Mapping Multiple Change Journeys 66

Your Learning Journey 70

IV: Thriving Through Change: Strategies for Success

15. Tips for Travelers 73
16. Be an Active Participant 81
17. The Leader's Toolkit: Navigation, Motivation, Connection 85
18. The Guide's Process and Troubleshooting 99
Your Learning Journey 109

V: The Four Drivers of Change

19. Organizational Growth and Development 113
20. Human Consciousness and Organizations 122
21. The Environment and Climate Change 132
22. Technology and Intelligence 143
Your Learning Journey 153

VI: Designing + Leading Change: Strategies for Executives

23. The Formula for Success 157
24. Phases 1–2: Decide and Lead 163
25. Phases 3–4: Evaluate and Design 169
26. Phases 5–6: Announce and Implement 174
27. Know When to Quit 180
28. Mergers and Acquisitions 188
Your Learning Journey 196

VII: The Path Ahead: Final Thoughts

29. Final Thoughts on Change 199
Synthesize Your Learning Journey into Action 200

References + Resources 201
Acknowledgments 210
About the Author 211
Learn More 213

INTRODUCTION

"Change is one of the most powerful professional development tools available."

Glenn Llopis, author, *The Innovation Mentality*

I wrote the first edition of this book in 2017, just after LinkedIn acquired the video training company Lynda.com, where I served as the chief learning officer. At the time, it was one of the largest and fastest tech acquisition deals in US history, allowing LinkedIn to add learning to its suite of services for working professionals.

Overnight, I was thrust into a massive change experience that altered everything about my world. Literally, ev-er-y-thing. I was reassigned to an office 500 miles away. My projects stopped. My supervisor switched. My colleagues shifted. And my career plan became obsolete.

My exploration into the neuroscience of change began three months later, as I watched myself and my colleagues experience things that were not accounted for by all the well-known models and theories about change—yes, the very models I had previously taught like Kotter's 8-step process, McKinsey's 7S model, and Prosci's ADKAR framework.

Now granted, I was going through one of the biggest change initiatives you can experience professionally—a sudden and uninvited change with no ability to plan for it. But I was still struck by how much the models couldn't account for what was happening. And I would be remiss if I don't point out that I was lucky because this change was one I was excited about and it left me employed and insured, unlike the thousands every year who get laid off or fired.

But clearly, something was amiss in what we know about change, so I set off to learn more because my book on the neuroscience of learning had just come out and it was natural to carry over that research into the topic of change. I also knew there was value in dissecting change from inside my own experience because I would find lessons that would apply to other organizations.

What I discovered astounded me. Several structures in our brain are actually designed to protect us from the potentially harmful results of change. Humans are wired to resist change, and we are working against our biology at every turn. As a result, I created the Change Quest® model based on the latest findings from a variety of academic and corporate studies, as well as interviews with leaders from all kinds of organizations.

This New Edition

I did not expect that first edition to become a bestseller, nor to be inundated with requests from learning professionals to create a certification so they could bring the model and training to their organizations. Nor did I expect that during the COVID-19 pandemic, an e-course I offered at the time would take off, becoming a tool that helped thousands of people around the world navigate the months of confusion and chaos of lockdowns, layoffs, and the trauma and grief we all witnessed.

Change comes in all kinds of forms, from the small and annoying to the epic and earth shattering. As you will learn, we can assess the impact of change by how long it takes to get acclimated to the new normal and how much disruption it creates in our daily lives. The pandemic was both highly disruptive and took months to go through and will take years, if not decades, to fully recover from.

I found myself inundated with work as organizations and executive teams brought me in to advise them during those turbulent times. It was gratifying to share science-based principles and practical actions people could use every day to navigate the pandemic, while also increasing their change readiness, agility, and resilience moving forward.

Since then, I have brought the Change Quest model to hundreds of organizations around the world. Using this research and these tools, I helped executive teams navigate major culture transformations, product launches, technology adoptions, and acquisitions.

This new edition is born from those experiences and the tough conversations about change that happen every day across industries. It includes several new chapters on the main drivers of changes and pressing issues challenging organizations of all sizes, including technology and artificial intelligence (AI), the growing impact of change fatigue and burnout, the environment and climate change, and shifting workforce demographics pushing organizations to become more purpose-driven. It also includes a greatly expanded section for executives and senior leaders with updated strategies for these modern times.

I added a new chapter on mergers and acquisitions (M&As) after interviewing several executives who played a central role in some of the biggest deals of the past few years with Nestlé, Microsoft, Amazon, Starbucks, T-Mobile, McDonnell Douglas, and Cisco.

I also invited people to submit their own stories of change and was thrilled to receive stories from around the world representing all kinds of organizations and changes. And, of course, I have updated previous sections with new research and findings on the neuroscience of change

How to Use This Book

This book is written for working adults everywhere. Whether you are on the leading or receiving end of change, you'll find useful tips and strategies you can implement today. The truth is that change affects us every day, both at work and at home, so I synthesize my research into practical takeaways to use anywhere they're needed. Knowing how we are wired to resist change and, more importantly, how to overcome that resistance to become more adaptive and resilient will serve you throughout your life. To that end, this book is organized into seven sections:

I. We'll begin by understanding what change looks like in today's organizations.

II. Next, we'll dive into the brain science of change and why it drives fear, fatigue, and burnout.

III. Then I'll introduce you to the new Change Quest model that synthesizes all the findings into an effective framework you can apply to changes of all kinds.

IV. This section offers tips and strategies for employees to successfully navigate change as well as for managers who are responsible for leading others through change.

V. Then we'll explore the four big drivers of change and how they impact organizations where you work, as well as others you engage with as a customer or community member.

VI. This section focuses on several strategies and best practices for executives and senior leaders to prepare you factors that will drive change in your organization for years to come.

VII. We'll end with some final thoughts on change, you'll synthesize your learning journeys, and I'll share my acknowledgments as well as the references for every study I mention.

Throughout every section, you will find stories about change, first-person narratives from 20 individuals from around the world. They answered an open call for submissions and represent a wide range of industries, as diverse as finance, manufacturing, hospitality, education, technology, and healthcare. Each person tells their own story of moving through a change journey, some of which were smooth and successful while others were filled with struggle. Each story is set off in a box with this mountain icon. Consider this first story:

Change Journey 1
Industry: Manufacturing
I owned a sign manufacturing company. We did great work with a high level of satisfaction with our customers. Our staff was well trained and happy in their positions, and we finally started to make money two years after we opened.

At the time, we were mainly pursuing real estate and construction firms, who gave us a lot of business. However, we didn't pay attention to the warning signs of the market and that the "bubble" was about to burst.

Despite coaches advising me to change direction and our employees making recommendations for tapping into other markets, I did not shift fast enough. Subsequently, the next year I moved my entire operation from our storefront to my home basement, and then into oblivion by October.

My staff became disappointed and disillusioned as they lost their livelihoods. And I ultimately had to file for bankruptcy and go through foreclosure. Unfortunately, I made several mistakes. I did not set a clear

> vision, nor allow my team to engage in shared decision-making. I had an unwillingness to change because I was focused on our current success and unable to look to the future. Ultimately, I let ego get in the way and it cost me everything.

My Research Process

I have been studying, synthesizing, and writing about the science of success in books and other media for 20 years. All thoughts, beliefs, and behaviors originate in the brain and neuroscience offers unique and valuable insights into how we can bring out the best in people and organizations.

I read several books about change and change management, but primarily focus on neuroscience, reading journals like *Neuron*, *The Journal of Neuroscience*, and *Social Cognitive and Affective Neuroscience*. Inevitably, these studies led me to other disciplines and studies in biology, psychology, business, and education. I reviewed research from many branches of business, economics, and environmental studies. I also conducted a content analysis of the personal stories submitted to identify common themes and experiences.

Another important part of my research process is mapping what scientists find in their labs to issues that impact today's workplaces. I leverage research by data giants like Deloitte, Gallup, Gartner, and McKinsey, as well as professional organizations like the Association for Talent Development (ATD), the Association of Change Management Professionals (ACMP), and the Society for Human Resource Management (SHRM). Many of these global studies yielded fascinating insights about change.

To be clear, I am not a neuroscientist; my PhD is in education, leadership, and organizations, and my career has focused on the intersection between effective leadership and learning. Because I am an active practitioner, designing and delivering learning experiences out in the field, I can see where lab studies do and do not translate to how people experience these concepts in the real world and especially at work.

I used this research to build science-based training programs that are proving to be exceptionally effective. If you want to learn more, visit www.BrainAwareTraining.com.

Take a Learning Journey

Before I wrote this book, I taught this content to live audiences and used these strategies with executive teams.

Engaging with concepts in a personal way helps the brain learn and retain material and, more importantly, it's where any meaningful shift in actions starts. To help you gain the most from this book, you will find this light bulb icon marking an element called "Your Learning Journey" at the end of each section. Each includes instructions for applying the content to your experiences.

To make this easier, I have created a free downloadable PDF for you to fill out as you explore each concept (www.BrittAndreatta.com/Wired-to-Resist). To maximize your experience, I also recommend you find a partner, as social learning boosts long-term retention, and when you work in partnership you gain the insights of each other's experiences. So, ask a friend or colleague who is also moving through change (hint: that would be anyone with a heartbeat) and explore together.

A Note about the Cover Design

In science, the symbol for change is Δ, or delta. When I was in college, we used Δ in our lab reports but it's also used as shorthand in notetaking to represent the concept of change or difference. In addition, the triangle is the shape of road signs that convey some sort of warning and it also represents a mountain that can be climbed. It seemed appropriate to riff on these concepts to convey the neuroscience of change, our biological resistance to it, and our ability to successfully move through a change journey.

UNDERSTANDING CHANGE

"It is not the strongest of the species that survives, nor the most intelligent, but the one most responsive to change."

Charles Darwin, biologist and author, *On the Origin of Species*

1. The Costs of Change Gone Wrong

Failed change is costing trillions of dollars per year. Some of these failures are so spectacular or widespread that we all know about them. Consider the failed attempt by OpenAI's board to remove CEO Sam Altman, which cost nearly $100 billion and a three percent drop in Microsoft stock value. Or the return-to-office (RTO) mandates driving high turnover and difficulties recruiting new employees. Or consider David Zaslav's drastic cost-cutting measures at Warner Bros Discovery that alienated some of the world's legendary filmmakers and ultimately galvanized the Writers Guild of America and Screen Actors Guild to strike. These failed changes made headline news for weeks.

Other equally expensive changes die quiet deaths in organizations all around the world, known only by the people who work there. For example, one global pharmaceutical company invested millions of dollars to implement a new enterprise resource planning (ERP) system and still has not achieved success after three attempts. And a high-tech company had to scrap an expensive overhaul of its performance review process after a last-minute change in executive support.

Failed changed initiatives affect every industry and at all levels of an organization. They can occur in every function from marketing to human resources, and from production to legal. Studies at Harvard show that 50 to 70 percent of change initiatives fail and another study found that, depending on the type of change, the range is 40 to 80 percent. Think about how astounding that is. Change initiatives are not just spontaneous whims thrown together by idiots. They are carefully designed, and expertly crafted by leaders and subject matter experts. Reports are written, data is analyzed, and rollout plans are built.

Even so, many will fail... expensively and sometimes spectacularly. Change can fail for a wide variety of reasons. According to McKinsey, a global consulting firm, there are three forms of failure:

- **Failure to launch,** which happens when there is too much resistance to get the planned change off the ground
- **Failure to sustain,** which happens when a good idea gets launched but never gets sufficient adoption to become part of the day-to-day work or culture of the organization
- **Failure to scale**, which occurs when the change cannot transition successfully as the organization grows

Another study found that only 43 percent of employees say their organization is good at managing change. And only 25 percent feel that managing change is a strength of their senior leaders.

Unintended Consequences

The cost of the failed change is not the only consequence. Failed change initiatives can generate a ripple effect that harms customer satisfaction as well as employee loyalty. In fact, mismanaged change, if it's systemic, can cause employees to lose faith in their leaders and the future of the organization. As a result, many employees leave, contributing to labor shortages in nearly every industry. Gallup estimates that 52 percent of the global workforce is actively seeking a new job.

This is certainly an issue in the United States where the Chamber of Commerce states that companies are, "facing unprecedented challenges trying to find enough workers to fill open jobs." US Bureau of Labor Statistics shows that there are more job openings than unemployed adults—if every person who is unemployed found a job, millions would still be unfilled. And several industries are struggling under intense talent shortages for specific skills or roles.

It's happening around the world too. The World Economic Forum is predicting that by 2030, there will be a net growth of 78 million jobs worldwide, even accounting for anticipated job displacement by technology/AI and other trends. Many of the fastest growing jobs are highly technical, which means that critical shortages are anticipated even with aggressive efforts to upskill workers.

Before employees quit, they disengage. Gallup, known for its global research on employee engagement, estimates that it costs the world economy nearly $9 trillion, or 9 percent of global GDP. In the US, engagement has declined the last few years, hitting the lowest scores in a decade, correlated with decreases in mental health and well-being. Disengaged employees cost organizations over $550 billion per year in the US alone.

As described in their recent *State of the Global Workplace* report, Gallup identifies three levels of employee engagement (see table for regions):

- **Engaged** employees "are highly involved in and enthusiastic about their work and workplace. They are psychological 'owners,' drive performance and innovation, and move the organization forward."

- **Not Engaged** employees "are psychologically unattached to their work and company. Because their engagement needs are not being fully met, they're putting time—but not energy or passion—into their work."

- **Actively Disengaged** employees "aren't just unhappy at work—they are resentful that their needs aren't being met and are acting out their unhappiness. Every day, these workers potentially undermine what their engaged coworkers accomplish."

	North America	Latin America	APAC	EMEA
Engaged	33%	32%	24%	18%
Not Engaged	51%	58%	63%	64%
Actively Disengaged	16%	10%	13%	18%

Other talent development researchers like Gartner, Blessingwhite, and Deloitte identify employee engagement as a critical issue that impacts organizational success in every industry.

The financial cost of actively disengaged employees shows up in tardiness, missed work days, decreased productivity or quality, and shrinkage (theft of supplies and other resources). Gallup calculates that each disengaged employee costs $3,400 for every $10,000 in salary, or 34 percent.

When I consult with executives, I help them understand the real cost of disengagement by showing what Gallup's analysis means for their organization. All I need is their headcount and median salary to show them this compelling data (see two examples below).

	Company A US Offices	Company B Denver Office
Headcount	5000	150
# of disengaged (US avg 16%)	800	24
Median salary	$75,000/yr	$75,000/yr
% Cost of disengagement	34%	34%
Cost per disengaged employee	$25,500/yr	$25,500/yr
TOTAL COST	$20.4 Billion/yr	$612,000/yr

An example of calculating the costs of disengagement in the US

	Company C India (APAC)	Company D Brazil (LATAM)
Headcount	500	500
# of disengaged (region avg)	65 (13%)	50 (10%)
Median salary	$5,000/yr	$1,750/yr
% Cost of disengagement	34%	34%
Cost per disengaged employee	$1,700/yr	$595/yr
TOTAL COST	$110,500/yr	$29,750/yr

Calculating the costs of disengagement by global region

When leaders see the overall and real costs of disengaged employees, they get focused on creating an engaging work environment. Using Gallup's data, I can also show the impact of disengagement in certain industries, like advertising, or in a sector like state or federal government.

What does change have to do with engagement? Quite a bit, actually. As you'll discover in future chapters, humans are biologically wired for constancy and can find chaotic or rapidly changing environments to be quite stressful.

While we might first respond by focusing and working harder, ultimately our brain will push us to check out emotionally, and even physically, becoming the sleepwalking and unhappy employees that Gallup describes.

We'll also learn that when employees can't find their way through change, they are more likely to quit. While losing a disengaged employee might be a blessing, the truth is that you're more likely to lose your best people. And replacing good people is much more expensive than leaders often realize.

Research by the Society for Human Resource Management (SHRM) finds that the cost of replacing an employee is 50 percent to 250 percent of their annual salary plus benefits. This takes into account the cost of recruiting and hiring a new person, the lost productivity of the role until it's filled, and the time it takes for the new person to get up to speed and fully productive.

The range of percentage is based on the employee's skill level. Entry-level positions will cost 50 percent of their salary plus benefits to replace while a position of leadership or high level of skill (for example, IT or engineering) will be closer to 250 percent. Turnover rates vary by industry with a low of 18 percent for government organizations to a high of 79 percent for hospitality—the average is 41 percent.

This can seem abstract so I find it helpful to calculate the costs so leaders can see the real impact. Use data from HR and industry sources to create a sense of the real hit to your bottom line. Look at this example below—losing 20 frontline employees can cost half a million dollars while 20 technical employees can cost more than $17 billion!

	Entry Level Employee	Technical/ Leader Level
Annual Salary + Benefits	$50,000	$350,000
SHRM Percentage	X 50%	X 250%
Cost to replace employee	$25,000	$875,000
X Total number of employees	20	20
TOTAL COST	$500,000	$17.5 Billion

Costs of replacing employees

The website Bonusly.com has an online "cost of employee turnover" calculator that allows you to enter your data and see more details. Again, leaders are genuinely surprised to see how much attrition is actually costing them. We'll explore more on the costs of failed change in chapter 23, but it's clear that getting change right is a major competitive advantage.

It's not like people aren't trying to fix this problem. Hundreds of books have been written on managing change and thousands of consulting firms offer their services. You can find whitepapers and articles galore, all attempting to address this critical issue.

Clearly, there is a lot of opportunity to improve our understanding of today's change. Few people are exploring the neuroscience of change and even fewer know how to translate that knowledge into actionable strategies for employees, managers, and executives. This is what we'll cover in this book.

Change Journey 2
Industry: Construction
Our organization suffered a massive upheaval when the board decided to fire one of our senior leaders, prompting the Executive Director to resign in protest. This left the organization suddenly up in the air and those in middle management were left to keep things on track.

The board did its best to "right the ship" by installing a temporary director while searching for more permanent leadership. But unfortunately, they chose someone who was not invested in the organization's future, nor were they respected or prepared to lead the organization out of the quicksand. Ironically, there were many qualified leaders who were ready and willing to step up, but the board's choice led to disaster.

Instead of adding stability, the new leader was disorganized and created chaos. They immediately pushed sweeping changes that caught many off-guard, miscommunicating the goals and mission while moving staff around to different positions within the organization.

The toxic environment only festered and a wave of resignations followed. The organization continued to bleed resources—both human and financial—to the point that they had to cut salaries, close locations, and suspend services.

After a year of this, I decided to leave. I was burned out, stressed, feeling like there was no real leadership, goal, "journey," or optimism. Luckily, that career move worked out for me, but I hear from former colleagues (who stuck it out) that the organization is still toxic, has high turnover, low trust, constant conflict, and a bad reputation, making it difficult to attract new employees.

It is truly sad, but also totally avoidable—if the board had communicated better, involved the employees in the change, and not pushed so much radical changes in a short window of time, it could have been a success and I probably would have stayed!

2. Change in the Modern World

There is no getting around change. It happens every day in every type of organization. But the nature of workplace change has definitely shifted over the last 30 years, driven by a few key factors.

First, the pace of technological innovation has increased. When you map our generation's advancements in technology on a timeline, the space between them gets smaller and smaller. And the time until 25 percent of the US population is using it gets shorter and shorter. Each innovation has the power to radically shift society, including how business is done. As you can see, the advent of smart phones and tablets drove very rapid adoption rates and generative AI tools like ChatGPT and DeepSeek are exploding at even faster rates.

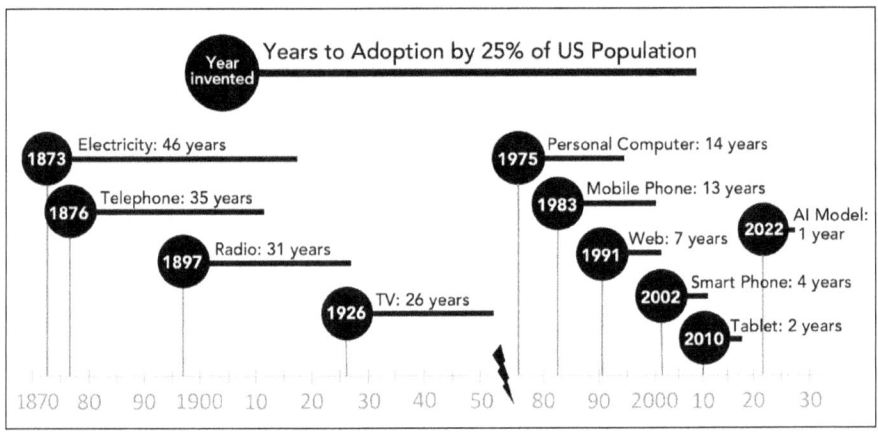

Adoption of new technology over time

Just think about how much your day-to-day work has changed with the immediate demands for information and communication. And how the widespread use of smartphones is pushing more demand for mobile access, so that you have everything you need in your pocket, 24 hours per day.

In addition, technology is big business, and innovation by the makers of computers, smartphones, and software creates a fast-paced, competitive market that drives unending upgrades and versions. If your organization has no change initiatives beyond keeping up with technology, you are still likely plenty busy with those.

Second, technology has enabled global communication and global business in a way that means that work is often 24/7, 365 days per year because, somewhere, you have an employee working or are trying to reach a potential client or supplier. Even if you are a small mom-and-pop business working traditional hours on Main Street, you cannot buffer yourself from all this change because it impacts your employees and customers.

Third, and finally, capitalism drives a relentless surge of growth and improvement. The market is filled with potential disruptors, especially because technology has made it so easy to create new businesses in this digital economy. For companies to survive, they must be striving for the newer/faster/better thing that distinguishes them from their competitors.

Change is constant, it is fast-paced, and it is relentless, much like ocean waves that pound on the shore. You might duck under one but when you look out, you just see sets of waves building and heading your way. Some might be small and others might be whoppers that can kick your butt if you aren't ready or don't have the right skills.

How does all this change show up in the average employee's life? It takes many forms in today's modern organizations. It can be a relatively small, like a new phone system, or sweeping, like a total redesign of the organization or its products. Consider which of these common change initiatives you experienced over the past 12 months:

- Different or new job or role
- New manager or new leader over your function or organization
- Switch to a different work station or work place
- Transition on your team (the loss or gain of coworkers)
- Shift in a process, policy, or procedure
- Implementation of new or different technology
- Drive to capture a new client or market
- New global territory with different cultures, languages, and laws
- Merger or acquisition
- Geopolitical shift that affects the your market or supply chain
- Climate emergency such as a natural disaster or pandemic

These work changes may drive big personal changes as well: moving into a new home, settling into a new neighborhood or community, and perhaps moving your kids to a new school.

You can see that change is happening in many ways and that we are moving through multiple change initiatives simultaneously.

Five Types of Change

While they can differ in size and impact, there are essentially five types of change. Identify which types are at play right now in your organization:

1. **Strategic (how the organization will fulfill its mission):** This includes redesigning products or services and targeting new markets. For example, when LinkedIn acquired Lynda.com to add learning to its suite of services. While the company had previously focused on helping professionals find opportunities and build their network, adding learning allowed them to help people close skill gaps to be more qualified for certain roles.

2. **Structural (the organization's internal set up):** This includes its divisions or functions, its org chart of authority, and administrative procedures. Changes might include reorganization of teams or depart-

ments, hiring growth that adds layers of hierarchy, or expanding locations. Every time German grocery giant Aldi opens a new store within an existing territory or expands into a new country, they are making a structural change.

3. **Process (how the organization maximizes productivity and workflow):** This includes optimizing manufacturing processes, implementing new software to support sales, or shifting technology such as implementing a new email system or mobile access. For example, when Amazon, T-Mobile, and American Red Cross implemented Salesforce, they engaged in a process-oriented change.

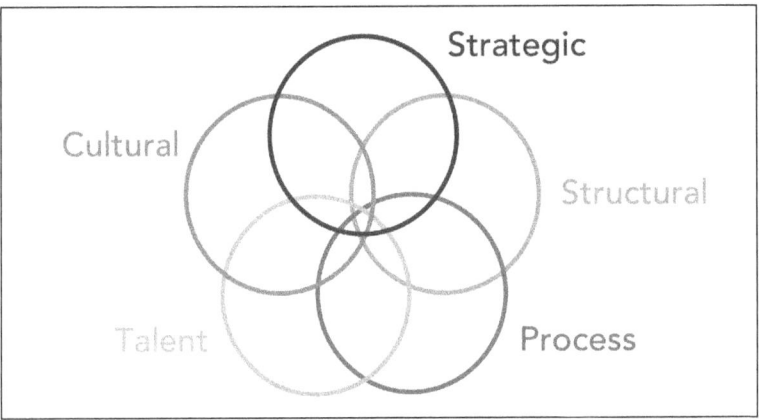

The five types of change at work

4. **Talent (maximizing employee skill and performance):** This involves initiatives affiliated with every aspect of the employee lifecycle including hiring, supervising, coaching, and training. Many organizations are shifting how they do performance reviews. Adobe was one of the first to do away with the annual rating process and many have followed suit, including GE, Gap, Accenture, Netflix, and Deloitte, to name a few.

5. **Cultural (shifting the attitudes, values, and behaviors of people such as employees and customers):** This might include revising core values, branding, or how people engage with a product or service. For example, when Satya Nadella took over as Microsoft's CEO, he launched an intentional cultural shift toward continuous learning and improvement, based on the growth mindset principles espoused by Dr. Carol Dweck.

But not all change is created equal. Large changes often include more than one of these types, creating a domino effect across the organization, and all can potentially impact others outside the organization—such as suppliers, customers, and shareholders—creating an intricate web of potential effects and consequences. Other changes may be small, and barely register as a blip in the organization. This got me thinking about what distinguishes one change experience from another and whether these differences might help us analyze change readiness or predict potential problems.

Change Journey 3
Industry: NGO/Nonprofit

I worked for a local non-governmental organization (NGO) as a grants program manager. We embarked on a journey to change the mission in response to various pressures. We had an extensive history of positive humanitarian work, but faced ongoing challenges due to a stigma surrounding "Islamic" in its name. Originally founded to advocate for a marginalized sect in the vulnerable community, the NGO has since transitioned to pure humanitarian efforts, with employees and board members representing diverse religious backgrounds.

One of the challenges we faced was that despite receiving funding from reputable international organizations, misconceptions persisted regarding our affiliation with religious and political entities, hindering our efforts to secure grants and funding. But we committed to overcoming the stigma.

The transformation of the NGO from its original sectarian roots to a purely humanitarian entity was primarily driven by its commitment to addressing the needs of marginalized communities and promoting social cohesion and inclusion. This shift was also influenced by evolving global standards and best practices in humanitarian aid, which emphasized the principles of humanity, impartiality, independence, and neutrality.

Additionally, the dedication and perseverance of our leadership, staff, and volunteers played a crucial role in navigating the challenges and complexities associated with this transition. By prioritizing the well-being of the communities it served and maintaining a steadfast focus on humanitarian principles, the NGO successfully embraced its new identity as a credible and respected humanitarian actor.

The evidence of our successful transition lies in our extensive track record of impactful projects and collaborations with reputable international NGOs like Acted, British Council, Catholic Relief Services (CRS), Expertise France, and the German Agency for International Cooperation (GIZ). Last year, we reached 52,927 beneficiaries with 1,755 being people with special needs. Our Primary Health Care Center alone serves up to 7,000 services per month, demonstrating significant outcomes.

Further, letters of recommendations from UNICEF, United Nations Development Program (UNDP), and CRS among others attest to our commitment to humanitarian principles. Our dedication to serving marginalized communities and upholding humanitarian values remains unwavering, underscoring our continued impact in the field.

3. Change vs. Transition

The concept of change encompasses two large and very different entities, and it's vital to understand the difference. On the one hand, you have the change itself, which is factual and structural; a thing you execute. It can be encapsulated in a detailed change plan written with measurable goals, milestones, and deadlines. And then there is the transition—the human psychological response to change, which includes humans' emotional reactions when confronted with change and how motivated they are to move through it. Transition is a process, largely driven by our biology, so it is something that requires adjustment rather than execution.

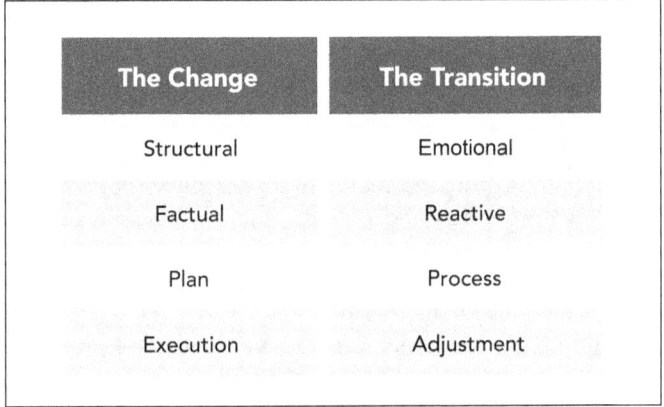

Change versus transition

Dr. William Bridges, author of *Managing Transitions*, argues that, too often, leaders in organizations make the mistake of focusing only on designing and executing a change plan without preparing for managing the transition.

I believe mismanaging the transition is the reason so many change initiatives fail. All changes require people to get on board and participate. All the detailed change plans in the world cannot overcome people who are resistant, reluctant, or downright oppositional.

The good news is that it doesn't have to be this way. With the right assessment and planning, leaders can be ready to successfully navigate the transition and, more importantly, help their people do the same.

Mapping Change Difficulty: Disruption and Acclimation

From all the various change initiatives I have witnessed in my years of consulting, I have consistently seen four factors influence outcomes. The first two:

- **Disruption:** How much disruption does the change create for employees? Some completely disrupt the day-to-day workflow while others have a negligible impact. So there is a continuum of disruption from very low to very high.

- **Acclimation:** The time it takes to acclimate or get used to the change is another factor. Some changes can be acclimated to very quickly (hours or days) and others can drag on for months or even years. This would be another continuum from very little time to a lot of time.

These two factors allow us to plot the impact of different types of changes into quadrants. Changes that are low disruption and require a low amount acclimation time fall into the bottom-left, or green zone: changes that are easy to adjust to quickly. For example, if you upgrade to eco-friendly lighting or if you switch to a different vendor, employees might not even notice the difference.

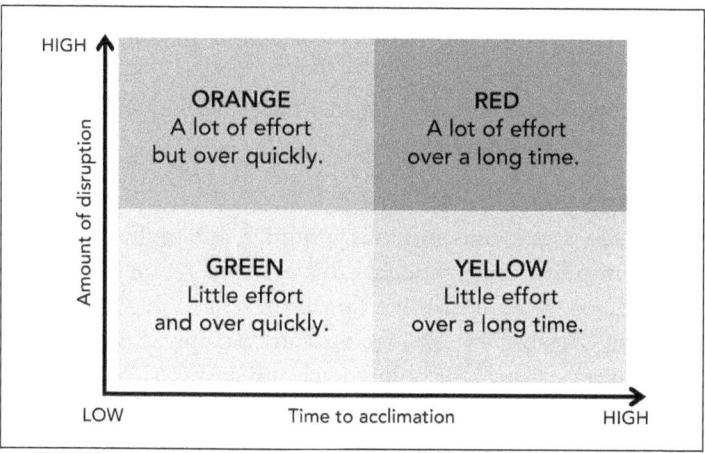

Matrix of disruption and acclimation

If a change falls into the bottom-right zone (yellow), it doesn't cause much disruption but will require stamina, since the adjustment period will take longer. For example, the slow preparation to meet a new regulation that goes into effect in two years.

The upper-left zone (orange) represents changes that are quite disruptive but are acclimated to quickly, such as converting to new email and calendar software or implementing a new customer relationship management (CRM) system like Hubspot or Salesforce. Almost inevitably, changes that impact how people communicate, manage their time, or close deals will be disruptive for a bit. Usually conversions like this are implemented over a weekend, although months of work were going on in the background up until the date of conversion.

Finally, the upper-right zone (red) represents changes that are high in disruption and time to acclimation. Examples include a complete revision of an organization's products and services, or a merger or acquisition with a company with different values, leadership structure, etc.

This matrix provides a quick way to assess changes. For example, Facilities might decide that they need to switch the faucets in the bathrooms or resurface the parking lot. Depending on the situation, those things might fall into the green zone—unless the organization has limited bathrooms and parking spaces, in which case this change may require people to alter their routines (disruption) for many days (acclimation), putting these changes into the orange zone.

When working with leaders on change initiatives, I have them use this matrix to consider the impact proposed changes will have on employees. It's a good predictor of how much resistance and upset a change is likely to cause.

However, the change-difficulty matrix does not yet tell the whole story because two more factors play a significant role in how employees respond to change:

- **Individual choice:** Do the employees *choose* the change or will it be put upon them?
- **Desire:** How much do the employees *want* the change, or again, is it being put upon them?

These two factors are the most important because they shape key psychological aspects of how humans are wired.

Mapping Employee Motivation

Choice and desire impact our emotions, attitudes, and motivations, as I am sure you have seen in your own experiences. It's easier to get on board with changes that you choose or want, even when they represent more disruption or longer acclimation time. Again, these two factors can be mapped against each other as a grid against "yes" or "no" for both choice and desire.

When you both desire and choose a change (yes and yes), you are likely to be happy about it and experience it with enthusiasm and energy. For example, you really want a job and you accept the offer. Your motivation would probably look like you are running toward it and celebrating the win. Even though this awesome new job may represent quite a bit of disruption in your life and acclimating to it may take time, your motivation will be very positive, which is why we need both matrices to really understand change.

The same for if your team has been pushing to redesign a service or update the marketing campaign. If this change is approved, you'll be excited even if it is a lot of work.

If you really want a change that you did not choose, you are likely to see it an unexpected but good opportunity. This is how I felt about the acquisition of Lynda.com—while I didn't choose it, I was excited because I was a big fan of the buying company and I admired their CEO. My motivation looked like me walking toward it, feeling good about embracing the unexpected opportunity.

The next quadrant—a change that you did not desire but did choose—is tricky, and probably represents some kind of "should" or intentional sacrifice, like accepting a lower position rather than being laid off or relocating because it might lead to more opportunities down the road. These are a bit harder to get excited about, so motivation is lower because you are enduring or accepting the conditions. It might feel like you are trudging along and could include feelings of resentment or disappointment, even if you are trying to make the best of it

Finally, in the fourth quadrant are changes that you did not choose nor did you want (no and no—or sometimes "Hell no!"). Obviously, without natural motivation you are likely to feel a lot of resistance toward this imposition, perhaps needing others to push or drag you along. Depending on how badly you feel about it, you might even actively fight the change, digging in your heels.

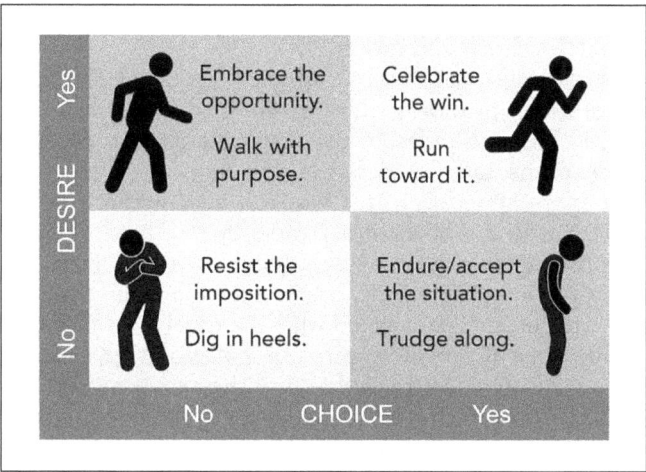

Mapping choice and desire

When you begin mapping change initiatives against these four factors—disruption, acclimation, choice, and desire—you'll find you have a much better way of predicting when people (employees, customers, constituents, etc.) are likely to resist.

You will also have a better understanding of how much skill leaders and managers need to help people through the related challenges. An inexperienced or ineffective manager can probably do just fine leading an eager group through a green or yellow change. But it's going to require many more nuanced leadership skills if you have trudgers or resisters and are taking them through a highly disruptive change.

This assessment helped a chief technology executive completely revise his approach to change at one of the world's top research universities. He had been hired to accomplish a major shift in how technology services were provided across the whole campus, serving students, staff, and faculty. In addition, he had inherited a team of experienced professional staff who had been in their roles for years.

He needed to roll out several major change initiatives over a three-year period, most of which would be disruptive, first to his team and then the various constituents they served. By mapping these four factors, he gained valuable insight that helped him shape the timing, messaging, and method for each of the initiatives. He also was able to define who needed what kind of training to best prepare them for success.

Change Journey 4
Industry: Healthcare/State Government

I worked for a state agency, which was launching a grant program to increase the number of healthcare providers in schools. The rationale was that student outcomes would improve since health is a crucial determinant of success in life, school, and career.

A grant was to be disbursed to an initial group of 67 school districts and local education providers with the aim of bringing them together to collaborate. In order to measure the collective impact, providers had to agree to collect the same data points and share them so they could be aggregated at the state level. This required a significant change because providers were used to working independently.

As the consultant leading this effort, I had to identify the forces keeping the system in its current state. First, I gathered information about past efforts and current pressures. Next, I asked what the ideal outcome was and what would be different if all providers were truly collaborating. I also established relationships with providers to understand their motivations, desires, and concerns about how this change could disrupt their current operations.

There were several barriers keeping providers working in silos, competition, and distrust. First, providers considered the state as a compliance enforcer who lacked an understanding of their reality and operational constraints, such as limited staffing and resources, as well as children with challenging life conditions. As a result, providers believed that the state could not appropriately use their data fairly when comparing providers to determine who should receive resources. Second, the providers often saw each other as competitors for funding. In the past, data had been used as a tool for punishment and/or funding cuts, so providers kept their data confidential.

I organized a planning retreat for 10 representative providers to help them define their common goal and strategize the best ways to bring about impactful change with the allocated funds. By the end of the retreat, providers had a solid plan based on their collective motivations, and it was grounded in the reality of their work. They left with a strong sense of partnership and trust, and they agreed to collect and share the same nine data points to measure success.

At the end of the first year, all grantees were collecting and sharing common data points, which provided valuable insights into how state funds were impacting access to healthcare and reducing negative outcomes for students. The program has been so successful that it is ongoing, with 186 grantees and over $30 million in funding disbursed. This success has enabled the state to tell a compelling story, supported by aligned data, demonstrating that the investment is effective.

Change is often met with resistance due to various reasons such as past failures, fear of the unknown, or fatigue from previous attempts. However, by understanding the reasons behind the resistance, both providers and the state were able to work collaboratively to overcome these challenges.

4. The Change Curve

The change curve is a classic model that has stood the test of time. I have found it a useful tool to help leaders understand the transition, the emotional aspect of change.

The change curve is built off research by Dr. Elisabeth Kübler-Ross, who studied death and dying. She found that people went through predictable stages of grief and acceptance when faced with a serious health crisis. Several researchers noticed that the model seemed to apply to all kinds of personal change situations. The application to business occurred in 1990 when Dottie Perlman and George Takacs were studying change in a healthcare organization and realized that employees were exhibiting the same reactions Kübler-Ross identified. Finally, in 1998, David Schneider and Charles Goldwasser published a formal model for business applications in *Management Review* and hundreds of studies have followed since.

The change curve shows that change can be represented as a graph that maps time along the horizontal axis, and productivity and morale on the vertical axis. Before you initiate a change, the group or team is running along at their "normal" level of productivity and morale. This level could be higher or lower than other groups but it's their everyday state.

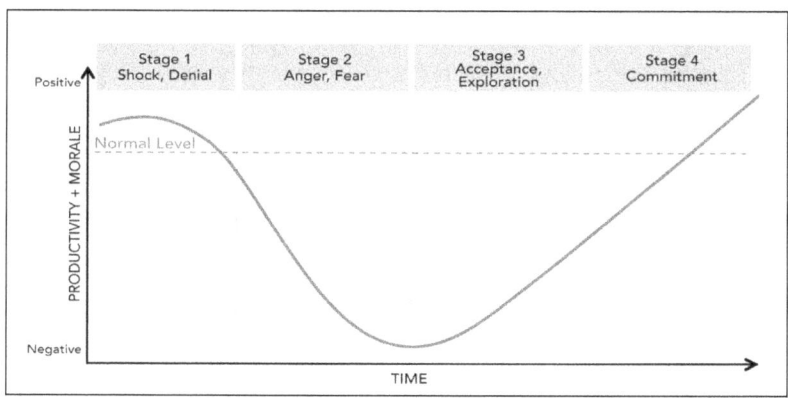

The change curve

Research on the change curve shows that when introduced to change humans go through a predictable pattern of emotions. And a big part of leading change is being prepared for the emotions of the transition and having patience and empathy as people move through the change curve.

At first, these emotions affect both productivity and morale but over time people tend to work through them until the change becomes the new normal. Here's the general pattern:

- **Stage 1:** Change is announced, disrupting the status quo. This might result in feelings of shock and denial. Employees tend to question the change or even ignore it and not take it that seriously. You might hear people say things like, "I can't believe they're doing this," or "They'll never go through with it," and ask questions like, "How will this impact me?"

- **Stage 2:** Change is met with anger and resistance. In this phase, people realize that the change is not going away and they can get angry about it. Comments here might be, "This isn't a good plan and it won't work," or "Why are they doing this to us?" "It's unfair!" and "I don't like it."

- **Stage 3:** Reluctant acceptance sets in. At the bottom of the curve, people start to accept that they cannot avoid the change. You are likely to hear comments like, "It seems like this happening so I better get on board." At this point, you might notice people trying to negotiate a compromise that makes the change more favorable. They might make suggestions like, "How about if we just do this instead?"

- **Stage 4:** Change is embraced with commitment. People continue to move forward with the change, understanding what is needed and getting involved with the change. When you see evidence of hope and engagement, and hear things like, "I think this just might work," people have begun embracing the change. Because people are now on board, they get creative, often offering suggestions for how the change could be improved. And they might even become impatient, wanting the rollout even faster now that they feel ready. This commitment continues until the change is completed. At first there is excitement about the accomplishment, and you'll hear things like, "We did it!" And "How did we ever get by the old way?" Then things settle down and you are back to the status quo . . . until the next change initiative is announced.

The change curve provides a map through transition—and there is really no getting around it. Ignoring the messy feelings that change brings up won't make them go away and, in fact, will make things worse. Good leadership can shorten the length of time or lessen the height of the curve but it won't disappear completely because we are biologically wired to resist change. Leaders often need help preparing for the messiness of the process because they can become disheartened when they see how people react. In sections IV and VI, we'll explore skills that better equip leaders and managers to make the change and transition successful.

While the change curve model is useful, it doesn't entirely capture how change unfolds in the modern workplace.

First, it doesn't account for the four factors of disruption, time-to-acclimation, desire, and choice. As a result, the change curve does not address the full range of emotions that employees exhibit. For example, when change is announced employees might feel excitement and hope if it's something they want and they choose. If they don't want it or choose it, you might see frustration and resentment. And employees often experience stress, anxiety, confusion, and even depression as the change continues.

The first half of the curve is difficult because people naturally focus on the past and potential losses the change might bring. This is a biologically driven response (which we'll explore in more depth in section II), but it's natural and a normal part of our species' survival instincts. This is not something that people can override or overcome. I often tell leaders, "They are not being difficult. They are being human."

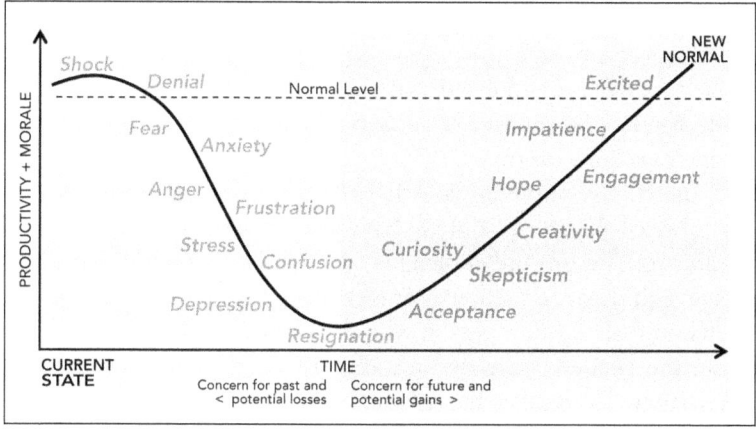

The emotions of transition

When people hit the bottom of the curve, I have witnessed three types of resignation, which are not accounted for by the change curve.

1. Employees might literally resign from the organization, quitting their jobs and thereby quitting the change, too.

2. Or, the employees might make the psychological shift and resign themselves to the change, thus getting on board emotionally.

3. Or, leaders surprised by unexpected "drama" might decide to stop the change initiative rollout, quitting the change instead of having patience for the bottom of the curve to turn.

This psychological shift occurs because people are able to turn their focus to the future and look for potential gains. This is a pivotal moment because it ushers in more positive feelings like creativity, and excitement which carry through to the end of the change. Once you see acceptance, you will start to see a slow progression through more positive and forward-focused emotions, such as curiosity (with some healthy skepticism thrown in). People will also start asking more questions. Leaders often find that they have to repeat information they have been saying for weeks once people start accepting the change, because instead of fighting against it they are actually listening.

The second way the change curve doesn't capture how change unfolds in the modern workplace is that we aren't just going through one change at a time. Employees are often moving through several change curves simultaneously, perhaps at different stages on each one. You could be finishing up a change in your email system, for example, when you're told that you are getting a new supervisor. And a new policy might be implemented right in the middle of your move to a new work location or team.

You rarely get the luxury of neatly arriving at the end of one change curve before you are launched onto one or several new ones. And what happens when you are starting to embrace one change, having feelings of hope and excitement, when a new change is announced that you feel resistance about? Do you back-slide a little on the first change? My observations say yes, and yet current change models don't account for that.

Third, the change curve implies that all change is experienced the same by every member of the group. But we have already seen that factors like disruption, acclimation, desire, and choice play a key role. Doesn't it make sense that if you have high desire and choice for a change, you may have a different emotional reaction than another person who does not want or choose that change?

Fourth, the change curve doesn't account for a person's capacity to take on more change. Each of us has a bandwidth for change, which is how much change we can hold and still function effectively. If you just had a baby, I suspect your bandwidth is pretty full already and there's not a lot of room to take on more. Or if you are going through an acquisition, it might not be a good time to remodel your kitchen.

This happened to me: In the middle of a major kitchen remodel and dealing with an ailing parent, my company was purchased. If the LinkedIn CEO had called me and asked if it was a good time for me, I would have told him that I'd prefer he waited a few months. My bandwidth for change was pretty maxed already, thank you very much.

But of course, that didn't happen, and I found myself dealing with so much change that if I had possessed a bandwidth meter, it would have blown out the top. It was a difficult period, both physically and emotionally.

In this example, the acquisition, the kitchen, and my mom's health were all changes that were high in disruption and time-to-acclimation. But your bandwidth can also fill up with lots of small changes. How many yellow changes is too many? And what happens if you add a red or an orange change to the mix?

In addition to bandwidth, most people have a preferred style for approaching and addressing change. According to research by Dr. Chris Musselwhite, people respond to change on a continuum, particularly in how they view the necessity for change and their own interest in participating.

On one end, you have the conservers, who are more cautious about change in general and tend to resist the unknown. When faced with change, they need a lot of information and a lot of time but are steady, reliable, and consistent. They prefer gradual change and they prefer to make small changes, retaining the current structure, rather than big shifts. Conservers ask good questions and keep people from making impulsive decisions, designing change that can gently transition the organization.

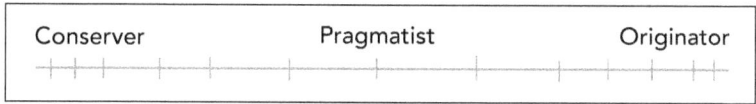

The change style continuum

At the other end of the continuum are originators, who enjoy risk and are comfortable with change. As the creative thinkers or innovators in a group, they often propose change with a "Let's try it out" mindset. They serve as the visionaries for change and often create new ways of doing business. However, they often need support thinking through the realities of implementation. They prefer change to be quick and radical and one that challenges the current structure.

In the middle, you have the pragmatists, who embrace change when they believe it is absolutely necessary. They are practical and reasonable but sometimes noncommittal. Because they sit in the middle of the conservers and originators, pragmatists often function as mediators between the other two, facilitating cooperation and communication. They prefer change to clearly serve a function and are willing to explore the current structure.

Most workplaces are filled with a fairly even mix of these change types, even at fast-growth tech start-ups, where you might expect to find a higher percentage of originators. (If you want to learn more, take Dr. Musselwhite's change-style-indicator assessment, found at MHS.com.)

The change curve assumes every person approaches change the same way when that is clearly not the case. Doesn't it make sense that originators might have a different psychological transition than conservers? I have certainly found this to be true.

All of these issues came together at a leading online travel booking website. The executives wanted to streamline their hiring practices so that all 100 of the recruiters were using the same strategies and processes. The VP of the recruiting function created a plan to shift everyone to a shared model. It was well designed and the company invested $100K in the process and related training. Once the change began rolling out, the recruiters experienced the typical emotions of the transition. They were adapting to the new process and adjusting.

However, the Chief People Officer was more cautious about change in general and was surprised to hear complaints. While the VP explained that this was a normal part of the process, the CPO's discomfort grew with every grumble. Soon, 90 percent of the team turned the corner and were doing fine but one small group of less than ten people were struggling. They continued to complain regularly to the CPO, whose own discomfort for change and lack of understanding about transition, gave greater weight to their concerns. Eventually, the CPO pulled the change, claiming that it was not working. This cost the company not only their investment and hours of staff time but ultimately their competitive advantage.

There are a few other change models that have shaped my understanding. In 1995, Harvard Business professor Dr. John Kotter developed an 8-step model to guide organizations through successful change.

1. Create a sense of urgency by articulating the risks for not acting.
2. Build a guiding coalition of leaders and influencers to lead the effort.
3. Form a strategic vision and initiatives that outline how you will get there.
4. Enlist an army of volunteers by communicating the vision to all levels of the organization.
5. Enable action by removing barriers that block progress, including outdated systems, resistant leaders, and inefficient processes.
6. Generate short-term wins with visible results to build momentum and commitment.
7. Sustain acceleration by using credibility from early wins to tackle bigger changes.
8. Institute change by anchoring it in the organization's culture, performance metrics, and leadership development.

Another often-used model is Prosci's ADKAR, created by Jeff Hiatt in the late 1990s. This model focuses on individual change as the foundation for successful organizational change. ADKAR is an acronym where each letter represents a key milestone an individual must reach for a change initiative to be successful:

- **Awareness:** People must understand why the change is necessary, including the consequences of not changing.
- **Desire:** The personal motivation to support and engage in the change by making the choice to participate.
- **Knowledge:** Knowing how to change, and having the necessary information, processes, and systems to succeed.
- **Ability:** Having the skills, capability, and confidence to implement the change, achieved through training, practice, and coaching.
- **Reinforcement:** Making the change stick through recognition, rewards, feedback, and continued support to prevent backsliding.

While useful, all of these models were created before neuroscience brought a deeper understanding of biology and how humans are wired to resist change. Insights from neuroscience provide more context for why the people side of change can be so challenging, and more importantly, the strategies that will prove to be most effective in making change stick.

5. The Rise of Change Fatigue and Burnout

A new development in the modern workplace is change fatigue, which is a sense of frustration, apathy, and resistance that arises among employees subjected to frequent, ongoing changes in organizational structures and processes.

It occurs when people just cannot keep up with the pace or volume of change coming their way. As McKinsey states, we have entered "the age of perpetual organizational upheaval."

A recent study by Gartner found that smaller scale, personal changes—such as being assigned to a new manager or moving to a new team—are two and a half times *more* fatiguing than larger transformational changes like mergers or adopting new technology. For small initiatives, the physical and psychological effort might be low but as more changes begin to overlap, a person's ability to successfully cope can become strained.

What are the signs of change fatigue in the workplace? From the front lines to the top executives, you might see several symptoms, including disengagement, exhaustion, absenteeism, confusion, conflict, and cynicism. You will also see increased stress and/or anxiety along with a decline in performance across the group, even among your top performers. Gartner found that change fatigue also negatively impacts psychological safety, inclusion, and intent to stay.

Change Fatigue at Work	
Disengagement	People become apathetic and emotionally "check out"
Exhaustion	Lack of energy, staring into space, sleeping at work
Absenteeism	Leaving work early or taking more sick days
Confusion	Poor judgment and decision-making
Conflict	Tension and conflict between individuals and groups
Cynicism	Increased complaints, skepticism, and resistance

Symptoms of change fatigue

In a study published in the *Journal of Organizational Change Management*, researchers found that change fatigue predicted increased strain, burnout, and intention to leave. Further, change fatigue negatively impacted teamwork, performance, job satisfaction, and organizational commitment. In another study in healthcare, the researchers found that change fatigue was negatively correlated with psychological resilience.

Researchers at Oxford and Birmingham universities found that change fatigue makes us less patient and also more averse to exerting effort, either physically or on tasks that require thinking or decision-making. Further, fatigue creates changes in the lateral pre-frontal cortex.

Recent studies show that 47 percent of senior executives and 45 percent of HR leaders believe that change fatigue is a problem in their organization.

Gartner found that the average employee now experiences 13 or more organization-wide changes per year, up from just 2 per year in 2016. It's no surprise that employees' willingness to support change has dropped to 44 percent, down from 74 percent in 2016. Gartner calls this the "transformation deficit."

According to Dr. Janet Fitzell, change fatigue occurs when people feel both burdened by relentless change and powerless to stop it. She says it's brought about when the workplace has "become one unending change initiative with staff spending an increasing proportion of their time reacting to change instead of getting the job done."

In my work as a consultant, I have seen many examples of change fatigue. One multinational company was facing some financial struggles and started reorganizing. But they would barely complete one reorganization before they would start on the next. One function was especially impacted with employees being moved to new teams and supervisors every couple of months. I met several workers who'd had six or seven new managers within one year! Naturally, they were not only fatigued, they were starting to become disengaged and the company saw more and more of their best employees leave.

This example specifically shows *chronic* change fatigue. Borrowing from medicine, chronic indicates an ongoing issue from which the patient does not improve. Those employees were experiencing a series of ongoing changes that created chronic change fatigue because they could not get out of the cycle.

Compare that to *acute* change fatigue, which occurs suddenly and is intense but fairly short-lived. For example, when you start a new job and everything about your work environment has changed. You are meeting new people, getting to know your supervisor, and learning about your responsibilities, and projects. And if you are an executive, you're also learning about the business strategy, building rapport with the other executives, and gaining information about the inner workings of your function, your organization, and the market.

Any new hire will tell you that those first few weeks are exhausting, both physically and emotionally. But fortunately, things get easier within six to eight weeks and you recover from the exhaustion and start to feel like yourself again.

Change fatigue is real and impacting organizations in every industry around the world. More and more studies are being done on change fatigue and its effect in the workplace. Tyler Durham, former president of Ketchum Change states that more leaders need to "recognize the exhausting effect that continuous change and volatility has on employees and how that exhaustion can lower employees' productivity, reduce their engagement, and damage retention rates."

You can completely overwhelm a team with the right combination of yellow-, orange-, and red-zone changes strung together without sufficient recovery time in between. In fact, like the proverbial straw that broke the camel's back, even one or two ill-timed green changes can also do damage.

The human body cannot sustain unending change. It's just too exhausting, so people begin to make choices. They may first jump into change with enthusiasm, working hard to be successful. But when more and more changes come their way, they realize they cannot put that effort in each time. So they begin to disengage. By caring less about their job and their workplace, they don't feel so affected by it. But sadly, this means they are not bringing their passion or motivation to work either. Dr. Dawn-Marie Turner says that this is when companies begin to lose their competitive advantage, because they are losing the productivity and innovation that engaged employees bring.

Employees can also learn how to "play the change game" by looking like they are participating but actually expending as little energy as possible. Jeanie Duck, author of *The Change Monster*, calls them change survivors. This threatens the organization's success because leaders get a false sense that change is happening but don't see the results that it should be driving.

I've seen this occur at a military base I consulted with. Every two years, a new commanding officer (CO) rotated in, bringing their ideas for change, and creating a cycle of upheaval where previous initiatives were suddenly abandoned and new ones launched. The permanently stationed staff had learned to "wait out" the changes by responding slowly while giving the appearance of activity.

There are five main strategies people can use to resist change:
- **Distance:** being unavailable to discuss the change
- **Delay:** avoiding taking action on the change, or missing deadlines
- **Diminish:** participating but doing as little as possible; giving the appearance of effort while not accomplishing the goals
- **Detract:** shifting the focus by claiming another issue needs addressing
- **Destroy:** actively seeking to sabotage the change to cause its failure

Burnout

Change fatigue exists on a continuum that ranges from engaged at one end to burned out at the other. When companies don't heed the warning signs of change fatigue, they can push their employees over into burnout, which brings a host of additional challenges and costs.

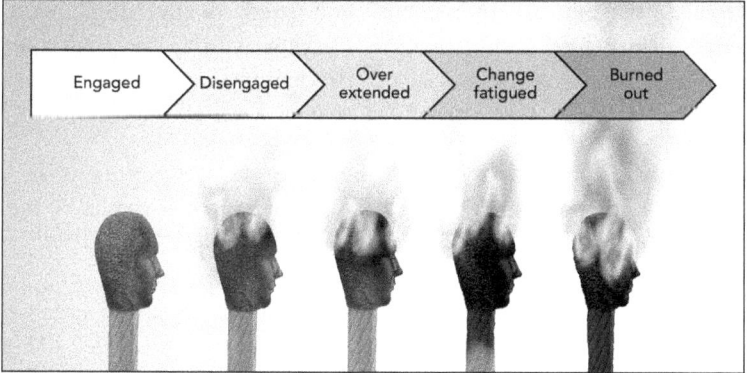

The burnout continuum

Burnout is a diagnosable state of emotional, physical, and mental exhaustion brought on by long-term stress. In 2019, the World Health Organization declared it a critical workplace issue and at that time, they estimated that 53 percent of the global workforce was burned out. When the COVID-19 pandemic hit, the burnout rate skyrocketed to 90 percent. Recent studies show that it has decreased but only to 77 percent, which is why employees' ability to cope with change is 50 percent of pre-pandemic levels.

Burnout is the number one reason employees gave for leaving their jobs during the Great Resignation—the time from March 2021 to June 2023 in which record numbers of people quit month after month. The second reason? Too much organizational change, clearly indicating a link between the two.

One study by Great Place to Work found that burnout more than doubles the chance that employees will look for new job opportunities. They identify that burnout typically occurs when an employee feels:

- Limited control of their environment and over their schedule
- Limited participation in decision making
- Lack of clarity in their work
- Communication is poor, especially with management

In their book *Burnout: The Secret to Unlocking the Stress Cycle*, Dr. Emily Nagoski and Amelia Nagoski, DMA, identify three components of burnout:

1. **Emotional exhaustion:** This is the fatigue that comes from caring too much for too long. Symptoms include chronic fatigue and, ironically, insomnia, putting sufferers in a cycle of accelerating exhaustion. This leads to impaired concentration or forgetfulness, anger, increases in anxiety and depression, increased illness, and physical symptoms like heart palpitations, chest pain, shortness of breath, GI pain, dizziness, headaches, and fainting

2. **Lack of accomplishment:** The second component is an unconquerable sense of futility, a feeling that nothing you do makes any difference. People experience feelings of apathy and hopelessness along with increased irritability. The projects that used to give them satisfaction or the teams they used to enjoy working with now make them feel, "meh" at best. This leads to a lack of productivity and, ultimately, poor performance.

3. **Depletion of empathy:** The hallmark of this component is detachment and depersonalization because the person has depleted their ability to give empathy, care, or compassion. Not just for others, but for themselves too. This leads to loss of enjoyment, pessimism, increased isolation, and disconnection. Joy and compassion seep away and even if the person realizes they need help they don't care enough to seek it for themselves. It's no wonder that burnout is a risk factor for depression.

Burnout has contributed greatly to the sharp increase in mental health issues that began during the pandemic and continue to this day. In fact, well-being has become a top priority for employees around the world and is now a focus of Gallup's research. In addition to measuring engagement, Gallup now asks respondents to rate themselves on a continuum from suffering to struggling to thriving. Globally, 34 percent of the workforce is thriving, 58 percent are struggling, and 8 percent are suffering. They also measure factors like their intent to leave their job and how much they experience daily negative emotions like stress, anger, sadness, and loneliness.

Gallup found that employees who strongly agree that their employer cares about their overall wellbeing are:
- 69 percent less likely to actively search for a new job
- 71 percent less likely to report experiencing a lot of burnout
- 36 percent more likely to be thriving in their overall lives
- Five times more likely to trust the leadership of their organization
- Five time more likely to strongly advocate for their organization as a good place to work

So, to properly interpret the change curve, keep in mind that it doesn't account for chronic or acute change fatigue nor burnout. It assumes that every trip through the curve will unfold like all the others but when people are physically and emotionally exhausted, they are just not going to respond like employees who are not fatigued. As someone who studies the biology of work, I found that neuroscience sheds light on understanding change, and more importantly how we better help people move through it.

Change Journey 5
Industry: Youth Organization
I recently left an organization that I loved due to change fatigue and burnout. I had volunteered with this national youth organization for 45 years after being profoundly impacted by it as a child. As a youth, I had completed the highest level of recognition for leadership and community service and knew that I wanted to contribute as I grew into adulthood.

I have been committed to my volunteer service, fueled by a lifelong dedication and love for the mission of the organization. The problem started with a lessening of standards over the past four decades, creating a gradual slide. But it then started to fall over the cliff about five years ago.

First, there seemed to be politics between the national office and local chapters. I was leading the implementation of a revised leadership course from National that encountered heavy resistance from other local volunteers, who stated, "Our local council knows better." This lack of support for the new vision from other "dedicated" adults was frustrating and ultimately, we could not get the new course off the ground.

> Around the same time, the COVID-19 pandemic impacted our organization, creating major changes in how we accomplished our goals through the limitations of lockdowns, social distancing, etc. Finally, the organization had been involved in several lawsuits, and ultimately had to file for bankruptcy.
>
> I consider my motivations to be selfless, but too much change in five years pushed me to the point of burnout and apathy, which caused me to lose my focus and dedication to leading youth and adults.

Your Learning Journey

Let's use these concepts to assess your own experiences. I recommend first reflecting on a change that you have already completed and then looking ahead to what else is coming. Consider these questions:

- How would you rate the amount of disruption and time-to-acclimation? Which quadrant best represents the change?
- What is your motivation for the change? Did you want it and did you choose it? Which stick figure best represents your motivation (runner, walker, trudger, or resister)?
- How well did the change curve map to your experience? What did the different stages look like for you?
- What level was your change bandwidth at the time you were going through this change? Did you have plenty of room to accommodate it or were you feeling maxed out?
- Did you experience any change fatigue during this change? If so, which symptoms did you exhibit?
- Have you also experienced any of the symptoms of burnout?
- What does well-being mean to you?
- Do you feel that your manager or workplace cares about your overall well-being?

THE BRAIN SCIENCE
OF CHANGE + RESISTANCE

*"Do the best you can until you know better.
Then when you know better, do better."*

Maya Angelou, poet and author,
I Know Why the Caged Bird Sings

6. The Brain on Change

Exploring the neuroscience of change was a natural continuation of my research on the neuroscience of learning. (For more information on that subject, see my book titled *Wired to Grow: Harness the Power of Brain Science to Learn and Master Any Skill*.) Neuroscience is the study of how the central nervous system (brain and spinal cord) and the peripheral nervous system (all the other nerves throughout the body) work together to shape our thoughts, emotions, and behaviors.

Medical technology has allowed researchers from a wide range of disciplines like neurology, biology, and psychology, to name a few, to explore the inner workings of the human body in ways never seen before. In fact, as I read study after study in various academic journals, it seems clear we are experiencing a renaissance of sorts and coming to know ourselves on an entirely new level. We have lifted the hood, so to speak, and are finally getting a real grasp on how our engines run.

While I am not a neuroscientist (my doctorate is in Education, Leadership, and Organizations), I feel very fortunate that my years as faculty and dean at the University of California trained me to decipher empirical research—and more importantly—draw connections among seemingly unrelated studies. It always strikes me that, because of their deep specializations, most scientists are isolated. So many of them are focused on a tiny niche of research, often studying one brain function or even one specific brain structure. While brilliant in their specialty, they are not looking across a wide range of disciplines, nor are they applying their work to solving today's workplace problems.

As a working practitioner in the fields of change management, executive development, and learning strategy, I serve as a translator, harvesting the latest findings and creating new brain-based models. In my cross-functional, multi-disciplinary review of the literature, I have found certain aspects of the brain are vital for understanding how change impacts today's employees. The studies about these aspects immediately shined a light on some major gaps in how we understand change, which is directly related to why so many change initiatives are doomed.

Simply put, we are working against human biology at almost every turn. In the most basic terms, human are designed to do three things, in ascending order: Survive, Belong, and Become®.

1. **Survive:** This is our most basic need to stay alive. Global conflicts and natural disasters highlight our primal need for food, water, and shelter. When we are not in crisis, this need expresses itself in our desire for job security because earning a paycheck is how we buy food and shelter. Anything that messes with our sense of job security, like a new boss, a performance review, or being assigned to a new team, can trigger these primal instincts.

2. **Belong:** This is our need to be part of a community and form meaningful bonds. Belonging is tightly interwoven with our need to survive because our chances of survival are greater when we're part of a tribe. Entire structures of our anatomy are dedicated to helping us understand and connect with others, and our health suffers when we experience loneliness and isolation. This need can be strained if workplace changes impact our relationships or our place in the organizational structure.

3. **Become:** Our deepest and greatest need is to become our best selves—to grow into our potential and make the contribution we are here to make. This is the "seeking" part of human nature and it distinguishes us from all the other living organisms on the planet. Our brains are wired to seek new levels of growth and we are called to identify and fulfill a sense of purpose. While this is a deep need, it can only occur once our survival and belonging needs are met.

This is my modified version of Dr. Abraham Maslow's famous Hierarchy of Needs, a model of human psychology and motivation that has stood the test of time. I find it interesting that even though the success of every organization depends on employees doing good work, and growing and improving over time, organizations often unintentionally threaten our need to survive and belong.

Change is often where and when that happens. When change initiatives are not handled correctly, they can work against our biology and keep people from performing their best.

Many brain structures relate to change but I believe these four in particular are crucial to understand: the amygdala, the entorhinal cortex, the basal ganglia, and the habenula. I have been sharing the results of my research with executives around the world and every single one immediately saw the implications for their organizations and their people. And each one could identify several key issues that were not being addressed in their change plans.

In sections IV and VI, I will show you how to weave these insights from neuroscience into effective strategies you can implement. You might also wish to check out my research on belonging in my book *Wired to Connect*, and on becoming our best selves in *Wired to Become*.

7. Amygdala: Our Voice of Fear

Many of us remember the story of Chicken Little who, after being bonked on the head by a falling acorn, ran around crying, "The sky is falling! The sky is falling!" This story actually demonstrates how one of our brain structures, the amygdala, functions.

The amygdala is largely responsible for our survival. According to Dr. Anthony Wright, professor of neurobiology at the University of Texas Medical School, the amygdala is connected to all of the major sensory nerves (optical, aural, olfactory, etc.). It's designed to detect threats in our environment. When a potential threat arises, like the smell of fire smoke, seeing an attacker, or hearing a gunshot, the amygdala launches the fight-flight-freeze response.

Within 200 milliseconds, our body is flooded with adrenalin and cortisol, which rush through the body to prepare it to survive the impending danger. Increased blood flow helps muscles respond more quickly while increased blood coagulants can help us survive an injury. Lung capacity increases, the body releases natural painkillers, and the neocortex (the "thinking" brain) shuts down, taking away advanced logic and self-awareness.

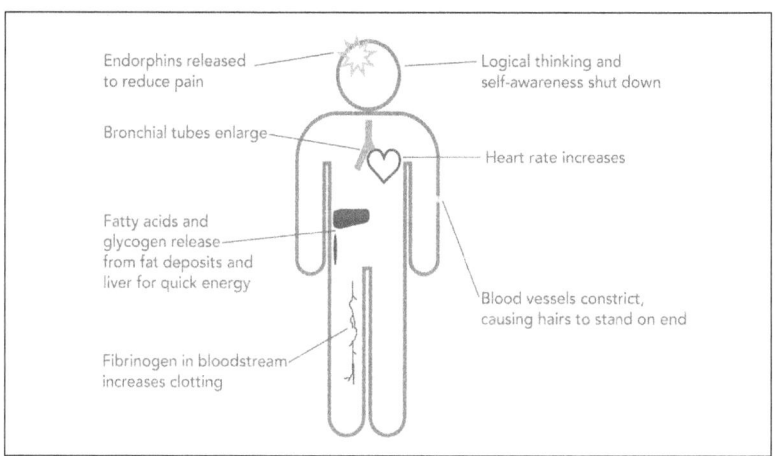

Impact of adrenalin and cortisol

Most of us have experienced this intense and powerful reaction, perhaps when another car has swerved near us or we have been attacked by an animal or a person. The emotional feeling of this response is first fear often followed by anger, so it is no surprise that we see those emotions at the beginning of the change curve.

It is interesting to note that the amygdala is wired to detect *change*—any change, even the smallest, most miniscule changes. This is because our species was most likely to survive if we approached our environment with caution and suspicion. Noticing that a bush looked different today could be the difference between life and death, because there might be a lion or an enemy lurking behind it. While it may have been a group of fluffy bunnies, we were more likely to survive to tell the tale at the campfire when we assumed the worst.

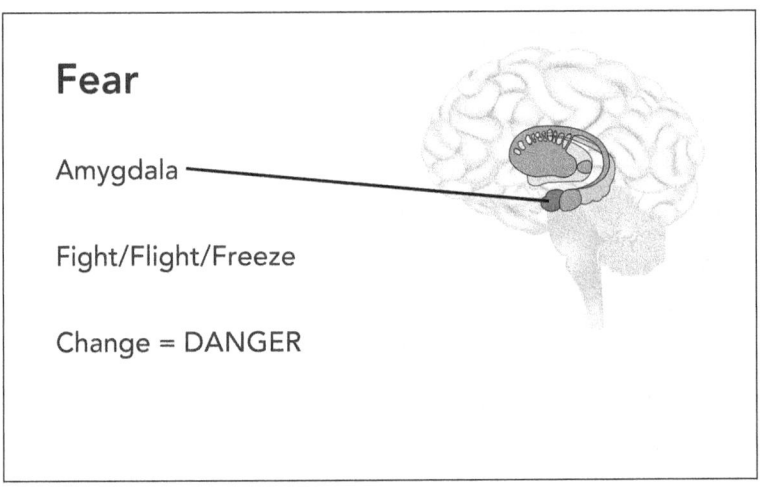

The amygdala and fear

From an evolutionary perspective, we who are alive now are descendants of the early humans who were most sensitive to change and most cautious in response to it. For a humorous depiction of this wiring, watch the animated movie *The Croods*. Nicolas Cage plays the patriarch whose motto is "Never not be afraid," and as a result his family survives while all their neighbors perish.

In today's modern world, our sensory nerves are constantly scanning our environment and when things are as expected, we feel calm. But when we detect change, we are wired to go on alert and assume the worst until proven otherwise.

In fact, our need to survive is so strong that others who have gone into fear easily influence us. The way Chicken Little's fear convinces her friends Henny Penny and Ducky Lucky that the sky is falling. When they ask her how she knows, she says, "Because it landed on my head," which is good enough to set off their amygdalas too, each one adding to the collective hysteria.

I have witnessed this in all kinds of organizations. One or two people can influence the rest of the group, spreading "doom and gloom" perspectives and amping up the group's fear and distress. Leaders are often surprised and frustrated at how easily this happens.

That's why it's important to assess how disruptive the change might be and how people will respond given their desire for and choice of the change. If you have a couple of trudgers or resisters in the midst of a group who is walking toward the change, they may not have much impact unless they are highly influential to the others.

It's also important to be transparent and share as much information as you can as early as possible. Psychologists have long known that in the absence of information, the brain fills in the blanks—but it doesn't just fill in any story. According to psychologist Dr. Janice Rudestam, the brain fills in the *worst-case scenario,* in an attempt to aid our survival.

This is how rumors of budget cuts and layoffs can run rampant in an organization. Employees usually sense that something is afoot and begin filling in the blanks with horrible possibilities. Again, this is part of our biological wiring—we are more likely to survive if we plan for the worst instead of hoping for the best. When people get anxious and start worrying about things that are not really an issue, they are not being difficult, they are being human. But they can only really shift perspective with information delivered by a trusted person.

Leaders and managers can address this by driving a clear and consistent narrative about the why and how of the change. I'll get more into the details in future chapters but for now, just understand that fear and anxiety are a big part of how humans respond to change. It's just the truth of our biology.

As you may have already guessed, the amygdala is responsible for the first half of the change curve. All those negative emotions are swirling around and people have lost their logical analysis and self-awareness, which can lead to poor choices. Most of us have learned to temper the raw intensity of the amygdala's fight-flight-freeze response, however. Rarely does it look like punching someone or running away. Instead, the modern fight response includes criticism, contempt, sarcasm, teasing, and shaming, in addition to aggression. And even aggression is likely to be contained to raising the voice, pounding a hand on a table, or slamming a door.

Likewise, the modern flight-freeze response is more often going to look like people getting quiet or withdrawn, or they may engage in defensiveness, stonewalling, making excuses, or blaming others. These are all attempts to shift attention to others.

As people engage in these challenging behaviors, like criticism and blame, they can affect each other and potentially strain or harm team dynamics. People are stressed and operating from a state of fear that can easily escalate. No wonder leaders are likely to see a decline in productivity and morale!

Like all good children's stories, Chicken Little has a message. As Chicken Little, Henny Penny, and Ducky Lucky continue their journey, they run into Foxey Loxey, who sees that they are distraught and hyped up on adrenalin. Sensing an opportunity, he takes advantage of their emotional state, offering to "help" but leading them to his den, where they are never seen again.

As this fable accurately depicts, heightened states of fear and anxiety can distract us, causing us to make unwise choices. While it's unlikely that we'll become someone's dinner, losing our self-awareness and logical analysis make us prone to injuries and accidents as well as producing defective or low quality work.

Part of leading change successfully is understanding, and being prepared for, the powerful fear response. When leaders and managers are ready for the side effects of the amygdala, they are much more likely to help their people through the change curve effectively and increase the likelihood of success for the change initiative.

In summary, if the amygdala could talk during change, it would say, "I'm freaking out!"

Change Journey 6
Industry: Education

I worked as a teacher in a K-12 school. New leadership arrived and wanted to make some changes, which was expected. Unfortunately, they did not thoroughly research our current state and chose to focus on something that was actually working successfully. When staff provided feedback that this was the not best use of time and resources, the new leaders seemed more focused on saving face than engaging in an authentic dialogue.

As the change unfolded and the staff experienced upheaval to a system that was working well before, distrust of the new leaders set in. In meetings, staff tried to point out what was not working but leadership then scrapped the Q&A segments of our meetings, essentially cutting off our ability to provide feedback. Further, the leaders seemed to gaslight the staff, stating that the changes were successful when the evidence clearly showed they were not.

Next, two prominent staff leaders were fired with no notice, which made many people feel scared. The leadership pushed forward with the changes, silencing any opposition. This caused a very unsettling work environment. What had once been a bustling, supportive community now felt like a ghost town. The biggest question was if leadership could dictate any change they wanted, what were they going to change next?

Needless to say, this approach to change created a lot of fear and stress and many staff handed in their notice, myself included. It's been heartbreaking watching this unfold when it could have gone so differently if the leaders had been willing to collaborate, rather than dictate.

8. Entorhinal Cortex: Our Personal GPS

As I explored the brain science of change, the Nobel Prize–winning work of Drs. May-Britt and Edvard Moser stood out as having important implications. They co-lead the Center for the Biology of Memory at the Norwegian University of Science and Technology and the Kavli Institute for Systems Neuroscience. The Mosers discovered that our brain has an internal geographical positioning system (GPS) that helps us navigate our way through physical space. Their fascinating research shows that the entorhinal cortex (EC), which sits within the hippocampus, is the brain structure responsible for our GPS capabilities. It contains a spherical cluster of cells that actually make maps of our physical surroundings and helps us successfully navigate our way through them.

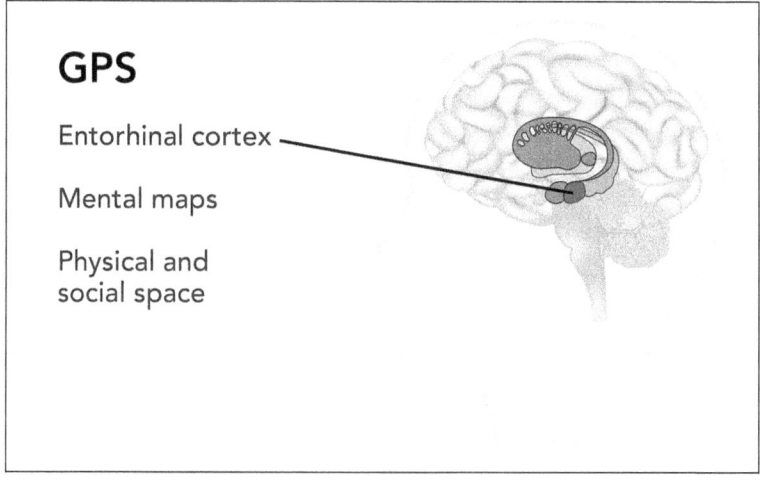

The entorhinal cortex and maps

The Mosers attached computer monitors to rats that showed the activity of the entorhinal cortex on a screen, creating a visual representation. And what they saw was mind-blowing: the sphere of cells was organized in a grid-like pattern, with the cells activating in a way that created a visual map. In other words, they could see the cells light up, one by one, as the rat walked around, showing accurate direction, distance, and even speed or pace. The cells even indicated a boundary when the rat encountered a wall. As the rat moved, the cells literally created an accurate map of the space—in all three dimensions. If that same rat was placed in a new location, the EC would build a new map. And if the rat was returned to the previous location, the existing map was "loaded," allowing the rat to quickly find its way around. If something in the environment had shifted, the mental map was revised.

This internal GPS system is vital to the survival of every species. It allows us to find our way back to sources of food, water, and shelter, and it reduces the mental and physical energy of having to figure it out each time.

We all have thousands of maps in our brains of various places we have lived and worked. Have you ever visited a neighborhood or school from your childhood? Or an old workplace? Your brain loaded up that old map, allowing you to find things you hadn't seen in years. And you probably could clearly see where things were different ("Huh, this is where the meeting room used to be"), evidence that your entorhinal cortex was updating your map.

Interestingly, the Mosers' research is shedding light on why Alzheimer's patients become disoriented. It turns out that this cluster of grid cells gets damaged early in the course of the disease, thus disabling their mental maps of the places they should know. Even though they are navigating places they have been hundreds of times before, the internal map has disappeared and along with it, their recognition of a place as familiar. In a 2023 study in *Trends in Neurosciences*, Dr. Kei Igarashi found that the entorhinal cortex often exhibits the earliest signs of Alzheimer's disease, with impaired neuronal activity preceding neurodegeneration. New treatments are focusing on protecting the EC.

These mental maps not only help us survive, they can create a sense of familiarity and belonging, something that we are biologically wired to seek. And some companies are able to harness this into long-term customer loyalty. For example, Waterfall Resort Alaska provides high-end sport-fishing adventures every summer. Started over 100 years ago, the lodge now regularly hosts guests who are the grandchildren of their original clients. These families make it a tradition to come back year after year because of their fond memories for both the location and the quality experience the staff provides.

Many of today's large hotel and resort chains also leverage our mental maps by creating consistent experiences down to the room layout, furnishings, and bedding. These executives know that traveling is stressful and many customers prefer to arrive at a place that feels familiar. By having a mental map that applies to multiple locations, it saves the traveler both physical and emotional energy.

I am often hired to work with executive teams, which means I visit an organization's headquarters multiple times throughout the year. To reduce decision fatigue, I book my travel with the same airline and hotel for every visit, even requesting the same room when I can. It's particularly helpful when I can count on a good night's sleep. This allows me to keep my mental energy focused on the things that matter.

GPS and Change

What does this mean for change in today's workplaces? Many changes may affect people's mental maps of their physical workplaces. We might move the location of an employee's workstation or office, or we might move certain services or resources, like food sources or the location of the tech support team. In the case of a relocation or acquisition, every single aspect of the work environment might be disrupted and replaced with something new and unfamiliar.

This is also true for every employee starting a new job. We have to build completely new mental maps of our work locations including how to get there, where we do our work, where colleagues sit, as well as resources like bathrooms, the copier, kitchen, and coffee. And if we moved our home to a new neighborhood for that job, then we must also build new mental maps of grocery stores, medical offices, restaurants, etc.

Fortunately, the brain will build new mental maps. But this process takes time and energy as the person navigates the new space. That's part of the reason we feel mental and physical fatigue when we start something new or go through a big change—the map-making part of our brain is doing some heavy lifting. And we're not just making maps of the physical space, but the social space too.

Social GPS

The Mosers are not the only researchers exploring the entorhinal cortex and the hippocampus it resides within. Research out of New York shows that these structures are also involved with creating social maps of people and relationships. Dr. Rita Tavares, from the Schiller Laboratory of Affective Neuroscience at the Icahn School of Medicine at Mount Sinai, states, "Beyond framing physical locations, the hippocampus computes a more general, inclusive, abstract, and multidimensional social map."

As we enter new social spaces, like a workplace or neighborhood, our brain scans for information and is actually able to map relationships based on power (which includes hierarchy, dominance, competence) as well as affinity (trustworthiness, love, intimacy). Functional neuro-imaging scanners (fMRI) show that the hippocampus is activated when we are navigating new social settings, proof that the mapping function is taking place.

As with physical space, social space is often affected by workplace change. An employee will unconsciously reassess and revise their current social maps when they get a new manager or leader as well as when coworkers and team members change. And if they are starting a brand new job or new location, they will have to build entirely new social maps of all of the coworkers and colleagues across the organization with whom they interact.

This is why the hiring and onboarding experience is so important. We begin building our social maps during the application and interview process and our feelings about the people we meet greatly influence our decisions to accept jobs. One tech giant in Silicon Valley was losing a lot of great candidates to their competitors. A deeper analysis discovered that many of the hiring managers were using a "trial by fire" philosophy during interviews, while the competitors were using a "welcome to our family" approach.

Our social networks matter because we are wired to seek safety and belonging. During change, people fear the loss of those connections. We spend quite a bit of time developing our professional and social networks, building trust and rapport over time through many interactions. Many workplace initiatives erase the results of that effort, forcing us to start over.

Now, our brains are made to do this, so we will make new social maps and will eventually build trust and rapport, but, again, it takes time and energy. This contributes to the very real issue of change fatigue. And if an employee is experiencing a series of changes over a short period of time (for example, several moves of their workstation), the exhaustion and fatigue may become chronic, driving employee disengagement and attrition.

It's vital that leaders consider the physical space and social network implications for change initiatives. When impacted by change, the phrase for the entorhinal cortex would be, "I'm lost."

Change Journey 7
Industry: Software/Technology
I worked as the Director of Implementation at a software company. The company had been struggling financially and decided to hire a marketing consultant to help with branding and marketing strategies. I took a leave shortly thereafter to care for my husband who was diagnosed with cancer.

During my time away, the consultant lobbied to remove the Chief Operations Officer, who had led the company for over 20 years. He had built deep trust with many clients over the years.

After he left, she stepped into his role. Somehow, she'd gone from designing our logos and fonts to running operations. I believe our CEO saw her as a "go-getter" and because the executive team was anxious to have solutions, they let the scope of a basic marketing project creep into operations.

Many customers were upset with the COO's departure and even more upset about not being notified of this major change in leadership, as he had worked collaboratively with them through a range of critical projects. All of a sudden, there was a new person who they didn't know and many found it disorienting.

In her new role as COO, the consultant redesigned the software implementation process, launching a major change without soliciting the appropriate input from stakeholders. As a result, two-thirds of the subsequent implementations failed, further angering our customers.

The consultant was highly emotionally intelligent, which I believe led the CEO to think that she could solve all our problems. But unfortunately, she did not have the skills to do so successfully and it cost us several long-time clients. I ended up leaving shortly thereafter.

9. Basal Ganglia: Our Habit Factory

Another brain structure involved with any change we experience is the basal ganglia, which is responsible for taking behaviors we do frequently and turning them into habits. You constantly experience the benefits of your basal ganglia. When you learn something new, like how to use your smartphone or a piece of software, it is the basal ganglia that changes the activity from something challenging that requires a lot of concentration to something easy that you don't even have to think about.

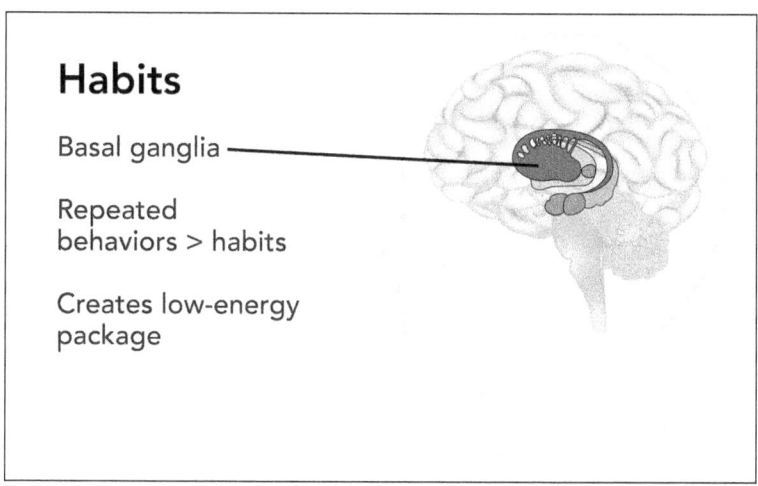

The basal ganglia and habits

Remember when you learned a new skill, like how to drive or ride a bike, cook food, manage your finances, or do a new hobby. All of these activities took focus and concentration as you learned them but after enough successful repetitions, you can probably do them on autopilot.

In work settings, some examples of your habits include how you manage your time, how you approach meetings, how you complete a project, and how you lead and manage others.

Researchers at the Brain and Cognitive Sciences department at the Massachusetts Institute of Technology discovered that the basal ganglia's purpose is to save energy, something that scientists can measure by the amount of glucose being used in the brain. Study after study shows that the more we do something, the less cognitive energy it takes and the basal ganglia is the structure that makes this happen.

Further, one 2023 study shows that as the basal ganglia manages longer chains of behaviors for complex tasks, it "allows access to the motor system in the correct order," thus reducing the likelihood of errors.

Consider how you use software or an app on your phone When you first started, you had to think about it. As the basal ganglia turns that routine into a habit, it frees up our brain and allows us to spend mental energy on other important tasks. Essentially, the basal ganglia turns repeated behaviors into habit loops. A habit loop has three parts:

- **Cue:** For example, getting in your car is the cue, or trigger, to begin the behavior of driving. Or walking into your kitchen at night is the cue to begin cooking dinner.

- **Routine:** The behavior itself. It's the act of driving: looking in mirrors, turning the steering wheel, stepping on the brake; or of chopping onions, pulling out a skillet, turning on the burner.

- **Reward:** The reward we get for completing the routine. With driving it's getting to our destination and for cooking, it's getting both the nourishment and taste of food.

Scientists have discovered that rewards are most effective when delivered immediately after completing a routine, like when we drive or cook. They get less effective the longer we have to wait after engaging in a behavior. This is why so many people struggle with getting in shape, eating healthfully, or quitting smoking. The new rewards of toned muscles, smaller clothes, or better blood pressure will be realized too far into the future, through incremental and often invisible shifts. From the brain's perspective, that's not very compelling, especially when eating healthy or working out might be a struggle at first.

Another interesting thing about rewards is that you don't have to use them forever, only until the habit loop is formed. Charles Duhigg, in his book *The Power of Habit*, shares one study of a group of people who wanted to exercise more. Split into two groups, both had the same cue (when you wake up) and routine (go for a run). But Group A was given a reward when they returned, a small piece of chocolate. They didn't do this forever; only until the habit was well formed. But the results were clear. Group A formed the habit and participants maintained the habit for far longer than those in Group B.

Think about how rarely we praise or reward people at work. Sure, you might get an annual performance review but it's likely to be a mix of praise and areas for improvement. And while it may come with a bonus, it's too removed from the completion of a routine to create a meaningful link in the brain.

James Clear, author of *Atomic Habits: An Easy and Proven Way to Build Good Habits and Break Bad Ones*, articulates what he calls the four laws of habits. The building and breaking of habits use these four laws in opposite ways.

	To Build a Habit	To Break a Habit
Law 1: Cue	Make it obvious	Make it invisible
Law 2: Craving	Make it attractive	Make it unattractive
Law 3: Response	Make it easy	Make it difficult
Law 4: Reward	Make it satisfying	Make it unsatisfying

He shares additional strategies, such as making your environment conducive to the habit you want to cultivate, and to "stack" habits by attaching a new behavior to a habit that is well-established. He also recommends investing in technology or tools that help you lock in the habit, as well as arranging an accountability partner until the habit is established.

We can all use these strategies in our personal lives, and organizations need to use them on a broader scale when trying to create behavior change among employees or customers.

The Importance of Repetitions

Another key factor is that habits are built through repetition. As you do the behavior over and over again, you build up the neural pathway to the point that scientists can see the neurons getting thicker with use. In fact, studies show that it takes 40 to 50 repetitions, on average, to establish a new habit. It's through repetition that the basal ganglia shifts the routine to be an automatic response.

Internationally renowned organist, Anna Lapwood, knows the value of repetitions and practice. Though at the top of her field, she rigorously prepares for performances and often posts videos on TikTok of the many repetitions she runs. She intentionally performs tricky sections of music multiple times until they become second nature.

If you need any more convincing about the importance of habits at work, consider the story of Rick Rescorla, a security guard who worked for Morgan Stanley at the World Trade Center in New York. After the WTC was bombed in 1993, Rescorla was upset about how disorganized the evacuation had been and he also worried that future attacks were likely given the iconic nature of the buildings. As a result, he insisted that all 2,700 employees, including senior executives, regularly practice evacuating from their offices, which occupied twenty-two floors of the South Tower. He would grab a bullhorn, and despite complaints from employees who wanted to focus on work, he would have them practice taking the stairs down.

He didn't just do this once or twice. He made them practice *every three months*. So when the unthinkable happened on September 11, 2001, and the first plane hit the North Tower, the 2,687 employees who were at work that day knew exactly what to do. Despite the terror and confusion, their practice kicked in and they got out safely. Those survivors credit Rescorla with saving their lives.

Habits and Change

Obviously, when we initiate change, we are likely to impact the well-developed habit loops that people already have in place. In all my years of consulting, I cannot think of a single change initiative that didn't require people to shift their behaviors in some profound way. Whether it's moving to a different email system, selling or marketing to a new type of client, or creating an innovative product, change involves building new habits and, worse, leaving comfortable, old habits that are easy to do and have predictable rewards.

Change requires people to focus and concentrate until they sufficiently learn the new cues and routines, which as we've seen takes time and a lot of energy, which can lead to change fatigue. In addition, we often expect people to build a new habit without offering compelling rewards for doing so. In fact, the new way usually (at least at first) takes more time and energy than the old way, which can seem more like a punishment to the brain. Is anyone really surprised, then, that so many change initiatives fail?

Let's take a common and costly example. Many companies have to make changes that affect their sales team, like shifting software or changing the way a product is marketed. Like any team, these changes will require new habits, which takes time and energy to develop. And the longer those new habits take to build, the more likely the company will see a dip in its own profit. This kind of impact may impact all the teams—engineering, HR, marketing—but for the sales teams, the potential consequence is even worse. Every minute of decreased productivity may also decrease their quota-based pay. In other words, they are likely to get paid less during the transition even while doing the same amount, or even more, work. Yikes—talk about a punishment!

For everyone, concerns about salary are likely to trigger the amygdala because money is key to our survival in modern times. We can't just go out and build a new shelter or hunt/forage for our dinner. Our paychecks allow us access to shelter, food, and water, so affecting an employee's ability to make money is not only a punishment, it's highly threatening to survival.

You would think that companies would help sales teams make the transition as quickly as possible by investing in quality training and coaching, things that help people build new habits and adjust to change. But the truth is that rarely happens. They may hold some training that provides information about the change, but not training that works with the brain to move people through the transition and develop the right habits quickly.

Habits impact your customers as well. Their habits include how they use your product, and any changes to that loop will impact how they feel about your brand, at least until they groove enough repetitions. Using the science of habit design, you can anticipate that you may hear complaints until they achieve 40 to 50 repetitions. And of course, customers may resist making the change altogether, which some companies have learned the hard way. When Target did away with their diversity, equity, and inclusion (DEI) initiatives, consumers boycotted, costing the retail chain millions. And Southwest Airlines lost many loyal travelers when they announced a new charge for luggage and the end of open seating.

We'll explore what kinds of rewards matter and to how to create effective training in future chapters but suffice it to say that the basal ganglia plays a major role in successful change, and ignoring how it works contributes to the dismal success we see with change initiatives.

During change, the basal ganglia would say, "I don't know what to do."

10. Habenula: Our Failure-Avoidance Center

Located deep in the center of our brain, near the thalamus, the habenula is responsible for decision-making and actions. It does this by creating chemical guardrails that moderate our behavior, so we don't repeat mistakes.

Our brain naturally releases dopamine and serotonin, the "feel-good" chemicals, when we do something right. This is part of the brain's reward system. You probably feel it when you accomplish a task or receive praise for a job well done. However, when we make a poor choice that does not lead to a reward, the habenula *restricts* the flow of those chemicals, cutting off the drip so to speak, making us feel bad.

The habenula's role is quite important to the survival of our species. In our hunter-gatherer days, it would help us repeat good choices like going back to the trail that led to a food source (reward), and making us uncomfortable about the trail that didn't have food. It's almost like a chemical game of "warmer/colder" or the reins on a horse, guiding us toward good choices.

In our modern world, the habenula helps us repeat successful behaviors like returning to a restaurant where we had a good meal or approaching a work project in a similar way to a previous one that turned out well. In fact, Dr. Qi Dai, a neuropsychiatrist at the University of Kyoto in Japan, found that psychological resilience is positively correlated with habenula volume.

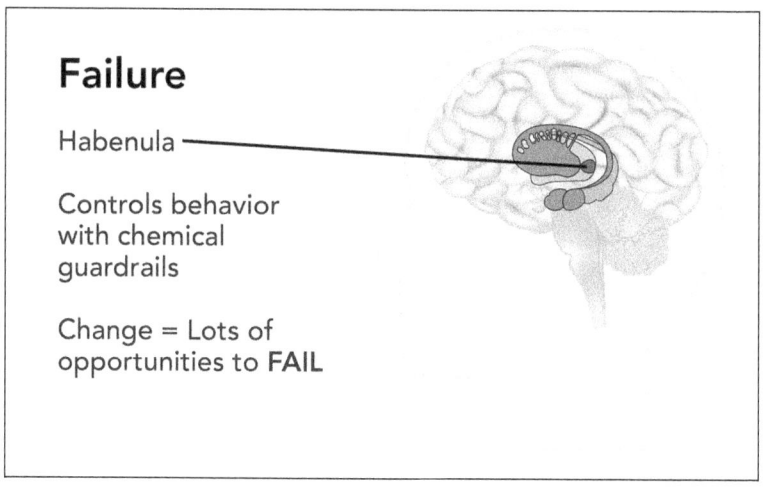

The habenula and failure

But the habenula does more than help us repeat behaviors that will bring rewards. It also helps us avoid punishment. According to Dr. Okihide Hikosaka, at the National Institutes of Health Laboratory of Sensorimotor Research, "Failing to obtain a reward is disappointing and disheartening, but to be punished may be worse." Studies have shown that the habenula is also very active when we approach a task where we have received a punishment. In fact, it suppresses not only our motivation but also our physical body movements by suppressing the motor-neurons. In other words, we don't want to do the behavior and it's more difficult to make our body do the behavior as well.

Scientists have also discovered that the habenula is hyperactive in people with severe depression, which over-restricts serotonin and dopamine so that they feel bad all the time. This is why sufferers mention having difficulty getting out of bed. It's not a euphemism—their muscles are literally struggling to activate because the habenula is suppressing the motor-neurons.

In one study published in the *2025 Current Behavioral Neuroscience Report*, researchers state, "dysfunction of the habenula plays a significant role in negative cognitive patterns, depressed emotional states, and a sense of helplessness that we attribute to an increased risk of suicide."

Stress also plays a critical role. When under sustained, uncontrollable stress, the body responds by inducing various immune responses such as increasing inflammatory chemicals. The body is essentially treating the stress as a physical threat and responding like it would to bacteria or a virus, like the flu, including suppressing motivation and motor movements. In other words, you feel tired all the time and have little energy or desire to get things done.

When we're physically sick, this response helps us to get better. It essentially forces us to rest, saving our energy so our immune system can overcome the source of the illness and return us to health. But in situations of sustained stress, it creates depression and lethargy that can go on and on.

When stress and the habenula's natural function to avoid failure come together, you can unintentionally create "learned helplessness," a concept first identified by psychologist Dr. Martin Seligman, who went on to found the Positive Psychology movement. He had been conducting experiments with dogs that were being classically conditioned by receiving a mild shock, a form of punishment, when they heard a bell. Once that conditioning was in place, he put the dogs in a room where they had freedom to move away from the source of the shock. But guess what happened? They lay down and gave up.

Seligman's research, and many subsequent studies, have shown that if we have enough negative experiences we become conditioned to expect failure and we just give up and stop trying—and here is the most important part—even when things have changed! In other words, we reach a point where we just can't motivate ourselves emotionally or physically to try anymore.

Many psychologists believe that learned helplessness is at play in all kinds of situations: people who cannot leave an abusive relationship, students who no longer try to succeed in a subject like math, people with health problems who continue to make the same unhealthy choices.

In the work setting, learned helplessness can affect people and teams. If conditions have been bad enough for long enough, change won't necessarily overcome the learned helplessness. I have seen numerous situations where a solution has been implemented, like a poor leader is replaced or more resources are provided, and the people involved don't shift to a healthier state. Clearly, this can be very confusing to leaders.

The habenula's function around failure can also be seen in a very common workplace process: the performance review. Dr. Markus Ullsperger and Dr. Yves von Cramon at the Max Planck Institute for Human Cognitive and Brain Sciences used MRI machines to view brain activity as people received feedback about their performance. When people were given negative feedback, a form of punishment, their habenulas were highly activated, creating another feel-bad experience.

No wonder employees and managers alike have come to dread the annual review process. The very process that is supposed to help people improve their performance becomes fraught with negative feelings. Performance reviews are known to kick off the amygdala's fear response as well.

Failure and Change

Understandably, the habenula is going to activate during change initiatives because change creates so many opportunities to fail. Think about all the potential "failures" for employees:
- Missing a milestone or deadline of the change plan
- Misreading new social dynamics in a way that affects a relationship
- Being tired and making mistakes in everyday tasks
- Having an emotional reaction that bothers others
- Not developing the new habits/behaviors fast enough
- Losing a job due to redundancy or poor performance

For the leaders and managers, the list includes those above as well as these additional opportunities for failure:
- Designing an ineffective change
- Miscalculating the change's costs or benefits
- Designing an ineffective change plan
- Undercommunicating or miscommunicating the change plan
- Miscalculating followers' change bandwidth
- Launching too many changes simultaneously or in succession
- Not allowing sufficient time for people to move through the change plan and the change curve
- Not preparing for the emotions of the change curve
- Not designing the right behaviors to support the change
- Not providing training that develops the right habits
- Not offering compelling rewards to motivate new behaviors and habits

Change brings opportunities to fail, and when we do, our brains and our bodies become more and more resistant to embracing future changes. I think it's likely that many of those initial negative emotions on the change curve are remnants of past failure.

Failure as an adult can also trigger some of our most painful memories of childhood failure and shame. As Dr. Brené Brown, an internationally recognized scholar on the effects of shame describes in her book *Daring Greatly*, "childhood experiences of shame change who we are, how we think about ourselves, and our sense of self-worth." Most often, children are shamed by parents and teachers when they make mistakes at home and at school.

Sadly, shaming doesn't stop when we grow up. I have seen managers attempt to "motivate" their teams by publicly shaming employees. And coworkers may use shaming as a defensive technique when their amygdala is activated. Dr. Brown's research goes on to show the profound and negative impacts of shaming in the workplace and how it harms creativity, innovation, collaboration, and productivity. If failure is combined with shame, the negative feelings will completely suppress both the motivation and willingness to try again.

I believe our previous lack of understanding about the habenula has contributed to the high failure rate of change initiatives. During change, the habenula's phrase would be, "I can't mess up."

Change Journey 8
Industry: Hospitality

I had been working as the HR Director for this small boutique hotel for almost 25 years when new, younger management came in. Instead of taking the time to learn from the existing staff, they launched several new changes that failed.

For example, they decided to move from using glassware to paper cups in the guest rooms. Not only did this create more waste, guests used many more of them during their stay, which affected the budget as well.

The new leaders also moved us to a different reservations system but did not provide any training. This set the staff up to fail, and sure enough, mistakes were made. Several guests arrived to discover that their reservation was missing, which obviously upset them. But it was also stressful for the staff who prided themselves in doing good work and now had to scramble to find a solution while managing their embarrassment that such an egregious error had occurred.

This same system impacted the housekeeping staff as rooms were often not on the list of those that needed cleaning. Again, the staff would scramble but guests were made to wait, which led to a series of bad reviews.

I was so angry because we lost guests who had been staying with us for years! It also drove a lot of turnover in positions that are not easy to fill. I ended up leaving because of the lack of communication and proper leadership.

11. The Dangerous Biological Cocktail

All four of these brain structures are individually powerful but change creates a situation where they are all likely to be activated simultaneously. The resulting biological cocktail is not easily overcome through sheer will power or inspirational leadership or training.

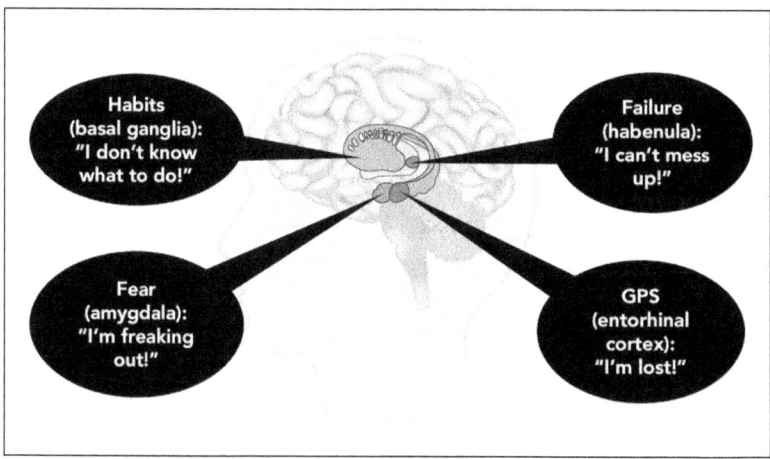

Four brain structures activated by change

It's important to remember that an employee's reaction to change is not an element of their performance. Anthony Onesto, chief people officer at Suzy, Inc., says, "Sometimes the people who are resilient and excited about a change are regarded as high-performers and leaders read the excitement as loyalty. A negative reaction to a change is biological—it doesn't mean the person is a low performer or are not committed to the organization."

Let's take a look at three very common change initiatives and how the brain plays its part. These are summaries of real situations from well-known organizations.

Scenario 1: A Thousand Small Changes

It's the second quarter and the sales team is working on its regular quarterly sales goals. It's business as usual and the team is rolling along. However, several departments in that organization have been working independently on changes that will be rolled out in Q2, each carefully designed for the lowest-possible impact on employees.

The IT department is rolling out a conversion to a different email and calendar system. While it's implemented over the weekend, it takes several weeks for people to develop the habits (basal ganglia) of the new system.

In the meantime, Facilities is continuing its yearlong rollout of new cubicles and the sales building is scheduled in Q2. While people will stay in the same building, their cubicle location and size will change as well as how much storage room they have. While the change occurs over the weekend, it still affects both habits (basal ganglia) and GPS (entorhinal cortex).

During the same quarter, Finance rolls out a new travel policy that affects meal allotments (decreased) and how receipts can be submitted for reimbursement. Several of the sales team travel to trade shows and must attend training on the new method. This change affects well-grooved habits (basal ganglia) and creates opportunities to fail (habenula), as well as a potential financial punishment for making a mistake.

The sales team, of course, experiences both change fatigue and stress as they worry that they won't hit their sales targets, affecting their income (amygdala, habenula). Collectively, all of these good changes created a negative impact.

Scenario 2: A Bunch of Medium and Large Changes

A competitor is gaining ground on market share and the executives are trying to correct the downward turn in revenue. Marketing and sales team leaders have been replaced, with the expectation that new leadership will help fix things. As a result, many employees are assigned to new managers. This disruptive change causes some anxiety (amygdala), shifts in social networks (entorhinal cortex), habits of workflow (basal ganglia), and performance (habenula).

In addition, the product team has been charged with completely redesigning the product while being reorganized into cross-functional teams. This changes supervisor relationships (entorhinal cortex), and requires embracing new ways of working (basal ganglia, habenula).

As expected, it takes time for the respective teams to adjust to these significant changes, which affects their overall performance. When the performance review process arrives, most of the affected employees receive a "meets expectations" evaluation, which impacts potential salary increases and bonuses (amygdala and habenula).

Scenario 3: A Huge, Career-Altering Change

A large global corporation purchases a small company and implements a thoughtful and robust transition plan. During the announcement, employees are both worried and excited (amygdala). During the first quarter, many redundant employees are let go and job titles are downgraded to match the acquiring company's system. Teams are split up and absorbed into different functions of the larger company, changing networks, locations, and reporting relationships (amygdala, entorhinal cortex, basal ganglia).

During the second quarter, many systems and processes shift over to those used by the purchasing company. IT switches employee computers, software, and phone systems. HR migrates to different payroll and time-tracking vendors. And Finance implements several new policies and procedures for purchasing, reimbursements, and travel. Most top-line managers are replaced with managers from the purchasing company, which changes reporting relationships and work expectations (amygdala, entorhinal cortex, basal ganglia, habenula).

By the third quarter, the purchasing company has rebranded everything with their logo, values, mission, etc., replacing coffee mugs, letterhead, and signage, and painting walls with approved brand colors (basal ganglia, entorhinal cortex).

As we consider how all of these brain structures work together, you can begin to see why, over time, people can become less flexible and adaptable to change and, worse, more anxious and worried about it. Our brains can begin to associate "change" of any kind with fear, failure, and fatigue so that it becomes a vicious cycle that impacts both employees and leaders. You could be rolling out the best-designed and most effective change your organization has ever seen, but its success depends on what else is happening or has happened in the past.

Given all this, it's actually surprising that 30 percent to 50 percent of change initiatives succeed, especially when we consider the real and compelling evidence that our brains are wired to resist change. But here's the good news: We can use the way the brain works to our advantage. The same structures that create challenges can be harnessed to create success, as we'll explore in the next section.

Your Learning Journey
Think about a few changes in your life and consider which aspects of the brain are likely to be involved.

1. Amygdala (Fear)
    - What might cause feelings of anxiety or worry?
    - What, if anything, could be perceived as threatening?
    - What can you do to create more safety?
2. Entorhinal cortex (GPS: physical space and social relationships)
    - How will physical work space or location be affected?
    - What are the impacts on relationships or social dynamics?
    - How can new physical and social maps be built?
3. Basal ganglia (Habits)
    - What new behaviors need to be developed?
    - What training/support will be provided to help build new habits?
    - How can you quickly get to 40–50 repetitions?
4. Habenula (Failure)
    - What opportunities to fail exist with this change?
    - What are the consequences of failure?
    - How can you create an experience that makes learning positive?

A NEW MODEL FOR CHANGE + TRANSITION

"Progress is impossible without change, and those that cannot change their minds cannot change anything."

George Bernard Shaw,
playwrite, *Pygmalion*

12. The Change Quest® Model: Mountains Instead of Valleys

From my research, it became clear to me that we needed a new model for understanding change that incorporated the various issues:
- The four factors: disruption, acclimation, desire, and choice
- The change curve
- Individual bandwidth
- Change fatigue and burnout
- The neuroscience of how the four brain structures respond to change (amygdala, entorhinal cortex, basal ganglia, habenula)

A comprehensive model would ideally be both diagnostic and predictive, helping distinguish between different kinds of changes and also clarifying which leadership skills are needed to successfully help people move through them.

I built the Change Quest® model to synthesize all the elements and studies we reviewed in previous chapters so that it accounts for the psychology and biology of the transition. You'll notice that my model keeps the change curve but makes three key shifts: First, I have flipped the curve upside down so that instead of looking like a descent into a valley, it shows the ascent up a mountain so its depiction better represents the physical and emotional effort that occurs when first experiencing change.

Second, the vertical axis has now switched from being a measure of productivity and morale to a measure of disruption and resistance, from low to high.

Third, in addition to integrating knowledge from several different tools, the Change Quest model is designed to be interactive, allowing you to adjust the axes (depicted as movable levers) to gain a clearer picture of how the change will be perceived and experienced by employees.

You can now dial along the vertical axis to indicate how disruptive the change is predicted to be. The more disruptive a change, the more resistance you are likely to get, and the higher the mountain, if you will, is likely to be.

The horizontal axis of time is something you can adjust as well to reflect whether a change will occur over a short (days to weeks), medium (weeks to months), or long (months to years) amount of time.

By sliding the levers, so to speak, you can more accurately diagram the disruption and acclimation elements that drive so much of the emotional transition process. You can now see that people typically move through four distinct types of change journeys that map to the red, orange, yellow, and green zones we discussed in chapter 3:
- The long, intense climb (red)
- The quick hike up a steep hill (orange)
- The long, steady trek (yellow)
- The pebble on the trail (green)

These change journeys are very different from each other, eliciting different emotions and reactions. Unlike the change curve, the Change Quest model shows variations in emotional responses for each of the major change journeys.

Finally, this model also allows you to estimate employee desire and choice, again allowing up to four options that represent their motivation. And you can also account for bandwidth and fatigue. Employees are considered travelers that leaders assist through the journey.

In this section, we'll take a closer look at each element and how you can use it to better predict and lead change.

1. The Long and Intense Climb

This hardest of the journeys most closely maps to the original change curve in terms of employee emotions. It represents a "red zone" change with high disruption and long time-to-acclimation. Examples of this type of change include a merger or acquisition or the design and launch of a new product. To employees, it might look like a steep, snow-covered peak that's hard to climb.

Because that change will be highly disruptive, it will drive more resistance so you will see the full range of challenging emotions plus the initial focus on the past and potential losses. At the peak, you have resignation, which still implies people quitting, getting on board, or leaders calling it off. If we are keeping with our mountain motif, employees would get off the top of the mountain via helicopter or gondola.

Once people make the transition of looking toward the future and potential gains, emotions become more positive and the descent contributes to more momentum and less effort.

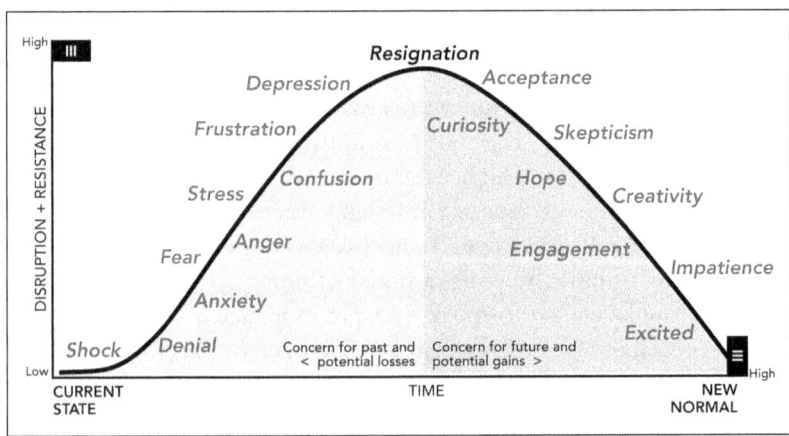

The "long and intense climb" journey

2. The Quick Hike Up a Steep Hill

This type of change still has a high amount of disruption but it will be over fairly quickly. It will require a burst of effort and focus, thus generating more resistance, especially if employees are already busy.

The sheer speed of the journey means you experience a flurry of intense emotions including resentment, overwhelm, and annoyance. But the speed also means that you can get to the peak of resignation and acceptance quicker.

Examples include migrating to a new sales software or responding to an unexpected emergency or crisis. On the backside of the peak, employees are likely to still feel overwhelm and will probably experience relief at the end.

The "quick hike up a steep hill" journey

3. The Long, Steady Trek

This type of change does not create much disruption but will unfold over a long period of time, thus requiring stamina. Because disruption is low, the workload is likely added to employees' regular duties. An example would be a new regulation that is going into effect in two years but you have time to get ready for it.

Notice that boredom is a new emotion and will need to be addressed as people can tire of the long timeframe. At the end of this journey, employees are likely to feel relief that it is over.

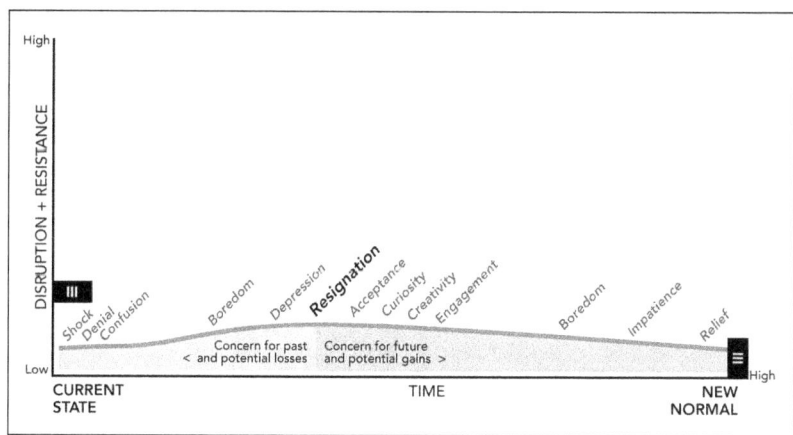

The "long, steady trek" journey

4. The Pebble on the Trail

Because it does not create disruption and is over so quickly, a pebble on the trail creates no emotional aspects to address nor does the focus on past losses or future gains come into play. An example might be that facilities changes the faucets in the bathrooms—people might not even notice that it happened. This is almost a non-event and practically invisible in the big scheme of things, unless it's added on top of several other difficult changes.

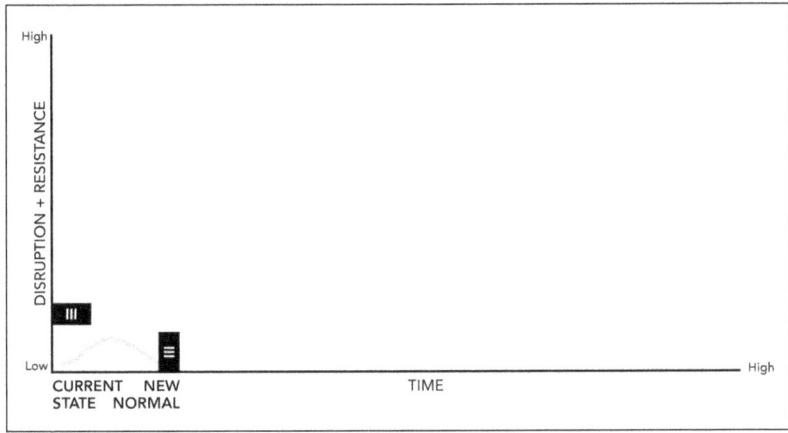

The "pebble on the trail" journey

By making this Change Quest model adjustable based on disruption and time-to-acclimation, we can now distinguish between four different types of changes. This can provide valuable guidance about the skills that leaders and managers will need to move people through that change journey.

Four types of change journeys

13. The Travelers of Change

The Change Quest model allows us to distinguish the roles and experiences of all the people involved in a change initiative. Certain people will decide that change is needed and lead the process, while others will be on the receiving end. I call them the travelers because they are going on the journey, no matter its form. Let's look at each group.

The Travelers

Several different groups can be the travelers. Perhaps you are taking your customers on a journey by making changes to your product or service, that will likely require some shift of their behavior. You might also be asking your vendors or contractors to go on a journey if you switch to a new payment processing system or implement a new policy for insurance coverage.

Your employees are the most common group of travelers. Employees play a vital role in how every change initiative unfolds. As we discussed in chapter 3, choice and desire have an important impact on employee motivation. We can almost see it as willingness to engage in the effort required and also their ability to generate and maintain forward momentum.

If employees want the change and choose it, you will have a group of people who are excited and willing to go on the change journey. They will be up for the effort required and may even run toward it with enthusiasm. It doesn't mean the change is any less disruptive or will occur more quickly, but their motivation and momentum will be self-driven and positive. Contrast that with a group who doesn't want the change nor did they choose it. They will have low motivation and momentum and will likely be resisting the change and perhaps even digging in their heels.

Managing these two groups will require very different skills and strategies. The Change Quest model allows you to assess employee motivation and convey it through the use of four people icons:

- **Runner:** Desires and chooses change (celebrating the win)
- **Walker:** Desires the change but didn't choose it (embracing the opportunity)
- **Trudger:** Doesn't desire the change but they did choose it (enduring/accepting the situation)
- **Resister:** Neither desires nor chooses the change (digging in heels)

As Peter Senge so eloquently states, "People do not resist change; they resist being changed."

Assessing employee motivation and momentum is crucial because it determines how the leaders should guide the entire rollout, beginning with how they initially communicate the change journey to their employees. The assessment should look at the group who will need to go on the journey and estimate which of the four types they will be. Perhaps they are 100 percent of the same type, like the walker who will "embrace the opportunity." Or you might have a mixed group where 50 percent are trudgers who will "endure/accept the situation" and 50 percent are resisters who will dig in their heels.

The Change Quest model helps you see how you need to engage your entire group, allowing you to better anticipate a range of reactions, attitudes, and inter-team interactions.

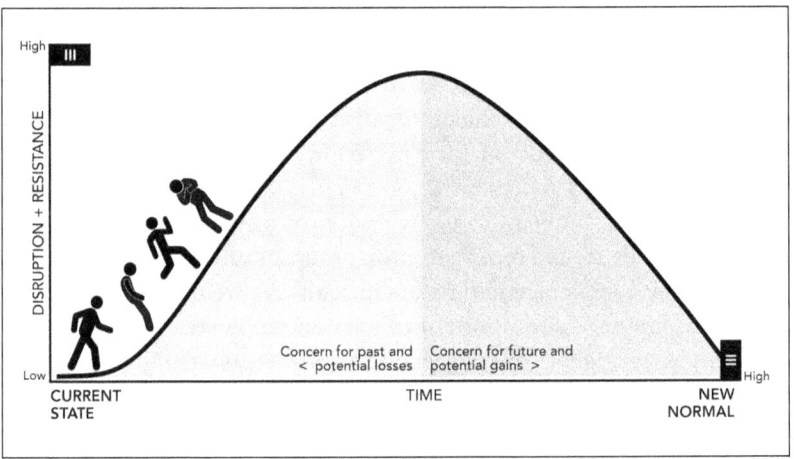

The four types of travelers on the change journey

Leader Roles: Expedition Designers, Trailblazers, and Guides

In every change initiative, a relatively small group of people are involved with both the design and implementation. Let's look at each of these key roles and how they intersect. In looking for an appropriate metaphor, my own experience on the California AIDS Ride, combined with my friend's summit of Mount Everest, gave me what I needed to clearly illustrate the differences.

Expedition Designers

The expedition designers identify that change is needed and begin to create the change. For example, the people who first conceived of the California AIDS Ride were expedition designers, and often they are involved in the early stages of fleshing out the idea.

At work, expedition designers are often the executives and senior leaders who are guiding the strategy for the future of the organization. While senior leaders/executives are often the expedition designers, they can be mid-level managers and employees, too, since sometimes ideas and plans for change come from the middle or front lines of an organization.

Expedition designers also include the people who develop the change plan. They identify the starting and ending points, plot the route, and work through all the details.

In most organizations, the designers are a group of people who collectively figure it all out. They might work together in a coordinated effort through a committee or task force, or they may hand off work to each other as they go. Obviously, designers do most of their work before travelers hear about the change. In fact, by the time a change journey launches, this group is already onto designing the next few change initiatives.

Trailblazers
Then there are the trailblazers who set the journey up for success. Trailblazers are crucial because they are responsible for putting everything in place that will allow the travelers to successfully complete the trek. For example, on Mount Everest, the trailblazers are Sherpas and every expedition has its own dedicated Sherpa group. They start their work before the travelers arrive, summiting the mountain several times as they lay the rope guides and ladders, carrying up vital supplies like oxygen tanks and food, and establishing the base camps and stops where travelers will rest.

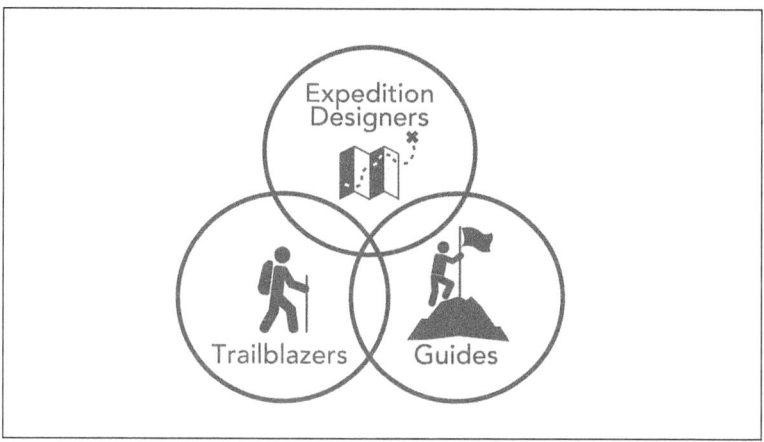

The three types of leaders for change journeys

The same system applies to, for example, a cycling event, like the California AIDs Ride or the Tour de France. The trailblazers work several months ahead of the actual events, getting everything arranged. Once the ride begins, they are several days ahead of the riders setting up the routes, signs, camps, shower trucks, medical tents, etc. Trailblazers also follow behind the travelers, dismantling and cleaning up.

In organizations, trailblazers take many forms but are mainly heads of functions and often involve key administrative services. Some change initiatives require the work of several trailblazers. For example, IT may need to do a lot of prep work to get things in place so the change initiative goes smoothly. Finance may be working with vendors, approving purchases, and allotting key resources. Learning & Development may be designing training, and Facilities may be preparing workspaces.

Guides
Finally, you have the guides, the people responsible for getting a specific group of travelers through a change journey. Whether it's a long, intense climb; a quick hike up a steep hill; or a slow, steady trek, the guides play a pivotal role in making sure their group successfully completes the change journey. Guides move with their travelers, tending to a specific group of people.

In most organizations, guides are the leaders or managers responsible for getting their team or direct reports through the change journey. Guides and trailblazers often work in tandem or side-by-side, and people in the administrative services might play both roles. For example, a director in IT or HR might be a trailblazer for the whole organization and then be a guide for their particular team of direct reports. This is difficult to do and requires a lot of effort and focus, which why some teams can experience more change fatigue than others because they are both supporting change and going through it themselves.

Each guide has a unique experience because his or her particular group of travelers has their own unique skills, competencies, and motivations. Good guides watch for and provide what their people need. I intentionally named this role the guide, rather than the leader, because sometimes guides will be out front but they are more often alongside or even behind their group, providing the right kind of support at the right time.

Leadership Failures and Successes
The success of all change journeys directly reflects how well people in these roles do their individual jobs and how well they communicate and collaborate with each other. Imagine what would happen if the designers, trailblazers, and guides on the Tour de France were not talking with each other or were not on the same page about the route and its core elements? And what if one of those key people dropped the ball and the water stations were spaced too far apart? Or cars were not blocked from driving on the route? It would be chaos and the riders would likely fail, or worse, you could have injuries and even deaths.

Many of these very issues have occurred during expeditions on Mount Everest—over 330 people have died on their way up or back from the summit. Perhaps the most notable occurred in 1996 when Everest claimed 15 lives of both expedition leaders and climbers (detailed in Jon Krakauer's *Into Thin Air* and *The Climb* by Anatoli Boukreev). Another deadly year was 2023 with 18 deaths spread across multiple expeditions.

While most organizational change journeys are not life threatening, the chaos that comes from poorly designed change or ill-prepared leaders costs billions of dollars, harms employee engagement, and can endanger customer loyalty. And some change initiatives, such as those in healthcare or manufacturing industries, can absolutely threaten life and limb.

Let's consider the tragic decline of Boeing, once an example of best practices for workplace culture and engineering excellence. In 2001, Boeing relocated its headquarters from Seattle to Chicago and underwent organizational changes that had profound implications for safety. Executives shifted focus to financial performance and launched cost-cutting measures that undermined the engineering-driven culture and ultimately impacted product safety and quality.

Two fatal crashes of the 737 MAX aircraft killed a total of 346 people traveling on flights with Lion Air and Ethiopian Airlines. This led to a 20-month global grounding of that specific aircraft and intense scrutiny at Boeing as several investigations and lawsuits ensued. Findings indicated several design flaws and insufficient pilot training. Besides the tragic loss of life, Boeing lost more than $80 billion between fines, legal fees, compensation, and canceled orders.

But troubles continued for Boeing in 2024 when an Alaska Airlines flight experienced a mid-flight incident as a door plug blew out of the 737 MAX-9. Inspectors discovered missing records and security footage, further highlighting concerns that Boeing had not made court-ordered changes. Boeing recently plead guilty to criminal charges for the deaths and the Department of Justice ordered them to fully fund an independent safety compliance program.

Fortunately, with insight and the right preparation, change journeys can be successful. Consider this great example from T-Mobile. The executives (expedition designers) wanted to become known for their customer service and set about to create an intentional culture shift that would drive the right values and habits among their employees. They planned to measure success by the number of JD Power Awards they won. Leaders drove a clear and consistent narrative with two transparent goals of increasing customer satisfaction and revenue.

One team of trailblazers across the organization supported the initiative. HR coordinated performance management, expecting every employee to have at least one quarterly goal that was customer focused. Leaders created accountability by expecting every director to spend two weeks per year in a call center and two more weeks in a retail center. These expectations were consistently enforced.

To create a culture of recognition, marketing printed blue poker chips that said "#1" on one side and "The Customer Is Why" on the other. Bowls of chips were visible in every office and people gave them to each other to acknowledge effort and improvement.

Extensive training for guides and travelers focused on the core values and behaviors that would support success. Every year, people could nominate employees who exemplified the values for the "PEAK award." The executives selected 150 annual winners who were treated to an all-expenses-paid trip to Hawaii where they celebrated together. Given this well-thought-out and executed plan, it's not surprising that T-Mobile not only hit their targets, they exceeded them. In 2024, T-Mobile celebrated their 27th award, winning first place in customer care for the 13th consecutive time!

Other recent examples of successful leadership:
- Many UK companies transitioned to the four-day work week, leading to 50 percent improvement in productivity, reduction in employee turnover, and an annuals savings to employees of £3,233.

- Executives at French advertising and PR agency, Publicis Groupe, launched a new technology strategy to upskill employees using AI tools and a centralized platform for data insights. As a result, they drove increased success for their clients, and achieved industry-leading growth (doubling their market cap from $10.5 to $28 billion).

- Medical device company, Phillips, is recovering from a massive recall by investing in improving processes and changing the culture. They are prioritizing product safety, leading to improvements in quality standards. As a result, they are retaining customer trust while minimizing long-term revenue losses.

- In 2015, Brazilian company Magazine Luiza (AKA Magalu), a chain of retail stores had lost 94 percent of its value. But it successfully transformed into a digital company, using an omnichannel strategy, creating unique shopping experiences like digital kiosks, a digital influencer (Lu), and streaming playlists for consumers. It's now valued at over $22 billion, an increase in stock price by 22,000 percent!

Leadership makes a difference and having people in the right roles with the best skills is paramount. In sections IV and VI, we'll focus on additional tips and strategies for both leaders and travelers.

Change Journey 9
Industry: Info Technology
Computers had just started finding their way into schools in Scotland. As the Head of New Technology in my school, I had just installed networks in three computer rooms and we were established as a new department, like Math and History. Like all the other subjects, we were timetabled to have the students in our labs for a one-hour session per week, to learn how computers were used in the real world.

Well, I thought that was rubbish—instead, I wanted to teach them how to use computers for real tasks. My suggestion to the senior management team was that instead of us boring the kids about how computers were used, we would simply act as a resource while the teachers of other subjects taught their regular classes in our labs. I proposed that my staff and I would facilitate, advising on features in the software being used, and sorting out small technical difficulties.

Unfortunately, this proposal was not embraced and if I wanted to succeed, I needed to assess the nature of the resistance and address it directly.

First, there was resistance among the leaders, who felt that having two teachers with one class was a waste of staffing resources. Next, there was staff resistance as many of the teachers did not want to give up one hour per week of their preparation time. Third, there was a lack of understanding of the benefits of the change, including my own IT staff!

I had to solve the last one first because, if I could get the benefits across, the other resistances would be easier to solve. I used part of an in-service day to present my plan to department heads including the benefit to students, the advantages to their departments/subjects, and how it would be implemented. Teachers really care about the learning and well-being of their students albeit through the lens of their own subject and their belief of its primacy of its importance in humanity. (Just try having a chat with a math teacher as to why factorising a quadratic might not be the most useful thing for a student who is clearly besotted with languages.)

That session resolved two of the issues, but management still didn't see the need to commit staff resources (teachers) to a job that was already covered by my staff. Then, a fortunate accident occurred.

I was speaking at the annual Management of Information Technology in Education (MITE) conference at a national teacher training college. I spoke on this same topic—the need to spread technology across the curriculum, the benefits for doing so, and the barriers in the way. My manager happened to be in attendance and, at the break, he thrust through a group of other senior managers who were patting my back while making job offers and said, "I understand now. Let's get this done tomorrow."

This new approach worked amazingly well. It was great watching the students drafting and re-drafting essays, creating amazing artwork, researching World War I for history, and a myriad of other fruitful tasks, rather than listening to boring old me telling them how to change a font or insert an image. Yes, those things were accomplished too, but only because the students wanted (passionately wanted!) to add some glorious finishing touches to their work.

Word got around and other schools adopted our method. As a result, I was appointed as a Staff Tutor for Glasgow, driving new initiatives across almost 50 schools. Looking back on this success, I believe the key elements in change management are:

1. Hearing the objections and understanding the stakeholders' points of view.
2. Addressing those issues in the context of how this makes the achievement of their core objectives easier and more successful.
3. Converting influential leaders to the cause.

14. Mapping Multiple Journeys

As you know, modern change is constant and fast paced, and in reality that means people are often going through several change journeys simultaneously. We can use the Change Quest model to map what that looks like as well: With time running along the horizontal axis, perhaps broken into quarters, you can map your team's changes. This allows you to identify possible problem areas.

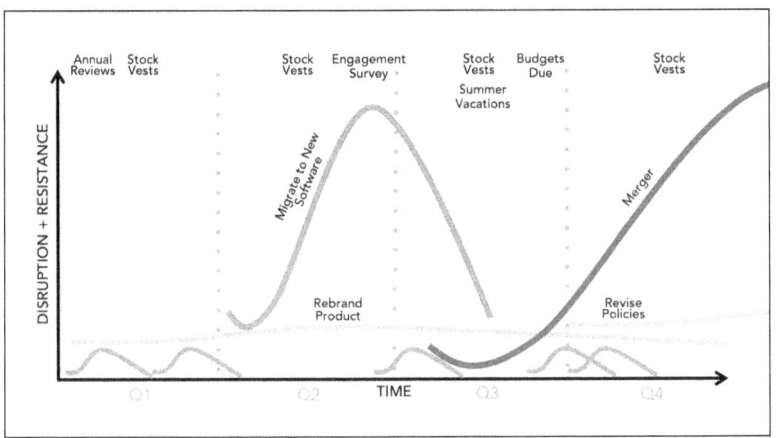

One team's multiple change journeys over a year

In the example above, the beginning of Q3 is going to be an intense time for this team. They will be cresting a quick hike up a steep hill; halfway through a long, steady trek; sidestepping a pebble on a trail, which might not feel so little at this point; and starting on a long, intense climb. And just a few weeks later, they will add two more pebbles and another long, steady trek just as resistance is building for the long, intense climb. This is important information for the leaders and managers of this team to see. They can now anticipate when the group might be feeling overwhelmed and likely to exhibit signs of stress and change fatigue. They can also see when their leadership and guidance will be most needed. Clearly, they should not be planning their vacations for August!

I recommend that leaders also layer on elements related to the rhythm of their business, such as peak production periods, performance reviews, engagement surveys, and stock vestitures. This brings additional insights that might cause them to rethink the timing of certain change initiatives or realize they will need to bring on more resources like staffing or administrative support.

For example, if they typically launch their major new product campaign in October, the leaders can see that the heavy lifting of that work will occur when the team is holding a long, intense climb plus two long, steady treks. If the team is experiencing change fatigue as well as high disruption and resistance, how creative can you expect them to be? It might or might not be an issue, but now it can be flagged and addressed.

The model can also be used to give you a view across the organization. By seeing the various types of changes rolling out for each function, you can identify potential challenges and where inter-departmental relationships or collaboration might be impacted.

Mapping change across the organization

It can also give you a sense of bandwidth. In this example above, the bandwidth of the product team is going to be pushed several times during the year. It is likely that January and February as well as April through August will be more intense for the team. Whereas the marketing team will be pushed July through November if these current changes stay where they are anticipated.

When teams are maxing on their bandwidth, you are likely to see more reactive emotions, which can create miscommunication and conflict. If these two teams have to work together in July or August, the leaders of both groups will need to provide a lot of support and guidance or better yet, shift some of these pressures beforehand to create better balance.

Change Traffic Control

This mapping exercise usually brings to light something really important. Most of the time, leaders are surprised to see how much change is happening at any given period of time. This is especially true for larger organizations where there are multiple departments driving change.

It's very typical that Facilities is rolling out space planning changes that affect where people work. This could include moving to a new location, remodeling to an open-concept work area, or changing lighting and desk height.

Separately, HR is driving changes for talent development, perhaps revising the performance review process or redesigning the org structure in ways that change who people report to. IT could be upgrading to a new data platform that everyone uses to track hours and vacation or switching to a different system of productivity tools for file sharing. Finance could be moving to a new purchase order system or vendor approval process. They could be adding or taking away perks and benefits or instituting new processes and procedures. Marketing might be targeting a new customer, with implications for global operation, languages, and currencies. The list goes on and on.

The point is, while these changes have been designed to help the business, poor timing might create a ripple effect of problems that undermine the very goals the business is trying to achieve, or the problem that it's trying to solve. We have all lived through examples of good changes gone bad. A key training is scheduled when the sales team is in their end-of-year push or IT changes the software a week before a major product rollout to customers.

This is why I recommend that your organization appoint a person to serve as the air traffic controller of change, much like the role at airports who keep planes from crashing into each other. If someone is responsible for tracking changes and considering possible challenges and unintended consequences, the more likely you are to stop an unnecessary disaster. This person should also leverage all available data analytics. For example, you already have a process for entering a new reporting relationship. What if that process could flag when a person or team has had two manager changes in a short period of time? You already have a method for tracking where people work and could flag excessive workplace shifts. You get the idea.

Once someone is tracking and mapping, it becomes easy to identify small shifts that can make all the difference. Sometimes, combining two changes together can be a great solution. Sometimes delaying or moving a change by a few weeks can have a profound effect on its success.

It's not unlike how we can track weather and create an early warning system. The change traffic controller can quickly become a vital role in every organization because she or he can help identify potential challenges—and help ensure sure that employees and leaders are prepared for what is coming.

Change Journey 10
Industry: Marketing

We are a fast-growing company and we have several capable leaders pushing out change in their part of the business. But when we took a holistic look at all the change happening in our organization, we were really surprised by what we learned.

We mapped several change initiatives that included a new enterprise resource planning (ERP) software launched by HR, a relocation of certain departments by Facilities, a switch to a different email by IT, and a new product launch designed to help us regain some lost market share. This is all in addition to our regular work of keeping the doors open.

We saw that our marketing team was going to be impacted by ALL of these changes within a span of a few weeks. And this was on top of the recent arrival of a new chief marketing officer who was already making big

> changes to their structures and processes. We realized that unless we made some shifts, this team would surely go into change fatigue and we could lose some of our best people during a very critical time for the business.

The COVID-19 Pandemic

To see the Change Quest model in action, let's reflect on the COVID-19 pandemic, as it was an experience we all shared around the world. Clearly, it was a change that we did not choose, nor did we want. And individually, we were all already in the middle of various change journeys, both professional and personal.

The pandemic qualified as both a Quick Hike Up a Steep Hill and a Long, Intense Climb. The immediate response to stop the spread of the virus and limit the death toll is the quick hike part. And it's also a long, intense climb because the aftereffects of the death toll, job loss, economic recession, and burnout lasted for months and will continue to for years to come.

When lockdowns were announced, people resisted the imposition that drastically changed daily life, and various levels of government responded with declarations and consequences to force compliance. While we largely acquiesced, we still went through all the emotions of the change curve, feeling some of them more keenly without the distractions of our daily routines.

But once resigned to the change, we started to look to the future and search for potential gains. Some people moved to be closer to family, others decided to change careers, and many used their freed-up time to pursue new hobbies like baking bread or home improvement. And many also focused on learning new skills with the explosion of online learning opportunities. Anant Agarwal, CEO of the edX platform stated, "We saw a 15-fold, not 15 percent, increase in the number of new learners."

Because the virus threatened our survival, our amygdala was highly active causing us to feel a lot of anxiety, fear, and even panic. For an intense time, we engaged in social distancing, disinfected our mail and groceries, and built temporary hospitals. To manage the unknown, many obsessively read the news, hoarded toilet paper, and overworked to the point of burnout.

However, because we are also wired to belong, we cared about others in ways we had not in a long time. We made sacrifices to protect the most vulnerable among us, and we helped each other in new and innovative ways. Sadly, many of us adapted to lives without our loved ones, lost jobs, and suffered the lingering effects of burnout, which impacted mental health.

But while we are wired to resist change, we are also wired to adapt and often disasters usher in a period of innovation and closer connection. In fact, our current hospital system grew out of the 1918 Spanish Flu pandemic.

I write in depth about how the pandemic reshaped the culture of work in my last book, *Wired to Become: The Brain Science of Finding Your Purpose, Creating Meaningful Work, and Achieving Your Potential.* When humans experience trauma, we can respond in one of two ways. Post-traumatic stress disorder (PTSD) occurs when the body gets trapped in a cycle of reliving trauma, often through ongoing fight-flight-freeze cycles that may bring on anxiety, flashbacks, and depression. Some respond by rejecting reality altogether, making them vulnerable to disinformation campaigns, conspiracy theories, and propaganda.

In contrast, post-traumatic growth, or PTG, is the other way people can respond to difficult circumstances. PTG is a positive psychological change that results from struggling with a highly challenging life circumstance. And during the pandemic, we saw a large part of the world population go through this healthy and adaptive response.

Studies show that PTG occurs on two levels: with a person, at the individual level, and at the level of the organization. It forces people and organizations to evaluate their priorities, creatively adapt in the moment to become stronger and more flexible than before, and to develop a greater appreciation for people.

Post-traumatic growth gives us hope that trauma, while both difficult and painful, can be a source of powerful growth allowing us to heal and thrive once more. In fact, it can even be the catalyst to becoming better than we were before—transformed in a powerful way.

Your Learning Journey

Take a few moments to apply these concepts to changes coming your way in the next 12 months.

- Map them out on a timeline. Which type of change journey best represents each of the changes you will be going through? Is it a pebble on the trail; a long, steady trek; a quick hike up a steep hill; or long and intense climb?
- Next, consider your motivation for each of the change journeys and give each one the stick figure that best represents your desire and choice. Are you running or walking toward it, trudging through it, or resisting it?
- Identify who the players are for each journey. Who designed each expedition? Which people are serving as trailblazers? Who will be your guide? And who are your fellow travelers?
- Consider how you might track and address the impact of too many change journeys arriving at one time. How could you create an "air traffic controller" system to prevent change fatigue and burnout?
- How did the pandemic impact your life? Did you find yourself reflecting on your values and priorities? Have you experienced post-traumatic growth as an individual? If so, how are you better or stronger than before?
- Have the organizations you work with experienced post-traumatic growth? Why or why not?

IV

THRIVING THROUGH CHANGE: STRATEGIES FOR SUCCESS

"Every great dream begins with a dreamer. Always remember, you have within you the strength, the patience, and the passion to reach for the stars to change the world."

Harriet Tubman,
American abolitionist and social activist

15. Tips for Travelers

Throughout your working life, you will be in the role of traveler many times. We all find ourselves on the receiving end of change journeys, many of which we did not choose and may not want. Even top executives must respond to requests by their shareholders and demands of the market, not to mention regulatory bodies and climate change.

But every traveler has the opportunity to thrive through change, even difficult changes that are foisted on you despite your protests. Let's look at how you can empower yourself to move through all kinds of changes with ease.

Do an Inventory

First thing, take stock of your situation. By taking a few moments to assess things, you will be better prepared to respond to many different changes.

1. Consider what kind of change is coming your way. How much disruption it is likely to cause? Does it impact how and where you will do your work? Does it impact your team of colleagues and relationship network? Will it require new skills and habits? Do you have to give up well-grooved habits? This information will help you plot along the vertical axis of the change journey and estimate how high a peak you can expect to climb. Look at how long it will take to acclimate to the change (not just getting over the major hump of the change but to complete it, getting to the new normal). It is weeks? Months? Or even years?

2. Add at least 50 percent to your estimate. I'm not kidding. Give yourself a good healthy cushion because even your leaders cannot accurately predict what the change is going to look like and if you estimate high, you won't be thrown when their estimates are off. It's not uncommon for workplace initiatives to take twice or even three times the estimated resources and time. If you've given yourself a cushion, you won't be thrown by it.

3. From your newly adjusted assessment of disruption and acclimation, determine which of the four change journeys you are embarking on. The long, intense climb (red), the quick hike up a steep hill (orange), a long, steady trek (yellow), or a pebble on the trail (green). Since it's likely that the small, slight obstacle of a pebble is not keeping you up at night, I'm only going to focus on the other three as we continue.

4. Map the next 12 months for all the change journeys you will be traveling. This includes those at work and those at home because we do not have two brains or two bodies. Your change bandwidth will be tapped into by all changes, professional and personal, so map them on the same timeline to get the bigger view. Don't forget to note some "rhythm of business" elements like annual reviews and budget submissions and some "rhythm of life" elements like birthdays, vacations, and taxes.

5. For each change journey, choose the stick figure that represents your change motivation: If it's something you choose and desire, use the running figure. If it's something you want but did not choose, use the walker. Or you can use the trudger or resister. This is also a great time to consider if you can shift your attitude about a change. Can you find something to look forward to, a possible gain that might motivate you? Will it be an opportunity to develop a new skill or make new friends? You can actually do a lot to shift your orientation by choosing to look for something good or positive. Try it and see if you can shift some of your stick figures from one type to another.

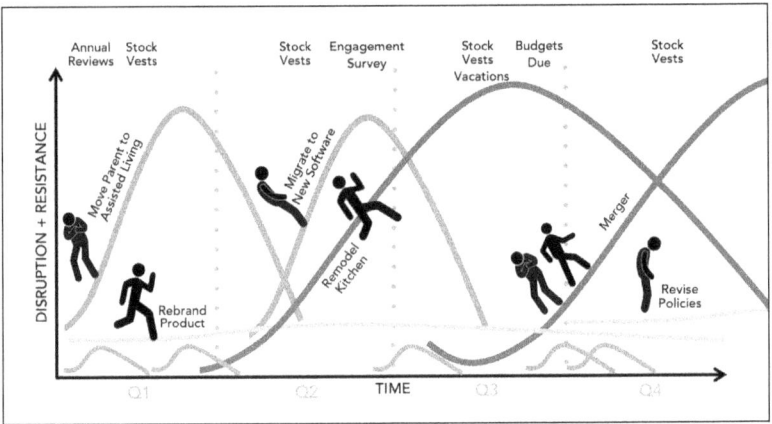

Taking stock of personal and professional changes

6. In the yearlong view, when will you be carrying the most changes (full bandwidth)? This is likely when you will experience change fatigue. Also, note when things will be lighter, as these are moments of possible rest and recovery. Most importantly, can you make any adjustments? I can't tell you how helpful this view has been for me and the groups I work with. Just by seeing the big picture, you can identify where things are stacking up and sometimes, you can shift something by just a few weeks, which makes all the difference.

7. After you have adjusted what you can, the final step is to circle or highlight the times when things are going to be the most intense. These are the times when you need to be intentional about how you support yourself so you can thrive.

A Powerful Troika of Support: Self-Care, Mindfulness, and Play

Once you have taken stock of your change journeys, you can intentionally mitigate the effects. Remember, the brain science of change tells us that our amygdala will perceive change as dangerous, kicking up fear and anxiety. Here comes Chicken Little! We might also feel lost, especially if the change will impact our physical space or social networks, causing our entorhinal cortex to do extra work to build new maps. If we have to learn new skills or habits, our basal ganglia will need some time to get enough repetitions to build a new automated habit. And finally, if we experience failure, our habenula is going to suppress good feelings and possibly even physical movement.

Keep in mind, change in general brings up some predictable worries for people. Dr. David Rock, of the NeuroLeadership Institute, created the SCARF Model that shows the five areas that people focus on, particularly when under stress. They are:

- **Status:** Our sense of importance in relation to others
- **Certainty:** Our ability to predict the future
- **Autonomy:** Our sense of control over events
- **Relatedness:** A measure of our trust of others
- **Fairness:** Our perception of how fair or equal things are

According to Rock's research, humans naturally sort for these, and they are wired to move toward experiences that improve these aspects and away from those that threaten them.

I had a firsthand experience of the SCARF model during the acquisition by LinkedIn. As I was feeling emotions like fear, excitement, anxiety, confusion, and hope, I realized that the source was status, certainty, etc. One minute, I'd be excited about my new role and the next I was worrying I would report to someone my junior. One moment, I would be curious about the team I was joining and the next I was stressed they wouldn't get who I am and what I bring to the table.

Even though I understood what I was going through (I teach this stuff!), I couldn't help myself from having these thoughts and worries. The power of our biology is stronger than education, experience, and expertise combined.

The only thing that got me through the crazy year was using what I call the powerful troika of support. Because I was going through an intense bevy of change journeys, I knew it was on me to take care of myself if I was to be my best through it all. That's not to say I was awesome, however. I had anxious and cranky days—but whatever state I was in, I know it was ten times better than I would have been without the troika of self-care, mindfulness, and play.

Self-Care

This includes the basics: good nutrition, sufficient sleep and exercise. We all know these are good things to do for our bodies but during times of stress, they become even more important.

As I mentioned in chapter 10 on the habenula, a body responds to stress as if it's being attacked and our immune system tries to fight the invisible foe like it would the flu. In fact, I liken starting on a change journey to the beginning of flu season. When flu season starts, most of us make choices to strengthen our immune systems. We eat more veggies and cut back on sugar. We exercise, which actually increases serotonin, the feel-good chemical. And we try to get more quality sleep.

Sleep should not be underrated as a tool in your self-care arsenal. Harvard Medical School has an entire division dedicated to "sleep medicine" and the profound effect sleep has on mood, focus, and mental performance among other things. The Centers for Disease Control and Prevention report that not getting enough sleep is linked to a range of chronic conditions including diabetes, obesity, and depression.

Further, a study published in *Science* magazine estimated that even one extra hour of sleep can boost happiness, especially for people who are not getting enough. Better sleep has been associated with weight loss, enhanced creativity, and better performance at work.

In her book *Brain Science for Principals*, Dr. Linda Lyman outlines the crucial role that sleep plays in how we move new learning into memory, a topic I also cover in my book *Wired to Grow*. In fact, the National Institutes of Health state "Sleep deficiency can cause problems with learning, focusing, and reacting. You may have trouble making decisions, solving problems, remembering things, controlling your emotions and behavior, and coping with change." Most change requires new learning so sleep not only helps us address the stress of change but helps us build new habits more quickly.

Beyond sleep, it's important to make sure that you're getting the various types of rest. Dr. Saundra Dalton-Smith has identified seven different types. You can learn more by watching her TEDx talk but here's a quick summary of the seven types she identifies:

- **Physical rest:** This includes all forms of sleep, including naps, massages, and active rest like yoga.

- **Mental rest:** Taking a break from thinking about work or life's worries. This can include taking a quick walk or vegging out with some TV.

- **Sensory rest:** This involves creating a calm and tranquil environment so we can get a break from all the sensory input (visual, auditory, olfactory, and kinesthetic) that we are barraged with every day, including unplugging from our digital devices.

- **Creative rest:** This is not about doing art or being good at it; creative rest is any activity that you do for enjoyment that lets you express yourself. It can also include appreciating beauty and art, and surrounding yourself with things that inspire you.

- **Emotional rest:** This happens when we take a break from people pleasing and just focus on being authentically ourselves. For some, this happens alone or with pets; for others it may include trusted friends.

- **Social rest:** We rest socially when we're with people who genuinely care about us and get who we are. After spending time with people you can socially rest with, you will likely feel recharged rather than drained.

- **Spiritual rest:** However you define "spiritual" for yourself, this type of rest includes things that open your heart, connect you with a sense of community, and give you a sense of purpose. For some this includes a religious tradition or a practice like prayer or mindfulness.

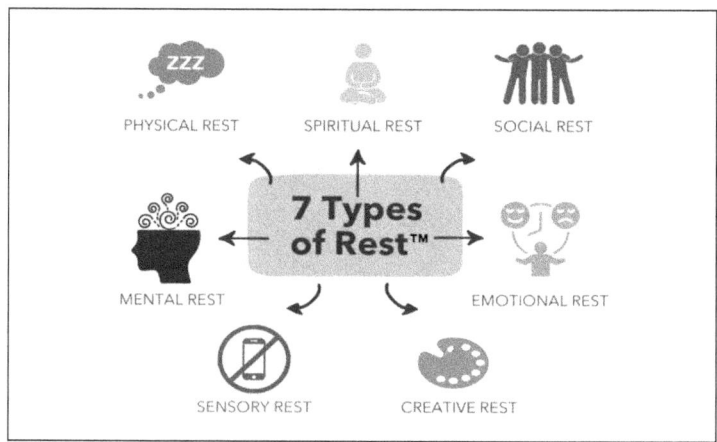

The seven types of rest

Mindfulness

Another way we prepare for flu season is getting a flu shot, which inoculates us against the harmful effects of the virus. Mindfulness inoculates us against the harmful effects of change and can be an antidote for the stress that often accompanies change. Whether it's meditation, yoga, being present, or expressing gratitude, mindfulness plays a powerful role in our brains. There is a reason that every wisdom tradition since the beginning of history purports some type of mindfulness practice.

Dr. Richard Davidson, Professor and Director of the Waisman Laboratory for Brain Imaging and Behavior at the University of Wisconsin, studies the effects of mindfulness on the brain. He uses MRI technology to compare the brains of long-time meditators, like Tibetan monks, to people who have never meditated, and those who have just done their first-ever meditation. The results are astounding. Meditating even one time permanently changes the brain in a measurable way. He details more benefits in his book *The Emotional Life of Your Brain*.

His groundbreaking research has shown that people who meditate are able to focus longer, they are less likely to worry about future events, and when something stressful does happen, they experience less distress in the moment and return quickly to their normal state. Another study by Dr. Sara Lazar at the Harvard University Medical School found that a daily mindfulness practice actually shrinks the amygdala, making it less reactive in as little as eight weeks.

In addition, several studies have shown that both gratitude and mindfulness make the brain more receptive to learning, which is vital during change, as we gain new skills and habits. Dr. Alex Korb synthesized some of the key findings on gratitude in his *Psychology Today* article titled "The Grateful Brain: The Neuroscience of Giving Thanks." Studies have shown that intentional gratitude practices boost attention, determination, and enthusiasm and reduce anxiety, depression, and physical ailments.

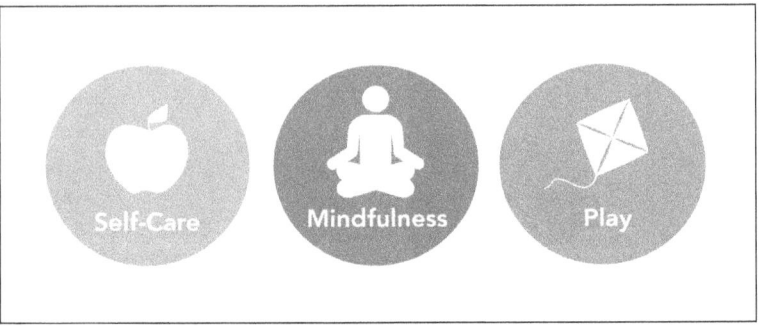

Powerful tools for thriving through change

Because of these and many other compelling studies, I also began a daily meditation practice of 15 minutes per day. I have seen a huge shift in my own reactivity and ability to manage all kinds of stress, including change. If you have not yet explored mindfulness, I encourage you to check it out. A simple online search will get you a list of local classes in your area, online videos, books, and apps for your devices. I personally use the 21-day series by Deepok Chopra as well as Desk-Yogi.com, which also includes videos on other important wellness topics. A lot of companies are buying Desk-Yogi for their employees so it's something you can suggest to your HR department.

Time magazine recently published a special edition completely dedicated to mindfulness ("Mindfulness: The New Science of Health and Happiness"), which compiled the latest studies on mindfulness practices with tips about how to incorporate them into your everyday routine. It gives the details on how mindfulness improves health, including lowering or reducing anxiety, blood pressure, and weight, and increasing or improving happiness and sleep. It also showcases companies who have integrated mindfulness into the workplace like Google, LinkedIn, and the Huffington Post.

Play

Studies show that people who play are more adaptive, innovative, and have more positive relationships. And the benefits don't just stop there. According to the National Institute for Play, play is vital for human health and well-being. It generates optimism, spurs curiosity, fosters empathy, cultivates perseverance, and leads to mastery. Conversely, societies, families, and other cultures that maintain a prolonged deprivation of play experience increased depression, stress-related diseases, addictions, and interpersonal violence.

Creativity and play also go hand in hand. When we play, we let ourselves move into a physical and emotional state that allows our creativity to flow more naturally. Our logical and analytical networks take a break so our brain can start making all kinds of insightful connections.

Neuroscience has demonstrated that playful environments powerfully shape the cerebral cortex, the part of the brain where the highest level of cognitive processing takes place. So, it makes sense that not playing much stifles creative energy. Dr. Stuart Brown, author of *Play: How It Shapes the Brain, Opens the Imagination, and Invigorates the Soul* has identified seven patterns of play. Consider your experiences with each, from childhood to adulthood:

- **Attunement play:** This occurs between infants and their parents/caregivers. As they look at each other, they naturally smile and connect, becoming attuned to each other.

- **Body play:** This occurs through movement and is how we learn to coordinate our bodies. Children naturally enjoy this process and, as we grow, we expand to more complex movement like sports and dance with increasing precision and control.

- **Object play:** This is how we play with things. It begins with simple things like banging on a pan or bouncing a ball and increases in complexity as we develop dexterity. Video games, painting, and cooking are forms of object play.

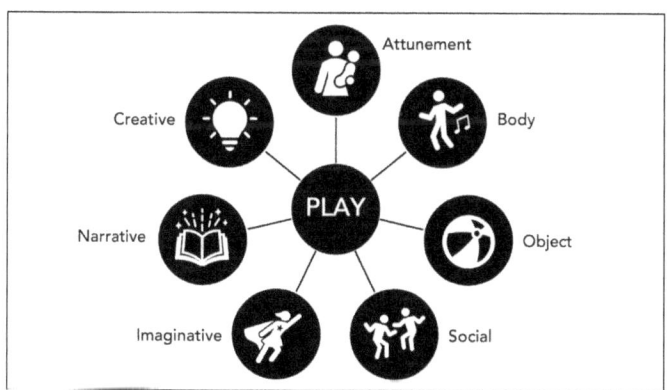

The seven patterns of play

- **Social play:** What we do with others for fun. From simple hide-and-seek and wrestling to complex group games, social play creates the base for interpersonal relationships, collaboration, and empathy.

- **Imaginative play:** This is the source of much creativity. It starts with simple pretend play in childhood, as we take on characters (for example, firefighter or teacher) and extends to fantastical creations of made-up worlds, friends, languages, and situations.

- **Narrative play:** This involves storytelling and is how we make sense of the world and our place in it. Storytelling is part of every culture and allows us to cross concepts of time and space as well as access various emotional states.

- **Creative play:** This occurs when we use our sense of fantasy or imagination to transcend or transform what is currently known to a new state. Musicians and dancers often use creative play to develop new works. Einstein was known for using this kind of play to consider unproven scientific ideas.

Play has healing properties as well. Charlie Hoehn, author of *Play It Away: A Workaholic's Cure for Anxiety*, used to suffer from intense and debilitating panic attacks. He found that play was a big part of his healing process.

So find a way to build more play into your life. It can be simple and solitary or complex and collaborative. The most important thing: make it fun. You should have a good play session at least once per week, and more is better.

If you need more motivation, consider this quote by Brian Sutton-Smith:

"The opposite of play is not work. It's depression."

16. Be an Active Participant

In addition to the powerful troika, one of the most important ways to ensure you thrive during change is to become an active participant in the journey. If you stay passive and let the change "be done" to you, the brain's natural resistance will take over. And that doesn't benefit you in the long run because it increases anxiety and fatigue, and decreases the feel-good chemicals. This harms your health and well-being both at work and when you're off the clock.

If you can find a way to turn toward the change with a "Let's do this!" attitude, you can now engage in problem-solving, turn on your creativity, and feel more empowered. You also can do a better job of getting what you need to thrive. If you need to develop skills in this area, read the book *Positive Intelligence* by Stanford professor, Dr. Shirzad Chamine. His science-based approach can help you master all kinds of situations—check out PositiveIntelligence.com.

While I would love to promise you that your leaders and managers are going to do a great job, we know that you might end up with an inexperienced expedition designer or an inept guide. (If you do, please buy them a copy of this book.) But don't let their competence get in the way of your experience.

Here are my ten tips for being an active participant in your journey:

1. **Learn about the journey:** Once change is announced, find out all that you can so that your brain can begin processing the news. The sooner you orient yourself to the journey and your role as a traveler, the easier it will become.

2. **Ask questions:** If you need more information, ask for it. If something is not clear, ask for clarity. In the next chapters I share things leaders can do to create successful change. I encourage all travelers to read those sections too because it will supply you with good questions to ask or suggestions to make, especially if your guide is not proactively addressing them.

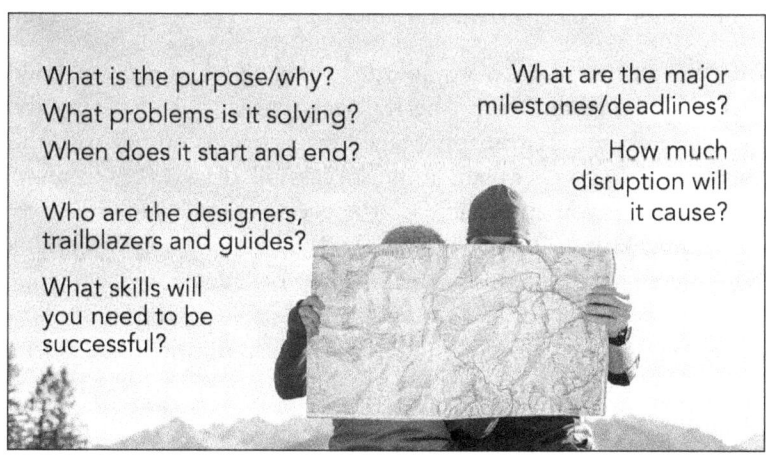

Ask questions to learn about the journey

3. **Find your own purpose:** Your ability to be motivated and happy will increase if you can create your own meaningful purpose for the journey. Find a way to convert the change to something that matters to you.

4. **Partner up:** You are not the only one going through this change so find a trek buddy or create a team. You will all benefit from sharing information, leaning on each other, and cheering each other's successes.

5. **Build a roadmap:** Most change plans are long, detailed documents that aren't really helpful. Create your own visual map of the journey. Draw the milestones, the steep sections, and the resting places. This can be fun (and enlightening) to do with your travel team as well.

6. **Gamify the experience:** The reward part of our brain loves games and prizes. Gold stars and high fives matter. Find a way to turn the journey into a series of levels that you earn points or stars for completing, and give yourself cool rewards for hitting milestones. This can be a great thing to do with coworkers. You can even turn a negative experience into something fun. For example, before the holidays my friends and I play "dysfunctional family bingo." We make a bingo card with all the things we hope won't happen like "Uncle George comments on my weight," or "Mom insults Grandma." Then as the weekend unfolds, we mark the squares and text each other. Later, we all go out for dinner and treat the winner. This tradition has made the holidays much more fun and the camaraderie makes it easier for us to love our families as they are. You can see the brain science working through problem-solving, finding success and rewards. If you are struggling with change at work, turn it in to a positive game. Perhaps you get a star for helping someone out, or you create a "no complaining" rule, with the first person to complain buying the others lunch. Maybe you create teams and have a friendly competition for the fastest or most creative solution. Find ways to gamify it and you will feel much better.

7. **Train for the trek:** Like any journey, training can help you build your strength and stamina before the trail gets difficult. And having the right shoes can help too. If you approached your change journey with the same idea, how might you get ready to be successful? If your organization offers training, be sure you attend, and maybe even get some additional coaching. If your organization doesn't offer it, look to other sources like books and online training sites like LinkedIn Learning or Udemy. Perhaps you invest in some new equipment like a good planner or a subscription to a support service. Maybe there are wise mentors you can speak with. Like most things, training can be more fun when done with a group, so consider how you can invite others to join you.

8. **Rest at the resting points:** Travelers often make the mistake of trudging on when they could rest, thinking something like, I'll get done quicker if I just keep going. Resting is a waste of time. But rest is really important for combating our brain's natural resistance. Every change journey has slower times or flat sections before the next steep hill. Take advantage of them. We live in such a busy culture now that we often don't know what to do with periods of quiet, so we fill them. We take on a project at home, or we push harder on something at work. But rest is vital, so give yourself permission to take a break. These are great times to double down on the powerful troika of self-care, mindfulness, and play.

Ten ways to be an active participant in change

9. **Ask for help when you need it:** Another mistake travelers make is not taking advantage of available assistance. They keep pushing through hoping things will just get better. But often they don't. If you are feeling overwhelmed or fatigued or confused, ask for help! Often organizations put various support systems in place. Make sure you note what they are and how to access them.

10. **If you need to, get off the mountain:** Occasionally, a change journey might just be too much. This usually happens when a person is carrying several intense change journeys at the same time, and likely a combination of things from work and at home. Life happens—you or a loved one might become ill or injured, or perhaps you just had a baby, or an elderly parent needs assistance, or you've been a victim of a crime. If you're unable to participate in the change, talk to your manager and HR to discuss your options. Perhaps you can sit this one out or play a less intense role. If not, maybe you can take time away. This is why organizations often allow leaves of absence, to take care of employees during times when things are just too much. Sometimes bowing out is the best thing you can do for yourself, your team, and your organization.

Overall, I hope that you can see travelers are not just passive passengers in the change journey. Even when many of the details are out of your control, there are lots of things you can do to ensure that you not only survive but thrive.

Change Journey 11
Industry: Advising Services

I have learned that change, while challenging, is often the catalyst for personal transformation. In 2013, I embarked on a profoundly meaningful chapter of my life, devoting myself to my children. It was a decision rooted in our desire to provide them with the nurturing they deserved.

Fast forward to 2020, amidst the chaos of a global pandemic, when I was inspired by my husband's career and decided to rekindle my own professional aspirations.

Despite the daunting prospect of an eight-year break, I pursued my career re-entry with the support of my family. Amidst a sea of applications, interviews, and rejections, an opportunity emerged in business development, even though my background was in packaging technology.

Assuming the mantle of partnerships manager at an online student advising website, I quickly had to adapt in this unfamiliar territory. I realized I needed to uplevel my own skills and enrolled in a prestigious course on career counseling at UCLA. I also joined a professional association for career advisors where I learned from experts on a variety of topics, including how to navigate change. This information not only helped me with my own career journey but taught me the importance of leading others through strategic planning and clear communication during times of transition.

These investments in myself equipped me with invaluable skills and allowed me to spearhead initiatives aimed at empowering students in their academic and professional journeys. My efforts led to improved student engagement, heightened satisfaction rates, and an increase in positive reviews on our platform. I also was able to expand our network and establish partnerships with educational institutions worldwide.

As a result, I quickly rose within the ranks to an executive position where I played a pivotal role in shaping the company's vision and strategy, driving growth, innovation, increased revenue, and enhanced brand recognition.

Looking back on my journey from homemaker to executive, I can see that by embracing each challenge as an opportunity for growth, I emerged stronger and more resilient. My mindset of gratitude and positivity kept me motivated through the emotional ups and downs of numerous setbacks. I became more adept at navigating the ebb and flow of life's transitions, empowered by the knowledge that change offers boundless opportunities for personal evolution.

17. The Leader's Toolkit: Navigation, Motivation, Connection

Based on my research on the neuroscience of change, I have created a leader's toolkit that will help you move your travelers through any kind of change journey. It works with the brain, particularly addressing the four structures of the amygdala, entorhinal cortex, basal ganglia, and habenula. This toolkit also accounts for the factors that influence a traveler's motivation and momentum.

The toolkit has three main types of tools: navigation tools, motivation tools, and connection tools, which can be applied together in different combinations to meet your travelers' needs on their respective journeys.

Navigation Tools: The Why and How of the Journey

The change journey is no different from any other traveling experience—it's an exercise in navigating through time and space. Travelers of all kinds are much more likely to get to their destinations safely if they have the right navigation tools. Hikers use geographic contour maps, compasses, and trail guides, while airline pilots use aviation charts and GPS systems. All of these tools should be incorporated into your change rollout and communication plan. There are four navigation tools.

The leader's toolkit for navigating change

Start with Why

Before you start on any journey, you should know why you are going in the first place. If you don't know the why up front, you are missing a key element to good decision-making and motivation. And the purpose should not only be clear to you. You need to communicate the why to your travelers. Simon Sinek's book, *Start with Why*, says it all: Travelers need to know why they need to make the journey at all. In fact, the why is the center of what Sinek calls "the golden circle" that includes the how and the what. But the why must come first.

From the brain science perspective, knowing the why helps the amygdala perceive change as less threatening and helps travelers look into the future and anticipate potential gains. In fact, the more you spell out the purpose and potential gains for them, the sooner they can shift their focus.

Map the Route
Once you know the why, you need to map your route. Getting from point A to point B requires you to identify each point's location and the best route between them. Most of today's change journeys are from a current state to a new, presumably better, future state. So the map might be expressed in gained revenue, decreased complaints, or any other metrics that matter to your business. However you explain it, as the leader you have to tell people where they're headed and place a beacon there to guide them.

Creating a map of the journey is critical to your travelers' success because it keeps them from getting lost and it helps them track their progress, boosting their sense of accomplishment. Like all good maps, it helps if you can add milestones and signposts along the way, again to help keep people on track and give them a sense of progress and accomplishment. And taking the entorhinal cortex into account, if the journey will affect your traveler's physical workspace or social network you will want to create literal maps of places and people too.

Build the Habits
It's highly likely that your change journey will require travelers to change their habits and behaviors in some way. This should be called out in your change rollout and communication plan. What, specifically, do your travelers need to be doing and saying? Get really crisp on the words and actions. The returns on developing this level of specificity can't be overstated, because it gives your travelers the right learning and training. Think about the new habits you need them to build. What is the cue, the routine, and the reward? This is all the work of the basal ganglia and we can either make it easier or harder for it to do its job of building habits.

Dr. Chuck Kalnbach, at the University of Oregon's Lundquist College of Business, states that managers should expect a lag in performance or productivity when employees are learning something new. He says, "Supervisors have to be okay with that lag and not punish the drop in productivity or employees will go back to the old way."

Remember, repetition matters. A neural pathway is built and strengthened through repetitions and a habit is formed around 40 to 50. Use the power of training and practice to get those habits built quickly. Practice is how we hone and improve our skills, developing mastery.

One of my favorite tools is video coaching by Bongo, which uses the power of interactive video to demonstrate ideal behaviors as well as create an environment for learners to receive authentic assessment and coaching. You can also use technology to create realistic practice environments for people. Explore the benefits of immersive training with companies like Mursion and Cubic. Check out the agility of adaptive learning with Amplifier and Area9 Lyceum. And consider the power of VR with Talespin and Strivr to upskill your workforce or industry-specific VR companies like Lumeto (healthcare), Apex Officer and XpertVR (first responders), and IMPROVR (sports).

Be a Steady Presence
Navigation tools should be reliable and consistent. Because change can be so disruptive, you want your navigation tools to become the new source of constancy for your travelers. Every great leader will tell you that this is what makes the difference—being a reliable and steady presence, repeating the key information over and over. You will need to repeat things more often than you expect and you might feel like you are a broken record sometimes. You will also find that you need to keep it up longer than you expect. So many leaders have told me that the biggest mistake they made was letting up after the group got over the hump of resignation. The travelers showed signs of embracing the change so they relaxed. And the group backslid. Think of your role like you are building a guide rope that they can hold on to whenever they need.

Motivation: Recognition and Rewards

The leader's toolkit also offers tools to motivate your travelers. Motivation is very important for combating the brain's natural resistance to change. It helps to address the various emotions that are part of the transition. Unless you are blessed with a group that has high choice and desire for the change, you will need to use these various forms of recognition and rewards.

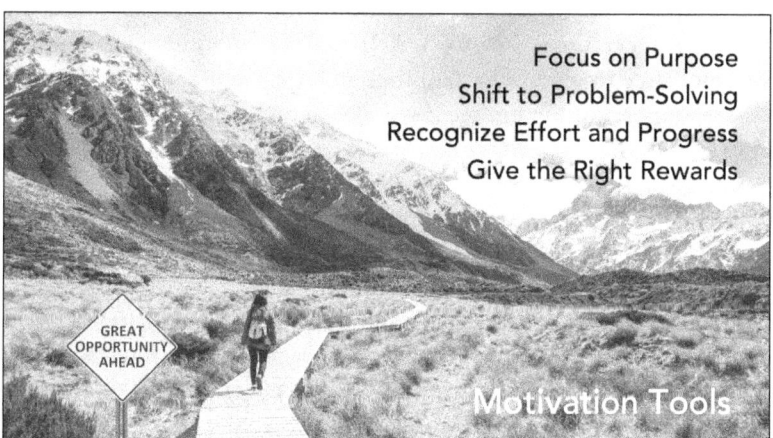

The leader's toolkit for motivating others during change

Focus on the Purpose
Humans are wired to seek purpose. This is part of the "become" aspect of our biology. In Dan Pink's book *Drive*, he synthesized many studies on human motivation and shows that people are motivated by three things: purpose, along with

autonomy and mastery (more on those below). People naturally want to make a contribution, so if you spell out the bigger purpose that the change initiative achieves, you'll naturally tap into your travelers' motivation.

In fact, purpose is so important that companies are shifting to be more purpose-driven. Books like *The Purpose Economy, Conscious Capitalism,* and *The Healing Organization* all share compelling evidence that both consumers and employees are seeking businesses that have a positive and meaningful impact in the world. My last book, *Wired to Become*, features the latest research on the science of finding your purpose, creating meaningful work, and achieving your potential.

In *Purpose at Work: The Largest Global Study on the Role of Purpose in the Workforce*, researchers state that connecting employees with purpose increased employee engagement, productivity, and profit. They found that purpose-driven employees feel 64 percent higher levels of fulfillment in their work, are 50 percent more likely to be in leadership positions, and are 47 percent more likely to promote their company as a good place to work.

The other two sources that Dan Pink identified were autonomy, the ability to be self-directed, and mastery, the opportunity to get better at things. Both of these can be threatened or decreased during a change journey, which makes purpose even more important. So, consider how you can connect the change initiative to a larger purpose, either some greater good the organization is trying to achieve, or to a personal value that the employee holds.

Shift from Goals to Problem-Solving
One way to motivate employees is to shift your focus from goals to problem-solving. According to Dr. Kyra Bobinet, a professor at Stanford University, "Goals are typically outcome-oriented, which means we either succeed in our attempts to achieve them—or we fail. If we 'fail' at something, the habenula kills our incentive to give things another go." Problem-solving works with the reward-seeking part of the brain. As we seek and find a solution, the experience becomes a success, something that works with both the habenula and basal ganglia. In addition, problem-solving is a type of design thinking, where we tinker and adjust as we experiment, getting better with each iteration.

Consider how most change plans are constructed. Most have rigid goals and milestones and rarely, if ever, do they unfold as expected, turning the change journey into a series of failures. To avoid this, frame each phase of the change initiative as an exercise in problem-solving. This allows your travelers to become active participants in the journey rather than passengers. And it's likely that their experience and perspective will improve the change initiative in countless ways.

Problem-solving also helps to shift employees from a fixed mindset to a growth mindset. Stanford psychologist Dr. Carol Dweck's research has examined what differentiates people who succeed from those who don't. She found that people who don't succeed tend to have a fixed mindset, meaning that they believe that their inherent traits or characteristics—such as their IQ (intelligence quotient) or people skills—are set once they reach adulthood.

A person with a fixed mindset thinks, I've got what I've got and I just have to make the most of it, but I can't change it. In contrast, a person with a growth mindset believes that they can always get better, that they can always learn something new, or practice something more, and that studying and effort are the pathways to improvement and even mastery. A person with a growth mindset thinks, I may not be able to do this yet, but I can work hard and get better.

The growth mindset yields several other benefits too. This chart compares the two mindsets at work—you can see that mindset influences how we view everything from effort, challenges, and feedback to the success of others.

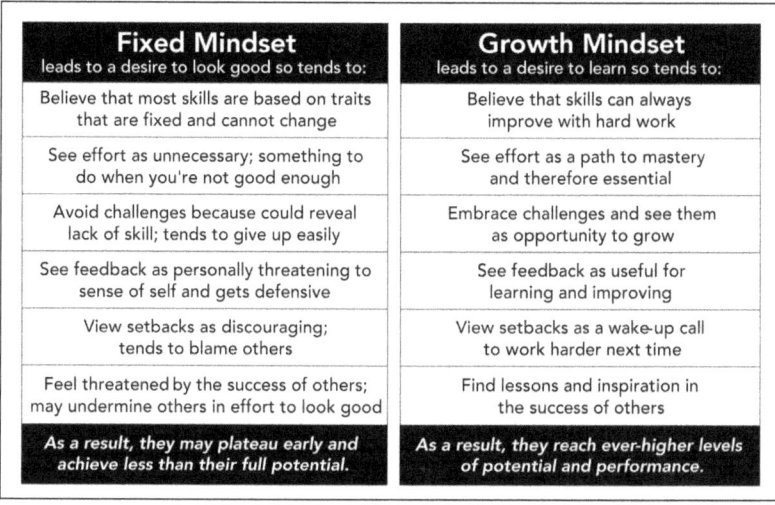

The two mindsets at work

Because of the compelling research on growth mindset, a lot of organizations are rethinking their performance review processes, moving away from ratings, and instead focusing on growth and improvement. When we rate people as "average," "excellent," or "poor," we essentially replicate the fixed mindset and say, "You are what you are." But when we move to evaluating growth and improvement, we activate motivation and, ultimately, potential, saying, "You are what you reach for."

In fact, the hallmark word of the growth mindset is yet. As in, "I haven't mastered that yet, but I will." It instantly turns a negative phrase into one of possibility and potential. As the leader of a change journey, harness the power of yet in your own messaging.

Recognize Effort and Progress
A key way to motivate your travelers is to recognize both effort and progress. Recognizing effort is part of fostering a growth mindset, which creates a culture of learning. Here are some examples for how feedback looks when it activates fixed and growth mindsets. Notice that fixed mindset tends to frame feedback in terms of a trait whereas growth feedback focuses on effort and improvement.

During a change journey, you will have lots of opportunities to recognize effort and improvement and doing so will give your team a boost. This can be especially helpful for the travelers who did not want or choose the change and might be trudging along or digging in their heels. The more their effort is rewarded, the more likely both the basal ganglia and habenula will respond in ways that assist the change journey.

Fixed (ability)	Growth (effort + improvement)
"Great job! You are so smart."	"Great job! I can tell you put a lot of time into that."
"You are really talented at this."	"You really applied yourself."
"You did high-quality work."	"I like the way you review and improve your work. That extra step makes all the difference."
"See, I told you it would be easy. You're a natural at this."	"You worked hard and did a great job. I think you're ready for something more challenging."
"You rocked it!"	"It was a long, complex project, but you stuck to it and got it done. You rocked it!"
"Nice job finishing the project."	"I'm really proud of you and how you kept trying even when it got hard. That persistence really paid off."

Feedback in both fixed and growth mindset forms

But don't ignore your walkers and runners if you are blessed to have them. They will also benefit from recognition, giving them a boost that may energize the entire group. In fact, researchers found that employee recognition boosted engagement, retention, wellness, safety, and employer brand.

You can recognize your travelers in many different ways as recognition is generally a type of reward that the brain responds well to. Certainly, a word from you, their leader, is powerful, so don't underestimate the power of your praise. According to Dr. Donald Clifton, co-author of *How Full Is Your Bucket*, not feeling appreciated is the number one reason employees leave a job.

In addition, a study by Workhuman found that organizations that invest just 1 percent of payroll into recognition experienced a significant reduction in flight risk and turnover. They state, "Well-recognized employees are 45 percent less likely to have turned over two years later." However, only 11 percent of employees say that someone at work has ever asked them how they like to be recognized for their accomplishments.

Officevibe's global study found the following results:
- 25 percent say their organization does not celebrate accomplishments or learnings
- 44 percent of employees are not satisfied with the frequency at which they receive recognition
- 75 percent say the feedback they receive is not frequent enough to help them understand how to improve

Gallup found that for employees, the most memorable recognition comes for their direct manager. But they also value recognition from a senior executive, a customer, and their peers.

Since being recognized by peers also matters, you can create opportunities for that to happen, perhaps in meetings about the change journey. See if you can create a culture where everyone is on the lookout for effort and improvement and make it a positive and playful part of the journey. Look for websites and apps to try out, or even go old school with high fives and gold stars if that works for your culture and context.

Marking progress is another part of this process. Like any journey, your team needs to know where they are on the map, what they have already completed, and what's coming next. Think again of climbing expeditions to Everest or the Tour de France. Every single inch of the process is mapped out and teams spend every evening discussing what happened during the day and plotting their strategy for the next. Climbers and cyclists need to know this information so they can manage their energy and make the right choices with food and hydration, or even when and how to nurse an injury.

Your travelers are no different. By communicating regularly about the roadmap and their progress, you empower employees to become active participants in the journey, especially if you view each leg of the trek as a phase of problem-solving. Also, progress needs to be celebrated! As your team crosses the milestones of the change journey, be sure you acknowledge each and every one with some sort of recognition. Even if you are behind schedule or over budget, you must find ways to mark progress and celebrate. Otherwise, the habenula is likely to code the experience a "failure" and your travelers will become resistant to future change initiatives.

This doesn't mean that you don't have honest conversations about performance and quality. You must have those too. But also be sure you build in moments that let people know they're making progress even though you're not there yet. Too many leaders give too much weight to the constructive and critical feedback and bypass the celebrations because they are busy or behind, leaving the brain with nothing to interpret as reward.

A process from *The Four Disciplines of Execution* by Chris McChesney, Sean Covey and Jim Huling is one of my favorite ways to ensure that progress is properly measured and recognized. It is very effective for driving all kinds of results, whether it's a change initiative or not. These are the four disciplines:

- Focus on the wildly important goals.
- Act on the lead measures.
- Keep a compelling scoreboard.
- Create a cadence of accountability.

This effective process helps leaders get clear on their metrics of success and "gamifies" them so that employees are both motivated to hit those metrics and take ownership of them. The process includes learning from failures (growth mindset) as well as celebrating successes.

Use the Right Rewards
Recognition and praise are definitely rewards but they are not the only ones. Remember, rewards play two vital roles in the neuroscience of change: (1) they help the habenula code an experience as a success, rather than a failure that it will try to avoid, and (2) they help the brain to want to replicate the behavior, because the basal ganglia sees rewards as the third component in the habit loop.

Charles Duhigg, in his book *The Power of Habit*, compiled and synthesized studies on habit formation from MIT, Columbia University, and other institutions. All kinds of rewards can work. Social connection is a powerful reward because we respond to acknowledgment and encouragement. Getting that "Good job!" makes the basal ganglia very happy. When human skin touches human skin—think high five, pat on the back, or hug—our brain releases oxytocin, a feel-good chemical the basal ganglia loves. And, of course, prizes, points, and chocolate can work too.

Managers benefit from learning how each of their employees best wishes to be appreciated. Research on "languages of appreciation" has identified four types of acknowledgment employees find meaningful: words of affirmation, quality time, receiving gifts, and acts of service. You can learn more by exploring the website AppreciationAtWork.com.

Rewards do not need to be big or showy, they just need to mark a success and be meaningful for your travelers. If you don't know what those are, ask them. By discussing rewards with them, you engage them in problem-solving and increase your change journey's likelihood of success.

Over the years, I've seen teams create all kinds of rewards. For example, ringing a loud gong when a goal is hit or earning a physical token, which become a symbol of pride. Gift cards are great too and can range from $5 to $5000.

The most successful models seem to have two levels. The first includes small tokens that mark recognition or success, like stars or chips, verbal "shoutouts" or electronic kudos. These should be given out abundantly but authentically. The second level includes larger, special prizes that are given to a few who show exemplary performance, like T-Mobile's PEAK achievement award (see p. 63). The latter requires a nomination and selection process because it's vital that the system feels fair and accurately acknowledge top performing teams and individuals. Again, all of this will be most effective if it reflects what is most meaningful to your travelers.

Connection Tools: Patience and Empathy

Connection tools are powerful because they help build rapport and collaboration between and among your travelers. As we know, change can be a disruptive and difficult process that can trigger worry, anxiety, and fear. And moving through change requires risk-taking and vulnerability. So, building a team culture of trust and empathy is key to bringing out the best in your travelers. There are four tools to use.

Start with Empathy

Because the transition aspect of change is such an emotional process, the biggest tool in your kit is empathy. Dr. Daniel Goleman, author of *Emotional Intelligence* and codirector of the Consortium for Research on Emotional Intelligence in Organizations at Rutgers University, identifies empathy as one of the core skills for building relationships with others. Emotional intelligence, or EQ, is what differentiates highly successful people from others.

According to Theresa Wiseman, a professor at the University of Southampton, empathy has four qualities:
- Being able to see the world as others see it
- Being nonjudgmental
- Recognizing another's feelings
- Communicating your understanding of that person's feelings

Dr. Brené Brown, author of *Daring Greatly*, says empathy is "feeling with people." In fact, she claims that empathy is often an act of vulnerability because in order to make an authentic connection with another person, we have to identify that same feeling in ourselves. That might be easy for feelings like hope and joy but much more difficult for feelings like anxiety, frustration, or fear.

Empathy can be learned, and as a leader you must learn it if you want to support your travelers and ensure their (and your) success. You can also help your travelers develop empathy so that they support each other. I weave empathy and emotional intelligence into all of my leadership development and manager-training programs, including those on change.

Empathy does more than drive positive relationships. It is one of the two key components that create psychological safety.

The leader's toolkit for connecting others through change

Create Psychological Safety
The tech company Google studied hundreds of its teams around the world and found that psychological safety was what differentiated the best teams from the rest. Harvard researcher Dr. Amy Edmondson defines psychological safety as "a sense of confidence that the team will not embarrass, reject or punish someone for speaking up—it is a shared belief held by members of a team that the team is safe for inter-personal risk-taking. It describes a team climate characterized by interpersonal trust and mutual respect in which people are comfortable being themselves."

Google's study further identified that the who of a team is not relevant—it's the how: not who they are but how they work together. A productive team builds psychological safety through empathy and making sure that all members contribute equally, allowing every person's ideas and thoughts to be heard, and contributing to the collective success of the whole.

If you are leading a change journey, help create psychological safety by making sure you build a culture of empathy. Model empathy when you engage with your travelers and help them do the same. In addition, make sure that meetings allow for each person to be heard and enable equal sharing. It's not enough to just ask if anyone has something to say. You have to make it safe and easy for even the quietest to contribute. If you need ideas, visit Google's re:Work site where they share best practices from their study.

If you need any more evidence, psychological safety also creates two more powerful effects. First, it allows for vulnerability. Dr. Brené Brown is most known for her research on shame and vulnerability at the University of Houston. Both of her TED talks are the most viewed in history. She states, "Let me go on the record and say that vulnerability is the birthplace of innovation, creativity and change." Second, psychological safety builds trust and camaraderie, two of the three core components of organizations that make the "Great Place to Work" list (the third is pride). If you want to unleash the real potential of your travelers, make psychological safety a priority.

Empower Social Connections
Camaraderie is a measure of social connection. We are wired to be social creatures. Entire segments of our biology are dedicated to forming meaningful bonds with others and as we learned in section II, change can often impact the social maps built by the entorhinal cortex. In addition, the amygdala is more reactive around unfamiliar people, who can be perceived as potential threats. It's vital to support your travelers in building social connections and camaraderie with each other as quickly as possible. And it will pay off on several fronts.

Some people scoff at team building, and I certainly have experienced my share of cheesy games. But when done right, team building is a powerful tool for building rapport, trust, and positive relationships. It can also begin a culture of psychological safety, and even protect people from pain as we are biologically attuned to our social status. Dr. Naomi Eisenberger, a professor at UCLA, studies this phenomenon and states, "Our research has shown that feeling socially excluded activates some of the same neural regions that are activated in response to physical pain." She goes on to explain that in the workplace, this reaction can be triggered by several common experiences:

- Being ignored or rejected
- Perceiving that you are being excluded from a group
- Starting work with a new team
- Being alone among strangers
- Working in cultures other than your own

Needless to say, these are all experiences that can happen during change journeys. As a leader, you need to identify when and where people's social connections are likely to be new, strained, or erased and help build them up as quickly as possible. This might include creating social experiences for the group to get to know each other in a relaxed setting, working together on a subcommittee or task team, or a formal team-building experience. Again, this can be made playful and fun and may even be enhanced through technology and apps. Many companies are now creating lunch meetups and providing fun team activities, like geocaching or game nights, to enhance networking and camaraderie.

Patience. Patience. Patience.
The last, and perhaps most important, tool in your connection kit is patience. Patience is crucial because leading a change journey can be hard work. Not only do you have your own experiences through the change initiative, you are now responsible for your travelers' experiences and success. You need to provide stability and guidance while expressing empathy and support. And sometimes your travelers will not show you the appreciation you deserve and they might even be snarky or grumpy.

Patience will be a tool that you use every day, particularly when you approach the peak of your change journey, and also near the end when everyone is running out of steam. Find ways to stay grounded and keep your sense of humor. Partner with another leader so you can coach and support each other, even commiserating when you need. And use the strategies from Chapter 16.

Change Done Right: Three Case Studies

To see some of these principles in action, let's look at some case studies.

Strategic Turnaround at a Manufacturer in Trouble
When former BP executive, Tufan Erginbilgiç took over at Rolls-Royce in 2023, he faced a struggling company he labeled a "burning platform." This British engine manufacturing company employs 50,000 people and serves the aviation, submarine, and defense industries.

Erginbilgiç initiated several changes like improving contract terms and supply chains, reducing duplication, and thinning out the middle manager ranks. In addition to cost-cutting measures, he made strategic investments in different parts of the business. In particular, Rolls-Royce builds engines for several airlines and by investing $1.29 billion for improvements, they have successfully built engines that can fly for much longer.

In just two years, the company's turnaround is now two years ahead of schedule. Profits are up 55 percent and Rolls-Royce is in the middle of a $1.27 billion share buyback. Under Erginbilgiç's leadership, shares have increased five-fold, a result that JP Morgan calls "outstanding."

His efforts have restored employee confidence, attracted new investors, and solidified or gained the loyalty of critical customers.

University of California: Merging Services in a Time of Budget Cuts
As a result of an ongoing state fiscal shortfall, the University of California experienced drastic cuts to its annual operating budget, which forced reductions at each of the ten campuses. To meet the goals at the Santa Barbara campus, the Division of Student Affairs needed to make unprecedented changes to the services it offered while maintaining quality support to the 20,000 enrolled students. In addition, it needed to move several departments into one building, combining staffs and services where possible. Anxiety was high as people worried about layoffs.

While this could have been a time when departments competed against each other for meager resources, the executive leaders decided to create an opportunity for enhanced collaboration. They first established some guiding values that became widely known by all of the employees. These were printed on posters, discussed in meetings, and people were recognized for living them.

Next, they empowered the directors to engage in joint problem-solving of how best to use the total building space and budget allotted, no longer "owning" a certain piece of it. To make the process safe, the executives made a guarantee that everyone would keep their jobs but now there were opportunities to innovate new roles, programs, and ways of working.

Directors then empowered employees to problem-solve specific challenges through cross-functional project groups. As a result, people made new social connections and built rapport, which led to new ideas for collaborations.

Every stage of the process was celebrated with group gatherings that featured humor, recognition, and ice cream. While the process was hard work, employees were positive, engaged, and ultimately created a new way of working that kept everyone employed and delivered better services more effectively.

Microsoft: Maximizing Global Resources
As this software giant grew, it built a global workforce in over 100 countries representing nearly as many languages and cultures. Over time, software development teams were operating in as many as four different time zones, making true collaboration difficult. It took longer to get products and features out the door in a timely manner, which impacted the customer experience.

Executive leaders empowered the directors to solve this problem. The directors met and identified a few clear objectives: (1) increase speed to market, (2) create a way to better partner across geographies, and (3) develop clear measurements of success.

Then they took a deep dive into the data together, learning the current state of the teams, and identifying the bottlenecks and assumptions that were driving current practices. They were held accountable as a group, which required them to let go of silos and territories and instead take ownership of the greater good of the customers and the company.

Together, they designed and implemented several solutions. Teams were reconfigured to better align with geographies and time zones. They developed a strategy that took advantage of where the best tech talent already existed, using it to shape key hiring initiatives and some targeted acquisitions. They also created a scorecard that rated teams on collaboration, leadership, and efficiency. All these efforts led to faster time-to-market and increased customer satisfaction.

In 2023, Microsoft redesigned their performance management process to clarify performance expectations and rewards like stocks and bonuses. A new rating system was introduced to foster a culture of excellence.

As you can see in these case studies, people in the leader roles can enable and empower travelers to move through a change journey successfully, no matter how steep it is.

Change Journey 12
Industry: Social Services

I worked as the HR director at an organization providing direct care for developmentally disabled adults. The agency was started by an immigrant from Africa who believed in compassion for all people and we ran several homes, providing a safe environment to live.

This organization became the place of choice for employees who had newly immigrated to the US, many of whom were refugees. As we grew from 65 to 300 employees, we intentionally built a culture of belonging.

Compassion, humility, and curiosity are the pillars that created an incredibly successful organization that tripled in size during my time. It remains my favorite workplace in my 25-year career. First, we focused on compassion. Hearing their stories of war, genocide, famine, and family loss made compassion across the organization run deep. When one of my managers unsarcastically said, "It has been a good day. No one died," it really put the job and daily life into perspective. I took interest in every person and would spend time at the front desk on paycheck Fridays just to touch base with everyone.

Humility and the willingness to learn became a core principle. The employees were learning a whole new country, new customs, new food, and new way of life after leaving the only home they had ever known. We learned together through positive experiences like organized potluck lunches, with staff bringing dishes from their home country to encourage education about other cultures.

We also learned through mistakes, like when I misstepped by having a "rewarding" staff and client barbecue during the holy month of Ramadan. The staff were so gracious when I went to those standing in the back not eating, explaining to me the time of year and their Muslim fasting requirements. That was the catalyst for a significant change in language use, adaptations, and new break offerings. We allowed staff to keep prayer rugs at the homes, had all of our employee benefits translated into the three dominant languages (English, French, Arabic), and allowed house staff meetings to be held in whatever language everyone understood.

Finally, we embraced curiosity and, without that, I do not believe we would have been as successful. Cultural challenges were systematically explored, discussed, understood, and absorbed into the company culture. For example, we discovered why it was best that competing tribal members of African countries be placed in different houses. Or that men who might normally view doing housework as women's work, would be willing to clean to help the clients. Or even when some male employees felt uncomfortable with female leadership, like myself, we'd find a way to talk it through and find a good solution.

It's the only workplace where I am still in touch with a large number of staff, even becoming their HR consultant when a few opened their own agencies. What was a good place to work became an incredible place because we intentionally built a culture of inclusion.

18. The Guide's Process and Troubleshooting

Change journeys are very much like the treks and hikes I use metaphorically throughout this book. Yet I am amazed how many guides embark on a change journey without the proper preparation. It's like going on a hike up Mount Fuji without training beforehand and leaving your hiking boots and sleeping bag at home. You might get up the mountain but it's unlikely that you will do so without challenges or injuries. No wonder so many change initiatives don't make it.

The guide's process is crucial to the success of any change journey. The goal is to get all your travelers up and over the peak and back down safely and, hopefully, happy. Using the tools we discussed in the last chapter—navigation, motivation and connection—will support your efforts.

Here's an overview of the guide's process:
- Preparing for the journey
- Readying the travelers
- Starting on the journey (resistance phase)
- Approaching the peak (resignation phase)
- Gathering momentum (embracement phase)
- Seeing the finish line (engagement phase)
- Dealing with the unexpected

Preparing for the Journey

The success of your change journey will directly reflect your preparation. For the small, quick changes (the pebble on the trail), preparation will be minimal. But for the other three types of change journeys (the long, steady trek; the quick hike up a steep hill; and the long, intense climb), preparation is crucial to your success. This might seem obvious but preparation needs to come before you start the actual change. Your travelers will be relying on you and if you're winging it, it's going to add to their distress rather than decrease it, activating parts of the brain that are not helpful for your overall goals.

Do what you need to feel so solid in your plan that you exude calmness and confidence. If you have ever taken a sporting lesson, or done any kind of guided tour, you know how important this is. If your leader seems scattered or rushed, it can freak you out. You need them to know what they are doing and make you feel like you can do it too.

There is actually a biological source for this. Within the brain, we have mirror neurons that fire in our brains as we watch another person do an activity or feel an emotion. Neuroscientists like Dr. Giacomo Rizzolatti from the University of Parma and Dr. Marco Iacoboni at UCLA have discovered that mirror neurons play a vital role in how we learn, how we understand another's intentions, and how we feel empathy. Seeing someone under stress, fires up your "stress-feeling" mirror neurons too, creating a sensation in your own brain for stress. And the reverse is true—when you see someone looking calm and confident, it lights up calmness and confidence in your own brain.

As a guide, your moods, words, and actions have a profound impact on travelers. So take the time to prepare yourself for the journey. Make sure you understand the why of the change and all the elements of the change plan. Test drive the elements of the change plan and practice your messaging. If parts are not clear, ask questions. If you think something is not going to work, speak up. And if you need more support, request it. Remember, the goal is to naturally exude calmness and confidence because you are genuinely prepared and ready to lead.

Another aspect of preparation is setting up the route. It should be ready for the travelers so that once they begin on the journey they can easily make their way through without stumbling unnecessarily. Many people think that change initiatives fail due to big and unforeseen circumstances. Yet the truth is that most fail for little reasons—things that easily could have been avoided or addressed if someone had done a better job of setting up the route in advance.

Everyone expects careful route preparation when people are riding in the Tour de France or attempting to summit Mount Everest. Long before the travelers actually arrive, mileage is calculated, maps are created, signs are hung, and stations for water, rest, and food are set up. The amount of support needed correlates with the physical exertion required and the length of the journey. For example, food and water stations are placed more frequently for a marathon than for a charity walk. For the California AIDS Ride, we had sleeping quarters, shower trucks, medical stations, and even entertainment spaced out and set up so that the riders were supported for success from the opening bell until the last rider crossed the finish line seven days and 550 miles later.

For workplace changes, this might translate to things like:
- Detailed action plans and timelines
- Signs and posters with key messages
- Websites and apps
- Large- and small-group communications, like emails and meetings
- Meeting agendas
- Training (in-person sessions, online videos, documentation)
- Coaching
- Recognition, rewards, and celebrations

Ideally, other leaders in your organization are thinking these things through and the change journey reflects thoughtful planning and the right level of support. If so, you just need to do your part and make sure you guide your group of travelers through the journey. You'll be most confident if you run the route ahead of them, making sure everything is ready. And then come back and lead with confidence. Or, if you discover that the right planning and support is not yet in place, speak up! Your preparation might just be the thing that triggers a better change journey for everyone.

And don't be bound by what is provided to you. If it's lacking, innovate some solutions. You can easily create your own maps and signs and support stations. You might even empower some of your travelers to help do this. Pick your stronger and more experienced folks to be a scouting team, thinking a few steps ahead on the journey. This turns it into a problem-solving experience for them and also takes some of the workload off of you.

Finally, preparation includes getting yourself ready for the journey too. You will also be taking the change journey in addition to the workload of leading, coaching, and troubleshooting. You will need emotional intelligence to manage the various challenging feelings that will arise and patience for the process.

Think about what helps you feel calm and grounded and do more of those things. Dial up your self-care and use the various tips and strategies from chapter 15 to ensure that you're at your best.

Readying Your Travelers

Another key element of preparation is readying your travelers. Before you head off on the trek, take a look at your group. What kind of shape are they in? Assess their motivation for this journey. Do you have people who will be running toward the change with enthusiasm and energy? Do you have a few who will be actively digging in their heels? It just doesn't make sense to ignore their motivation because it will actively impact the group every day.

You can also assess if they are carrying a heavy load that needs to be accounted for. Separate from our motivation, aspects of our personal lives also impact our ability to move easily through change. For example, an employee who is working through an illness or injury is likely to have less energy. As would a new parent who is in the throes of sleepless nights and overwhelm.

I think of these things as rocks in a backpack. I can't necessarily remove them but it helps to know who is under extra stress and carrying a heavier load than others. And if there is anything I can do to help lighten that load, I try. Sometimes, small shifts to projects, working hours, or resources can make all the difference. This is where you can also employ the buddy system. If people are paired up or put in small teams, they can help each other. If you do this, make sure that your people with heavy backpacks are paired with folks who have bandwidth to spare.

After you assess your team, consider what you can do to get them ready. For real hikes and treks, people train to build up their physical strength. They work out and practice and stretch. What does that look like for a workplace change? Perhaps helping them learn some time-management skills now will really pay off when you are getting close to the peak of the mountain. Perhaps doing some trust and rapport-building now will help them lean on each other when they are getting tired and frustrated. Perhaps encouraging people to take some downtime now and rest up will payoff tenfold in just a few weeks.

Consider the skills, habits, and relationships they will need to succeed and start building those now, before you start on the trail. And, when possible, let your team know about the journey ahead of time. If they know the destination, route, and timeline, they can become active participations in their own preparation, even innovating solutions that increase the success of your whole group.

Four Phases of a Change Journey

Let's look at the four phases and actions guides should take during each.

Starting Out: Resistance Phase

Starting out on the trail, keep some things in mind as you guide people through these early stages. (Just a reminder: we don't really have to worry about resistance with pebbles on the trail, the "green zone" changes. But for the other three journeys, be mindful of these key phases.) Usually, the beginning of the journey is when we will hit some resistance. Humans are wired to resist change so no matter how great of a job you have done getting ready, grumbling will still happen. They will question the change, focus on potential losses, and likely have strong emotions, especially if it's a steeper journey or if they are moving through several change journeys simultaneously.

Your best strategy is to communicate early and often, being as transparent as possible. Share the why, how, and when and treat your travelers as participants. If there is any part of the experience they can design, let them. This works so much better than when the leaders, trailblazers, and guides do it all. In fact, studies show that when people choose for themselves, they are far more committed to the outcome, by a factor of five to one. If they cannot choose the change, then let them choose as many aspects of their change journey as possible.

Some possibilities to consider:
- Creating a map and updating progress in a way that's visible to the team
- Identifying key milestones and designing the celebration events
- Creating meaningful rewards
- Building a sense of team identity, perhaps a team name or mascot
- Creating an agreed-upon way of handling conflict
- Gamifying the experience—can it be done faster or better?
- Designing ways to include self-care, mindfulness, and play
- To be determined (let them figure out what they want and need)

When they grumble, listen. And listen carefully, as they are likely sharing their worries about what they might lose. The more you know their fears, the better you can allay them. It's very common for people to worry about the issues we have already discussed like autonomy, mastery, and purpose as well as status, certainty, relatedness, and fairness. In her book *Rising Strong*, Dr. Brené Brown, says that during times of change, people have a fear of irrelevance. We all want to matter and we all want to be seen and heard.

So, see them and hear them. Let them know they matter. That doesn't mean making false promises but having empathy for their concerns will go a long way to helping them through the psychological transition. And it will help you build trust and rapport with your team.

I always remind leaders and guides that the travelers' grumbling is not a reflection of your leadership, it's just people being human. Modeling patience and empathy will go a long way to helping the group feel safer and calmer.

Provide consistent and reliable guidance, exuding calmness and confidence. Now is the time when you get them to trust the guide rope you are building so they can hold on to it during difficult moments.

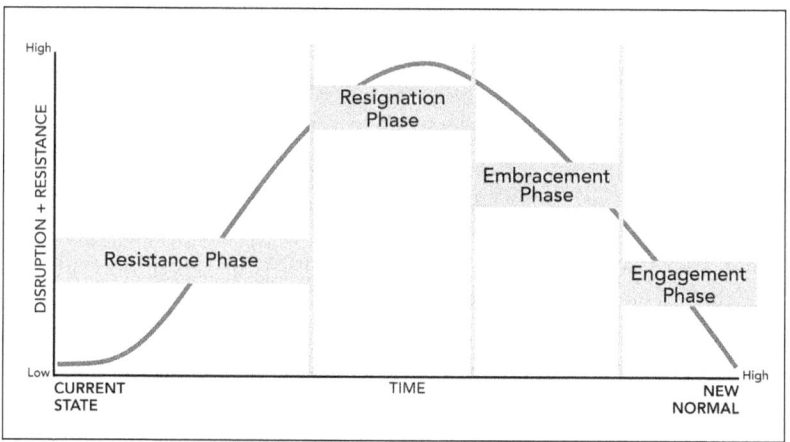

The four phases of the change journey

Approaching the Peak: Resignation Phase
At this phase, you have made it through the initial grumbling but as the climb gets steeper or takes a very long time, people may get frustrated and even depressed. They have not yet hit the peak where they see the potential benefits, so it can be helpful to remind people of the why and all the good things that are coming.

Your leadership at this stage is crucial and yet it can't be so out of step with their emotions that you seem insensitive or clueless. I recommend having a meeting or celebration that acknowledges how far they have already come. Recognize people and have them recognize each other, and find a way to do it that matches the tone of your group. If they are into silly, do silly. If they are more serious, do serious. If you are not sure, ask them.

This is a great time to ask people to share stories of what is working. These stories can be what's working with the change. Or what's working with how they are moving forward during a difficult journey. Or even how they have overcome an obstacle. Shine the light on all the good stuff you can find to enliven the group and create a positive experience for the brain.

This is actually a form of appreciative inquiry, a method that naturally brings out in the best in a group through a collaborative process. After you celebrate, let them know that they are getting close to the peak and ask what they need for this next push. Have them own their journey and brainstorm what would help them. Then do your best to provide it. You may also need a boost at this stage so consider meeting up with other guides and support each other and celebrate your successes too.

And always, be that steady and calm presence, that strong guide rope they can hold onto as they keep moving forward.

Gathering Momentum: Embracement Phase
By this time, you have gotten over the hump of resistance, which feels good but don't let down your guard. This is still a very vulnerable phase so you want to tend to the momentum as it continues to build.

Keep being the calm, steady presence, sharing the why and how of the journey. At this stage people often have a lot of questions, things you have likely already talked about. But since they have now psychologically gotten on board, they will have a new interest in what this change is for, how it's going to get done, and they may be ready to add their own ideas and suggestions.

Leaders and guides might get a little frustrated here because it's going to feel like people weren't paying attention to all the great communicating you have been doing. Breathe and dial up your patience. Remember, they're just being human. And it's really a positive sign, because the questions are evidence that they have made the turn and are now looking toward potential gains. Listen and respond. And don't worry that revisiting these topics will cause the group to backslide. In fact, this is a great time to listen even more attentively because they will often see issues that need to be addressed or have ideas that should be implemented. Some of the best innovations come at this stage of a change journey but only if the guides listen.

This is also the phase when you are likely to start implementing new behaviors. Be sure you use trainings to get those repetitions built. This is when people are likely to fail so create an atmosphere where it's okay to make mistakes and harvest the learning from those mishaps.

Somewhere near the end of this phase, have another celebratory gathering, recognizing people and calling out all the good work they did getting on board and moving forward. This helps the brain see another positive reward in change.

Seeing the Finish Line: Engagement Phase
By this phase, you might feel like you are done but you are not, so resist the temptation to turn your attention to other things. While your travelers are on board and gaining speed, keep the guide rope in place and make sure they complete the journey. Because the hard part is over, people can lose focus and take unnecessary risks, especially because the fatigue of the exertion is setting in. Sadly, most deaths in mountain climbing occur after people have summited and are heading back down.

You can certainly take on an air of celebration but keep your calm and steady presence in place. This is a great time to reorient people toward the finish line. Be clear on what it means to complete the change initiative and which metrics matter. Many change initiatives actually fail at this stage because they don't reach completion. Leaders erroneously assume that since the group is "this close" they will naturally keep on going.

But the reality is that by this point, the team has been tasked with other changes and has started on other journeys. And because this one seems "in the bag," the guides head to other treks and the trailblazers start packing up, which both threaten the success of the journey and denies the travelers the satisfaction of the final celebration. The brain needs that sense of completion to code change as a success. And if the change initiative falls apart at this stage, the organization will have invested time and money in something that did not succeed, and the travelers will be marked with a failure despite the great work they did. So, keep guiding until the last traveler crosses the finish line and the change journey is officially over.

Then formally close out the experience for people. Don't let it become something that never gets scheduled because it's an important element of the brain science of change. If there were failures and challenges, that is okay. Learning is an important part of how we improve, so have a meeting where you talk through what happened and what should have shifted. I recommend that you have a post-mortem meeting assessing the change and the outcomes. And a separate event to celebrate the journey and the travelers.

A note about celebrations. Celebrations can come in all kinds of forms from the casual break (think pizza party, shooting pool, or silent disco) to an offsite adventure (like bowling, geocaching, or glassblowing) to the elaborate and expensive (awards dinner or trip to Vegas or Hawaii). The most important quality is that they align with the culture and context of your travelers. Some of the most cringe-worthy scenes from TV shows like The Office or Superstore are when the boss is "celebrating" the team in a way that totally misses the mark. This is why I recommend that you ask your travelers to design the rewards and celebrations, because then you will know it will be right. Give them a budget and let them create what will make them feel honored.

Dealing with the Unexpected: Roadblocks, Storms, and Landslides

In reality, few (if any) change journeys roll along as planned. Even when the expedition designers, trailblazers, guides, and travelers all do a phenomenal job, unexpected things happen. And the best change leaders plan for the unexpected.

With the Change Quest model, you'll have already accounted for typical issues, like what's to be expected when taking a highly resistant group on a long, steep climb journey. Or having a group of travelers who don't have the skills they need to be successful on the trail ahead of them. The model allows you to assess and predict, which will help your expectations become more accurate. And the strategies I laid out in the previous section should help you address many potential issues. However, unexpected challenges often come from unanticipated sources and they may threaten the success of the entire change journey or the success of a group of travelers. I have observed that they seem to fall into three categories and your response to each should be a little different because the damage they do varies as well.

Roadblocks

Sometimes something drops onto the trail that prevents your travelers from moving forward until it's addressed. Roadblocks don't affect the overall change journey, so the goal and path remain the same, but you will still need to respond to the roadblock, possibly climbing over it or taking a short detour.

A roadblock's impact depends on your team and timeline as well as the size of the obstacle. I think of it as a boulder on the trail. Experienced travelers who are highly motivated for the journey might handle it before you even know it happened. If the block is large, they may need to stop and strategize the best solution for getting over or around it. But a roadblock may completely demoralize highly resistant travelers or those carrying heavy backpacks, causing them to backslide into some negative emotions. Depending on how long it takes to resolve, a roadblock can also impact the timeline, either pushing it out so the journey takes longer, or forcing a steeper incline.

Here are some examples of roadblocks:
- A supplier is delayed in delivering a component
- The cost of a necessary resource just increased
- Another team's process or product is not yet finished
- A key player or guide leaves the team or company
- A regional difference has not been accounted for
- A trailblazer did not adequately prepare a necessary resource

As the guide, you'll want to be a calm and steady presence. If you spot the roadblock on the horizon, the sooner you tell your team the better. If your team suspects you withheld information, it can harm your rapport with the group.

My favorite way to handle a roadblock is to turn it into a problem-solving challenge. Have your travelers take the lead on finding the best solution as they are likely to have great ideas and will feel more empowered if they are taking the lead. Once you get through the roadblock, celebrate the success and teamwork.

Storms

The second type of unexpected challenge is like a blizzard or sandstorm. Storms are something that come from the outside and descend upon the journey and travelers. Again, the parameters of the change journey don't change but the storm definitely affects the timeline because your travelers will need to hunker down and wait it out. One difference between a storm and a roadblock is time—storms take longer to resolve, so they tend to stop the group's forward momentum. The second difference is you and your travelers have no action to take, as you have to wait for others to resolve the storm for you.

Here are some examples of storms:
- A new policy or regulation goes into effect that needs to be addressed by the designers/leaders
- A person or group raises concerns about the change that needs to be resolved by the designers/leaders

- A process is not configured correctly and will take time to fix
- A shift occurs in the market but is likely to right itself in the near future
- A designer makes a significant change that needs to be worked through

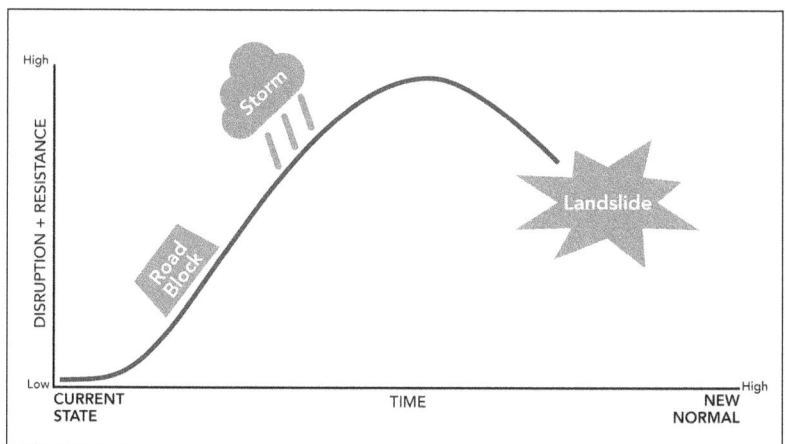

Types of unexpected challenges during change

When a storm hits, remain the calm and steady presence, talking them through it. As mentioned, the sooner you can let them know a storm is on the way, the better. Your value as a guide will be less impressive if you come bounding up announcing the storm when they are already buried under two feet of snow. Giving them warning helps them physically and mentally prepare.

The impact of the storm on your group really depends on how you handle it. The shared experience might bind your travelers together, but it's not unusual for added anxiety and strife to divide a group. Obviously, the former is preferred. Be transparent about what you know and how long you anticipate the storm to last, and address how this delay impacts them and whether it affects how their performance will be viewed. The amygdala is going to create anxiety about this change within a change. And the habenula might cause more concern about failure and blame. There is nothing more stressful to a group than to be prevented from being successful but still held accountable for the result. You will likely hear a lot of questions and comments to that effect so come prepared with the answers.

Luckily, you are unlikely to be on the side of a real mountain building an igloo to withstand a snowstorm. So your travelers can probably use the storm as a break in this particular journey to focus on their other work, especially since they may be on other journeys too. It might be good to help them figure out how to best use their time and energy until the storm passes.

When things start up again, reconvene the group to tell them what caused the storm (if they don't already know), adjusting the map and timeline accordingly. If a long time has passed, you may need to reorient them to the goal and assess their overall motivation since things might have shifted in the interim.

Reestablish your guide rope, mark where you are on the route, and get them started. Don't expect them to just pop right back to where they were before. They likely need to warm up and build some momentum again. If you can, acknowledge and celebrate their adaptability.

Landslides
The final type of unexpected challenge completely wipes your group off the mountain, creating a sudden end to the change journey. These are significant shifts in the landscape that will not only affect this change journey but likely several other things about your work environment.

Some examples of landslides include:
- The financial collapse of your organization
- A merger or acquisition
- An election, lawsuit, or regulation
- A natural or geopolitical disaster

Landslides are the most disorienting because they create sudden, seismic shifts so your travelers will likely be stunned. They put an obvious end to this particular change journey, and launch a whole new one.

Because your travelers are likely experiencing confusion and shock, it's helpful to bring them together and maintain your role as guide. Help them understand and process this shift and allow them to ask questions. You can leverage the team's connection and your time together to create some stability around the new, bigger change that caused the landslide.

It might be helpful to share the why, if you know it, and help them see the route or map. If you don't know or can't share, let them know that more information will be coming soon and ask them to have patience. Remind them that this might be a good time to use the troika of self-care, mindfulness, and play and, if possible, organize some options at work (e.g., games, meditation class, potluck) to take people's minds off the unknowns. And still end with recognizing and celebrating the team's accomplishments for the original change journey.

Change Journey 13
Industry: Sales
I was a senior leader at the time it was decided that our department would merge with another. Unfortunately, the whole thing was horribly mismanaged. I tried to advise the executives, but they plowed ahead and did irrevocable damage. It was like watching a train wreck in slow motion and feeling powerless to stop it.

The first mistake the executives made was telling both groups that "a big change was coming" but nothing more than that was shared. Very quickly, people in both departments started freaking out, assuming the worst—the most common fears were massive layoffs or bankruptcy. A few of us leaders were informed of the merge, but we were told that we could not say anything, and we were not given any specifics, so we found ourselves trying to calm people down without having any real information.

This went on for more than three months before the executives shared that the plan was to merge the two departments, but they still didn't have a timeline or specifics to share. By then, we had already lost two of our best leaders and a handful of top performers from both groups who didn't want to deal with the stress of not knowing what might happen.

Because no details were shared, both departments had more issues with people worrying about their projects and who they would report to. The rumor mill ran wild, and we were spending a lot of time trying to keep people calm. In addition, people started having strong opinions about what would and would not work. This chaos pushed the timeline even further.

At this point, I left because the stress and uncertainty made what had been a great place to work simply untenable. The irony is that a new executive came in shortly thereafter and paused the merge—that was three years ago, and it still has not happened but it has not been canceled either.

It was painful to watch every rule about good change management be broken and lose talented colleagues as a result.

Your Learning Journey

To help you thrive through upcoming change journeys, apply these tools to create your own personal change success plan:

- Do your inventory of the change. Capture key insights.
- Identify ways you can increase your self-care, engage in mindfulness practices, and schedule time for play.
- Explore the 10 options for being an active participant. Identify some actions you can take in the coming weeks to help yourself succeed.
- Whether you are a traveler or a guide, explore the tools for navigation, motivation, and connection. Identify a few tools from each category that would be helpful to you. Clarify how you could create or use them.
- Since psychological safety is so crucial to every group's success, identify a few ways you can help build more psychological safety with your team/colleagues.
- Whether you are a traveler or a guide, explore the guide's process. Identify a few strategies from each phase that would be helpful to you. Explain how you could create or use them.
- Read section V and identify how the four drivers of change might impact you or your travelers.

THE FOUR DRIVERS OF CHANGE

"When we are no longer able to change a situation, we are challenged to change ourselves."

Viktor Frankl, Holocaust survivor and author, *Man's Search for Meaning*

19. Organizational Growth and Development

Before we get into strategies for expedition designers/executives, it's important to step back and look at the bigger picture of what drives change. All four have direct implications for the future of your organization as well as your career. In addition, these four drivers shape aspects of your personal life as they impact every organization that produces the goods you consume, the educational institutions you or your family attend, the agencies that serve your communities, and the service providers you use to enhance your life.

When we look at all the drivers of change in any organization, they fall into four main categories: organizational growth and development, human consciousness, environmental change, and technology. We'll explore each in more detail in this section.

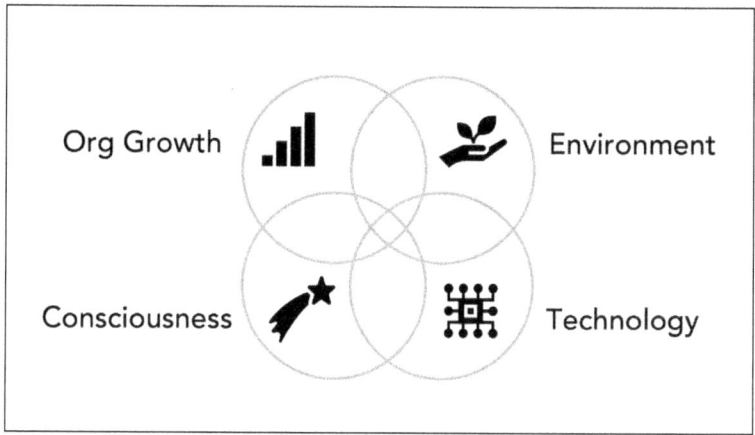

The four drivers of change

Anticipating Organizational Growth and Development

Change may feel relentless and chaotic, but there is method in the madness. Scholars have found that organizations grow in predictable ways, moving through stages of development and levels of consciousness. Each shift brings a host of predictable changes as the organization seeks to resolve common issues of growth. I have seen this play out so regularly in my consulting work that, like Bill Murray in the movie *Groundhog Day*, at times I can eerily predict what is coming next and when.

Dr. Larry Greiner, a professor at USC's Marshall School of Business, developed my favorite organizational growth model. He identified six distinct phases that organizations move through as they age and grow in size, each with its own set of challenges.

Identifying your organization's current stage of development and—more importantly—the stage it is growing into will help you anticipate the changes coming your way. But keep in mind that organizations move through the phases of the Greiner model at radically different paces. For example, a large, traditional financial institution will have a much slower and gentler progression than a fast-growing tech startup. Each phase may last from months to decades, depending on how quickly you are hiring and adding more employees, thus making your organization bigger.

Every stage ultimately leads to a crisis point when the current structure can no longer support what the organization needs to grow. These crisis points force transformation into the next phase. Now in a new phase, an organization may experience a period of relative stability, from months to decades. Until, inevitably, its growth pushes it to the next crisis point and resulting transformation.

As you read this overview of the six phases, see if you can identify your organization's current position on the Greiner model.

Phase One: Growth Through Creativity
The founders first come together and build an organization run by a small group of people who wear many hats. People work closely together, with spontaneous and informal communication that contributes to a work environment high in trust and psychological safety (and often playfulness and fun).

Since the small group is pushing for and designing the changes as well as implementing them, there is little resistance to change and, often, a high motivation for it. This team moves fast to solve issues, and almost never through hierarchical decision making or formal processes. During this creative and fertile time, there are fast failures and quick wins.

Over time, as the organization gets bigger and adds more employees to handle its growing success, it leads to the crisis point of leadership, where professional management needs to be brought in to help run the various functions like finance, marketing, and human resources. When the needs of the organization grow past what the original group can provide, this original team may be disappointed when the culture starts to get more impersonal, as the feeling of a small, intimate family starts to shift. In addition, activities that were once normal come under scrutiny as things get more formalized.

Phase Two: Growth Through Direction
Additional leaders are brought in to manage various functions. You are likely to see them drive a lot of change within their functions as each leader attempts to bring their part of the house in order and prepare it for future growth.

This can be a tender time for legacy employees who have been there from the start as they likely had ideas about what changes were needed. They may also feel demoted if they no longer report to, or have the ear of, the founders.

The new leaders tend to hire people that they have worked with before, which has its advantages but can also strain existing relationships. Since the organization is still small, leaders expect change initiatives to launch quickly, especially since they may feel an urgency to prove they can "whip things into shape." At this stage, it is important that these leaders remember they are changing processes their employees might have followed for years and even developed themselves. New leadership can help stabilize this stage by focusing on augmenting and enhancing rather than on pointing out what they perceive to be broken or outdated.

Simultaneously, while the organization focuses on developing new products and services, to gain enough market share for long-term viability, the original team tends to protect what they built—even if it isn't scalable, they may be reluctant to diversify their products and services.

At some point, again, months to decades later, the scale of the offerings gets too big for the leaders to monitor, creating the crisis point of autonomy where work and authority need to be delegated to others.

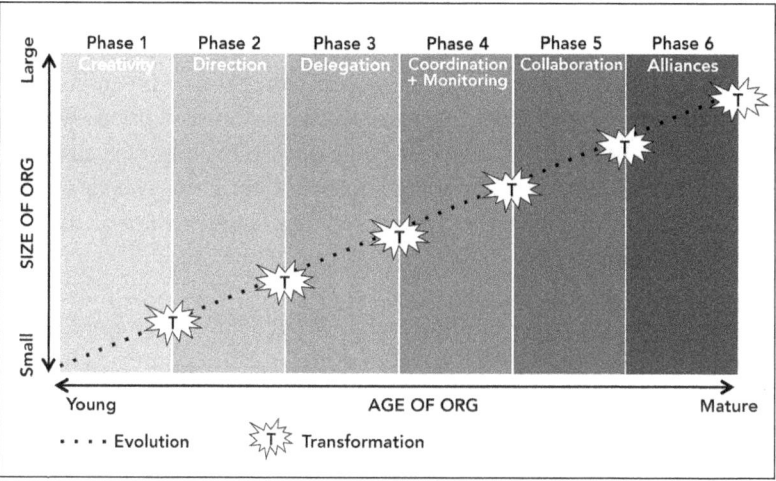

The six phases of the Greiner model

Phase Three: Growth Through Delegation
That leads to the third phase, where layers of hierarchy are added, and authority is delegated down the organization. Roles start to segment into levels like senior director, director, and assistant director. Top management becomes less involved in the day-to-day details and turns their focus to long-term strategy. At least, that's the goal but early in this phase, it can be rather messy as new leaders may not yet be ready to take the reins, or the top leaders are reluctant to let go and may micromanage their functions. When the growth and needs of the company outpace their current capabilities and leadership skills, some top leaders may need to shift into smaller roles or out of the organization.

Changes during this phase include organization redesigns and shifts in reporting structures, which drives change in many downstream administrative support functions like finance, HR, facilities, and technology, to keep pace with headcount expansion of employees.

Eventually, things smooth out and the organization settles into some stability that may last for months or years, depending on the pace of growth. But eventually, the sheer size of the organization stresses the current policies and communication channels, creating the next crisis point of control. To solve it, the different parts of the organization need to work together better.

Phase Four: Growth Through Coordination and Monitoring
This ushers in the fourth phase, which introduces new policies and procedures that give an organization structure and consistency across various functions. Changes may include creating companywide practices in managing teams, conducting performance reviews, budgeting, and project management. In addition, there is a transition to formal processes for a host of actions, as well as a drive to shared technology systems, and platforms.

At first, this effort helps establish reliability and consistency to the organization's broader scope. You might be gaining some efficiencies and economies of scale and addressing problem areas like performance review inequities. But people might also start to feel that things are becoming too rigid or "corporate" and many employees who prefer the wider range of responsibility and fast-changing pace leave at this stage, to find organizations still in phases two or three of the Greiner model. This exodus of employees in turn changes the makeup of teams and reporting relationships.

While policies are good at first, organizations often over-compensate by relying on them too much. For example, while 98 percent of the employees show up to work on time and use the corporate credit card appropriately, the company will react to the poor choices of a few people by creating overly restrictive policies—essentially "police-ing" all employees instead of dealing with the few bad actors individually. Combined, this trajectory leads to the inevitable crisis point of red tape, where bureaucracy gets burdensome, reducing the organization's agility.

Phase Five: Growth Through Collaboration
To solve this problem, the organization switches gears and moves to the fifth phase of growth: collaboration. Bureaucracy is replaced by a range of scalable and agile systems that support more flexibility. Instead of a rigid system for making decisions, emotionally intelligent leaders are trusted to use good judgment while managing complexity.

This phase requires a change of top leaders who can work in this more organic, fluid way. Naturally, this ripples through an organization's philosophy and style as well as structure. Such a dramatic shift from the previous stage ushers in a commensurate amount of new changes. It's not unusual for leaders to undo or redo changes, such as systems and policies, that employees had already moved through. Whether an organization spends months or years in this phase, as it grows, it eventually arrives at the crisis point of internal growth, where the organization must look outside itself for new growth opportunities.

Phase Six: Growth Through Alliances
In the final phase, organizations can only solve their challenges by partnering with other organizations, through actions like outsourcing, mergers, franchises, etc. Dr. Greiner termed these "extra-organizational solutions." These actions bring a whole new range of changes as complex entities try to integrate products, leadership styles, values, and cultures (not to mention policies, communication and technology systems, currencies, and regulations).

Top executives (and their legal teams) broker most ventures of this nature, which are kept secret until they are announced, much to the surprise of the employees. While they may take months or years to unfold, they often suddenly drive countless changes to the organization's environment, and the employees' psychological reactions to those shifts.

So, the organization expands, the various entities mix and merge together, diluting the culture and ultimately leading to the crisis point of identity—where the organization must refocus on its vision, mission, and strategy and revise it into a unified whole.

It's important to state here that when Dr. Greiner first published his model in 1972, he only identified the first 5 phases, adding this last stage in 1998. However, I believe modern organizations are diverting from Greiner's model because mergers and acquisitions (M&A) now can occur at earlier phases with Phase 4 companies acquiring Phase 1 startups or Phase 3 companies launching franchises, for example. We'll explore this more in the next section on rapid scaling and chapter 29.

I think it's very interestingly, however, that in his 1972 publication, Dr. Greiner contemplated what a sixth stage might be like, writing

> *"While there is little clear evidence, I imagine the revolution will center around the "psychological saturation" of employees who grow emotionally and physically exhausted by the intensity of teamwork and the heavy pressure for innovation solutions. My hunch is that the Phase 5 revolution will be solved through new structures and programs that allow employees to periodically rest, reflect, and revitalize themselves. We may even see companies with dual organization structures: a "habit" structure for getting the daily work done, and a "reflective" structure for stimulating perspective and personal enrichment. Employees could then move back and forth between two structures as their energies are dissipated and refueled."*

Greiner went on to list a few examples:
- Rotating employees into a reflective group that explores new possibilities, sharing their insights
- Providing sabbaticals to employees
- Moving managers in and out of challenging jobs/situations
- Establishing a four-day workweek
- Assuring job security

- Building onsite facilities that allow for relaxation during the workday
- Making jobs more interchangeable
- Creating an extra team so that one team is always off for training or rest
- Switching to longer vacations
- Offering more flexible working hours

It turns out his original instincts were accurate and predicted the rise of employee burnout. He seemed to anticipate that organizations would consider the well-being of their workforce as a top priority and vital for strategic success.

Embracing Your Evolving Ecosystem
So, have you identified your organization's phase on the model? More importantly, can you tell what crisis point and transformation is coming?

When I consult with leaders, I ask them to identify the overall phase as well as the phases for each function, to gain as much insight as possible. It helps them predict the next crisis point so they can prepare rather than just react. All kinds of troubling situations may be avoided with thoughtful preparation. I also ask leaders to reflect on their experiences and what they have learned over the course of their career. At what phases have they excelled? What aspects of their knowledge and skills need to grow?

As an employee, you may find that you enjoy a certain phase more than the others, something you learn with experience. working in different organizations. Use this valuable information to shape your career and future job searches.

As you become more familiar with the phases of organizational growth, it becomes evident that change initiatives are a natural output of development. How work gets done, what work gets done, and who does it shifts significantly from phase to phase, which requires precise interventions to address the various pain points like adding positions or creating policies. While our brains may be wired to want static and predictable companies, organizations are organic things, living ecosystems that shift and move.

Remember that though the Greiner model graphic depicts the phases as of equal duration, in reality, they may vary widely, depending how fast you're adding people. And the model is not strictly linear, as organizations may slide back into previous phases or be between two phases as they transition.

It is also quite common that the core part of the business is more developed and in a different phase than newer functions. For example, at Lynda.com, video production was the core product and it existed years before they added the sales function.

I find the Greiner model a useful way to help the people I work with embrace change as a constant, and even predictable, part of the growth process.

Rapid Scaling

Greiner's research occurred in the 1960s and 70s, yet his model has stood the test of time, even aligning with the trajectory of uber-growth tech companies like Google, Amazon, Facebook, and LinkedIn. In fact, Reid Hoffman, the founder of LinkedIn, PayPal, and an early investor in Facebook, has become especially focused on quickly scaling companies, in a process he calls "blitzscaling." He offered a class at Stanford University to help others through the same process he learned to navigate with no guidance.

In today's networked and global business environment, Hoffman states, "You have to move faster, because competition from anywhere on the globe may beat you to scale. Software has a natural affinity with blitzscaling, because the marginal costs of serving any size market are virtually zero. The more that software becomes integral to all industries, the faster things will move. Throw in AI, machine learning, and the loops get even faster. So, we're going to see more blitzscaling. Not just a little more, but a lot more."

Hoffman identifies three kinds of scale:
- Growing revenue
- Growing the customer base
- Scaling the organization

He found that this last one is often overlooked but crucial because without the right people and processes in place to execute on strategic goals, an organization may not be able to achieve the first two.

Hoffman identifies that growth occurs as a series of five stages, in magnitudes of scale with founder or family-run businesses from one to 15 employees—he calls this the "family" level. Next is the "tribe" level that occurs from 16 to 150 employees. It's followed by the "village" level with up to 1,000 employees, the "city" level with thousands of employees, and the "nation" level with more than 10,000.

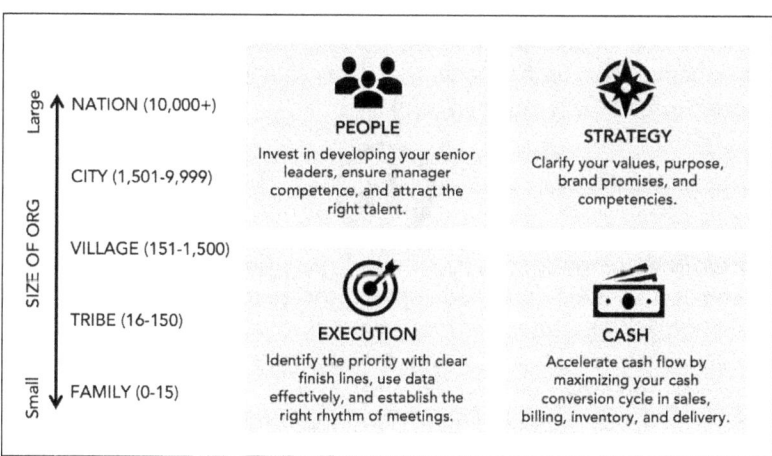

Critical elements for scaling a business

Blitzscaling usually occurs between the tribe and village levels but, in rare occurrences with a really hot market, it can start earlier. Hoffman has gone on to co-author a book, titled *Masters of Scale: Surprising Truths from the World's Most Successful Entrepreneurs*. He also launched a podcast where he interviews successful entrepreneurs, and a website with his classes—learn more at www.MastersofScale.com.

Another expert on scaling organizations is Verne Harnish, author of *Scaling Up: How a Few Companies Make It… And Why the Rest Don't*. He focuses on the specifics of scaling the organization with four critical areas: people, strategy, execution, and cash. He offers detailed tools and action items for each area, with many free resources on his website ScalingUp.com.

- **People:** Invest in developing your senior leaders, ensure manager competence, and attract the right talent.
- **Strategy:** Clarify your values, purpose, brand promises, and organizational competencies.
- **Execution:** Identify priorities with clear finish lines, use data effectively, and establish a productive meeting rhythm.
- **Cash:** Accelerate cash flow by maximizing your cash conversion cycle in sales, billing, inventory, and delivery.

Making the right choices with scaling positions the company to respond effectively to changes in the market, shifts in client demographics, and the rise of disruptors.

Before we move on to the next driver of change, consider how you have experienced organizational growth and development, the phases of Greiner's model, and the effects of rapid scaling. Certainly, consider your experience as an employee, but also as a consumer. Perhaps your favorite brand has shown a recent dip in quality or has announced some exciting new options. Maybe you've noticed a shift in customer service, or it's been announced that it has become part of a rival brand. This particular driver of change—organizational growth—shapes what is happening in every single organization you engage with, both professionally and personally.

Change Journey 14
Industry: Technology
I worked at a company that had experienced success, and the growth that follows. While the leadership was committed to updating business and manufacturing processes, it was a real struggle to get them to update processes and mindsets related to our people.

The executives expected the HR group to drive the same types of engagement with a diverse, international, and domestically distributed workforce as they experienced when the company was just a handful of employees all working in the same building.

During my tenure, I frequently stated that we still had a small company mindset, but we were now a mid-sized company. Ironically, I was ignored—

I was just one of the masses, which was exactly what I was trying to make them see.

As a company moves from small to mid-sized, there is a needed shift in mindset. People strategies and expectations must change just as much as the other aspects of the business, with more streamlined processes and procedures. The problem with a founder-led or family-owned company is that they are often resistant to feedback or hear legitimate advice as akin to telling them their baby is ugly. While their name is on the door and everyone's business cards, leaders must be willing to listen if they want their company to grow successfully.

When I decided to leave that company, I needed to find the right fit. I searched for large companies that had already bypassed those growing pains, where I could lead on a divisional level. I also looked for small companies, where my expertise and experiences would allow me to help lead as they grew. I was determined to avoid that messy middle.

In the end, I landed in a new industry at a bank with just under 100 employees. We are now branching into a new market for the first time, and I can't help but think that my previous experience will be beneficial during this phase of rapid growth.

20. Human Consciousness and Organizations

The Greiner model gives us a useful framework for understanding organizational growth but does not account for the influence of human consciousness, and how its evolution drives change in organizations.

Frederic Laloux wrote about his research and discoveries on this topic in his book *Reinventing Organizations: A Guide to Creating Organizations Inspired by the Next Stage of Human Consciousness*. His work caught the attention of Zappos CEO Tony Hsieh, who used Laloux's work to shift the consciousness of that company (so publicly that you may have heard of it).

Let's first explore human consciousness and then we'll delve into how this shapes organizations.

Human Consciousness

Human consciousness has been a focus of academic study for decades. For example, Stanford University is home to the Center for the Explanation of Consciousness and the University of Sussex houses the Centre for Consciousness Science. The Center for Consciousness Science is funded by the US National Institutes of Health and lives at the University of Michigan focusing on the neuroscience of conscious states. While the Division of Perceptual Studies at the University of Virginia investigates "the possibility of consciousness surviving physical death…and phenomena that challenge mainstream scientific paradigms regarding the nature of human consciousness."

One vein of this field studies consciousness as a mental state of alertness, ranging from unconsciousness (comatose) through decreasing levels of sleepiness, to highly alert and aware. Neuroscientists have mapped each level of alertness to different brain waves. Various learnable techniques, such as meditation, have been found to alter brain waves, which can help people achieve different levels of mental alertness.

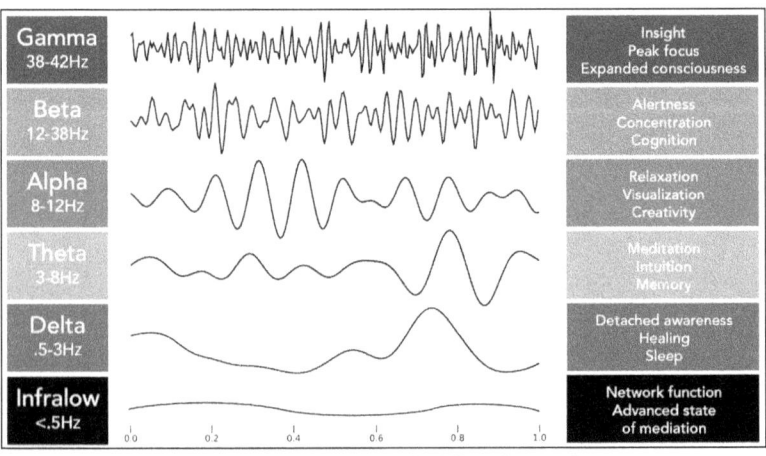

The range of brain waves and affiliated mental states

Another vein of research explores human consciousness as shift in awareness from self to one of connection to the collective. The continuum goes from egocentric, where the focus is solely on the self (AKA the "me" stage) to ethnocentric, where relationships shared with others brings awareness of common experiences, shared values and dreams, etc. (shifting from "me" to "us"), to world centric, at the other end of the continuum, where awareness expands to other groups and cultures around the world as well as to other sentient beings/species and the environment (from "us" to "all of us").

Other research explores the possibility that consciousness resides outside of the human body as a collective phenomenon shared by all living things. As Mark Gober, author of *The End to Upside Down Thinking: Dispelling the Myth That the Brain Produces Consciousness, and the Implications for Everyday Life*, frames it, "I've come to believe in nonlocal consciousness, or consciousness that originates outside our physical bodies and outside our brains. To me, this is the most scientifically sound explanation."

Scholars studying human consciousness from many disciplines—neuroscientists, biologists, psychologists, sociologists, and even anthropologists—have noted stages of development that they have associated with colors: infrared, magenta, red, amber, orange, green, teal, turquoise, indigo, violet, ultraviolet, and clear light.

Like Greiner's model, human consciousness also evolves in sudden transformations, where personal and world events create a challenge or pain point that must be resolved, catapulting someone to the next level of consciousness. Here are a few ways we often shift consciousness at an individual level:

Education
Learning about other people, places, and events can shift perspective. While much of K-12 education is centered around the core subjects of math, writing, science, and history, attending college exposes young adults to hundreds of fields of study. It often includes requirements for introductory courses across a wide range of disciplines, to expand their breadth of knowledge, and their academic major requires students to take several classes designed in increase their depth of knowledge in a specific field.

Experience
Lived experience is much more impactful than academic study. For example, in college, I took several courses on sociology and psychology. But a summer trip to Napa Valley with friends gave me a life-altering education. We rented a house for a week and were having a lot of fun. One day, at the grocery store picking up some things, we suddenly realized we had to hustle to make it to our reservation at a popular winery. Looking back as most of us got to the car, I yelled to my friend Carell, who was just coming out, "Run, Carell! We're going to be late!" His pace didn't change. The others joined in, "C'mon, Carell! We're going to miss our appointment! Run!" We watched in frustration as he slowly made

his way to the car. He calmly got in, turned to us, and said, "I am a black man. I will never run from a store. Ever. That's how you get killed because someone is going to assume that I have committed a crime." The rest of us, who are all white, sat there, stunned by the sudden insight. This was a pin-drop moment when I finally understood how much race mattered and that my experiences told me nothing of what other people experienced every day. We apologized to Carell and went on to the winery, but that moment set me on a path of learning about oppression and privilege, and listening to others' lived experiences.

Mindfulness
Practices such as meditation are designed to shift an egocentric view to one that's more detached. You become the observer of your own thoughts and feelings, which creates the opening to consider other views. While meditating, many people eventually experience an altered state of consciousness where they directly see or sense "collective" energy, or "all of us" state, but this usually occurs after developing an ongoing practice.

Spiritual Traditions
Many traditions, including religions and spiritual practices, are built around this journey. Spiritual experiences can raise a person's consciousness in profound and permanent ways.

Psychedelics
Studies show that certain psychedelic substances can alter human consciousness, allowing senses to merge, or creating feelings of sacred oneness. To learn more about the deeply researched medical and psychological benefits of using psychedelics therapeutically, read Michael Pollan's book *How to Change Your Mind: What the New Science of Psychedelics Teaches Us about Consciousness, Dying, Addiction, Depression, and Transcendence*.

Life Events
Painful experiences or trauma also have the power to shift our consciousness. Any cancer survivor will tell you that facing your mortality brings your values and priorities into sharp focus and increases your empathy for others who are suffering. People can experience a range of traumatic experiences including military combat/war, losing a loved one, being in an accident or natural disaster, having a chronic illness, surviving a sexual or physical assault, becoming a hostage or refugee, and also a global pandemic, such as COVID-19.

While this journey of human consciousness is individual and personal, scholars can also study the trends across the population, seeing where large groups are exhibiting similar levels of consciousness as well as when there are shifts in the bulk of the population.

We have currently entered a unique time, when consciousness is evolving more rapidly. The COVID-19 pandemic created a simultaneous and worldwide experience that greatly accelerated this pattern.

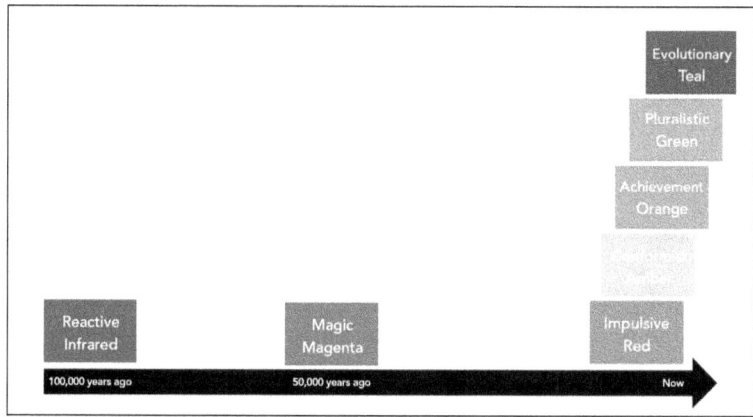

Timeline of human consciousness

Organizational Consciousness

Laloux discovered that organizational development maps to these stages of human consciousness and, as humans evolve, so do the organizations they build, with five levels of consciousness actively shaping organizations over the past 200 years. He wrote, "Every transition to a new stage of consciousness has ushered in a whole new era in human history. At every juncture, everything changed: society, the economy, the power structures…and organizational models." Laloux's work seeks to further define each organizational stage, mapping each to a corresponding color.

While it may seem far-fetched on its surface, he isn't the only one talking about the intersection of consciousness and business. Whole Foods CEO John Mackey partnered with Raj Sisodia to write *Conscious Capitalism*. Dr. Fred Kofman wrote *Conscious Business* and now consults with companies and governments around the world to integrate conscious practices.

And it's not just a feel-good exercise. Companies operating in the green and teal levels of consciousness significantly outperform others, according to *Firms of Endearment: How World-Class Companies Profit from Passion and Purpose* (by Rajendra Sisodia, David Wolfe, and Jagdish Sheth), a book that details a powerful study comparing over 65 companies to the companies featured in James Collins's bestselling book *Good to Great*. They found that *Firms of Endearment* companies outperformed the others by over 1,400 percent! Coauthor Raj Sisodia collaborated with Michael Gelb on another book—*The Healing Organization: Awakening the Conscience of Business to Help Save the World*—that examines the recent rise in purpose-driven organizations that align with the teal and indigo levels. We'll delve more into that later in this chapter.

In every place I have ever worked, whether as employee or consultant, I have seen evidence supporting Laloux's model, so I consider it an essential tool when assessing organizations. Conscious evolution is at the heart of many change initiatives, as well as shifts in what employees want from their workplaces. It's directly tied to employee recruitment, engagement, and retention. I will provide a quick summary here, but I strongly recommend you read *Reinventing Organizations* and view his posted videos and resources on ReinventingOrganizations.com. His rich research and detailed descriptions really helped me integrate this model in my work.

It's important to remember that no stage is better or worse than another. As Nick Petrie from the Center of Creative Leadership states, "There is nothing inherently 'better' about being at a higher level of development, just as an adolescent is not 'better' than a toddler. Any level of development is okay; the question is whether that level of development is a good fit for the task at hand."

Red/Impulsive
These organizations thrive in chaotic environments, like times of war or when competition for resources is high. These organizations are highly reactive and have a short-term focus. The constant exercise of power by the leader keeps people in line, and fear is the primary tool for control. The key breakthroughs of this stage are division of labor and command authority. Current examples in today's society include the mafia, tribal militias, and street gangs. Media headlines about events in the Middle East, Ukraine, and Venezuela show that this consciousness is expressed in times of intense survival.

Amber/Conformist
These organizations use top-down command and control as well as highly formal roles within a hierarchical pyramid. The goal is stability and consistency, which are often crucial to the organization's success. Leaders determine the "what" and "how" of the organization and members are expected to execute as instructed. Stability is achieved through rigorous processes and zero-tolerance for nonconformity. The core breakthroughs of this phase are formal roles, scalable hierarchies, and long-term processes. Current examples include military and law enforcement as well as public school systems and the Catholic Church.

Orange/Achievement
These organizations focus on profit and growth with the goal of beating the competition. Innovation is the key to staying ahead so this stage has driven much of modern capitalism. Leaders use management by objectives (MBOs) or key performance indicators (KPIs) to measure effectiveness and success. Peter Drucker has been a major voice of this stage. Organizations are guided by leaders using command and control but middle management has more freedom on how it gets done. The key breakthroughs of this rational/logical approach are accountability, meritocracy, and innovation. Current examples are global companies and charter schools.

	RED Impulsive	AMBER Conformist	ORANGE Achievement	GREEN Pluralistic	TEAL Evolutionary
Description	Thrives in chaotic environments. Constant exercise of power by leader to keep people in line. Fear's primary tool for control. Highly reactive, short-term focus.	Highly formal roles within hierarchical pyramid. Top-down command and control. Determines the org's "what" and "how." Stability highly valued and achieved through rigorous processes.	Goal is to beat the competition, achieve profit and growth. Innovation is the key to staying ahead. Management by objectives (command and control on the "what"; freedom on the "how").	Within the classic pyramid structure, focus is on culture and empowerment to achieve extraordinary employee motivation.	Org is seen as a living system with a direction of its own that needs to be listened to. Focus is on moving from ego to integrated wholeness and authenticity.
Key Breakthroughs	Division of labor Command authority	Formal roles (stable and scalable hierarchies) Processes (long-term perspectives)	Innovation Accountability Meritocracy	Empowerment Values-driven culture Stakeholder model	Self-management (based on peer relationships and roles, not job titles) Wholeness Evolutionary purpose
Guiding Metaphor	Wolf pack	Army	Machine	Family	Living organism
Current Examples	Mafia Tribal militias Street gangs	Military Most government agencies Public school systems Catholic Church	Multinational companies Charter schools	Culture-driven organizations (e.g., Southwest, Ben & Jerry's, LinkedIn)	Consciousness-driven orgs (e.g., Patagonia, FAVI, AES, Morning Star)
"Good" Decisions Judged by…	Achieving leader's desires	Conforming to social norms	Effectiveness and success Rational and logical	Belonging and harmony People/feeling process	Inner measure of rightness Being of service to world All forms of data from rational to intuitive Considers "both-and"

© Laloux

The levels of organizational consciousness

Green/Pluralistic
These organizations seek to stay competitive by harnessing extraordinary employee motivation and engagement, which research shows is a powerful driver of productivity, customer satisfaction, and retention. The definition of "stakeholder" expands beyond shareholders to include customers, employees, and communities. Green organizations focus on creating culture through attention to vision and values, aligned with purpose. We often hear through the media about culture-driven organizations like Patagonia, Zappos, Southwest Airlines, Google, HubSpot, Microsoft, Chewy, Adobe, SAP, ZipRecruiter, ADP, Ring Central, Workday, REI, etc. For more on the green stage, check out these books:

- *Delivering Happiness: A Path to Profits, Passion and Purpose* by Tony Hsieh
- *Firms of Endearment: How World-Class Companies Profit from Passion and Purpose* by Rajendra Sisodia, David Wolfe, and Jagdish Sheth
- *Conscious Business: How to Build Value Through Values* by Fred Kofman

In many organizations, I see a blend of orange and green consciousness. Many still set strategic and tactical goals using MBO or KPI terminology and measure productivity/success in terms of goal achievement. Most modern performance-management systems assess employees against goals, even if they are following the current trend of shifting traditional ratings and annual reviews.

At the same time, organizations are exhibiting quite a few green components as they compete for talent, especially among Millennial, Gen Z, and technically trained employees. They create values-driven cultures and focus on employee engagement, often offering all kinds of wonderful perks and benefits. They seek to foster a feeling of "family" within their organizations, with leaders who seek employee input of and strive to create an empowering environment.

Straddling orange and green stages at the same time is complicated—natural tensions inevitably lead to one superseding the other. For example, I often see organizations that present an outward-facing appearance of green elements (often overplayed to draw in good employees and paying customers) but with a solidly orange core to their day-to-day operations. Almost like green wrapping paper around an orange box. Employees drawn to a culture that appears green but is more orange in actuality are disappointed, which drives disengagement and turnover. I believe it is one of the reasons the average tenure of today's employee is a mere three years.

Teal/Evolutionary
Teal organizations started to emerge in 2012 but by no means were they all young startups. Laloux features eleven teal organizations in his book, ranging from 600 to 40,000 employees, across a wide range of industries, including apparel, manufacturing, technology, and healthcare. He depicts organizations as living systems with directions of their own that need to be listened to, which shifts the organizational structure from hierarchical to more localized and

collaborative teams. This shift ushers in new models of decision-making, job responsibilities, and performance management. Known as holacracy, key breakthroughs include self-management, wholeness, and authenticity. Current examples include Patagonia, Morning Star, and AES (a global energy company). In addition to Laloux's *Reinventing Organizations*, read *Holacracy: The New Management System for a Rapidly Changing World* by Brian Robertson, and *Conscious Capitalism: Liberating the Heroic Spirit of Business* by John Mackey and Rajendra Sisodia.

Note that while this is an evolutionary process, some organizations align with a certain stage because it best suits their mission and work. For example, the military will likely always align with the Amber/Conformist stage because it must succeed in often chaotic and dangerous environments where adherence to strict processes is paramount. That doesn't mean that it won't adopt some elements of other stages, but its core structure and way of working will stay amber.

Indigo/Transcendence

The hallmarks of indigo consciousness include self-transcendence, with a sense of purpose and meaning focused on being of service to others. This comes from an understanding that all things are connected, along with greater compassion for, and even cherishing of, others. Stakeholders now include suppliers, families of employees and customers, and more holistic views of communities and the environment. In addition, the tone changes from "do no harm" to focusing on ending suffering and creating healing. This shift naturally initiates a breakdown of old paradigms and structures, as many were birthed from previous consciousnesses and are no longer compatible with the new level of evolution.

As mentioned, Raj Sisodia studies purpose-driven organizations, documenting their rise since 2000 and tracking their continued outstanding financial performance. In their book *The Healing Organization*, Sisodia and coauthor Michael Gelb articulate four stages of purpose-focused businesses that exist on a continuum from profit-driven to healing-driven.

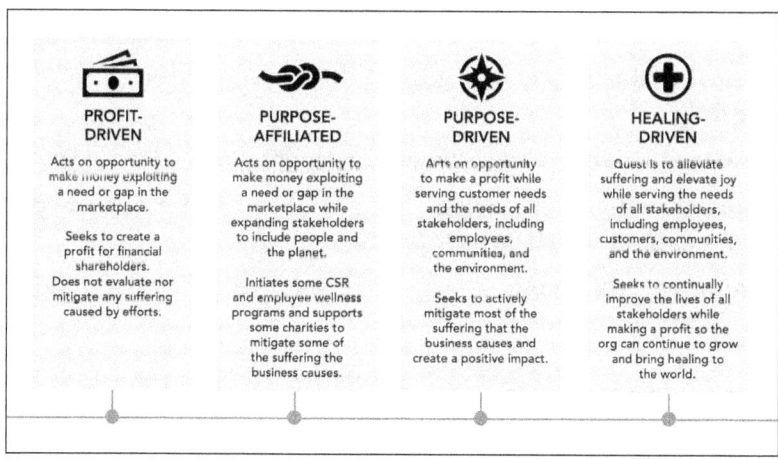

Continuum of purpose-driven organizations

From their data, Sisodia and Gelb highlight eighteen "healing organizations," which share these qualities:
- Their employees love coming to work
- Their customers are passionately loyal
- They have a strong and positive impact on the communities they serve
- They preserve and restore the ecosystems in which they operate

The major business researchers—McKinsey, Deloitte, Gallup, and Gartner—have all started publishing reports and feature articles on purpose-driven organizations. McKinsey released a report titled *The Search for Purpose at Work*. They found that 70 percent of people (all generations) say they define their purpose *through* work. In other words, people want their jobs to bring a "significant sense of purpose to their lives."

Certainly, the pandemic has clarified this. McKinsey's report stated, "One of the really interesting pieces that we found in the research is that nearly 7 out of 10 employees are reflecting on their purpose because of the coronavirus disease, or COVID-19. In fact, we found that, as a result of COVID-19, half of American employees are reconsidering the work that they want to do."

Other data supports this notion that profit-only is a thing of the past. Only seven percent of Fortune 500 CEOs believe their companies should "mainly focus on making profits and not be distracted by social goals." The new norm is the "triple bottom line," which Harvard Business School calls the three Ps: profit, people, and the planet. This philosophy is at the heart of most current MBA programs. As we see in the above diagram, the triple bottom line covers three of the four stages on the continuum.

As the focus turns to healing, it is natural to consider well-being and thriving or flourishing. Gallup has also turned their attention to well-being and now measures thriving along with engagement. They argue that well-being includes the following five elements:

1. **Meaningful work/career well-being:** Liking what you do each day and being motivated to achieve your goals
2. **Physical well-being:** Having good health and enough energy to get things done daily
3. **Social well-being:** Having supportive relationships and love in your life
4. **Financial well-being:** Earning a living wage and managing your economic life to reduce stress and increase security
5. **Community well-being:** Liking where you live, feeling safe, and having pride in your community

The US Surgeon General's report titled *Workplace Mental Health and Well-Being* released a new framework that identifies five essential elements: protection from harm, connection and community, work-life harmony, mattering at work, and opportunity for growth. These two frameworks are becoming more central to how organizations define their cultures and articulate what sets them apart from their competitors. This differentiation is highly appealing to both employees and consumers of all ages, but is particularly important to Millennials, Gen Alpha, and Gen Z, who care passionately about the environment and social equality.

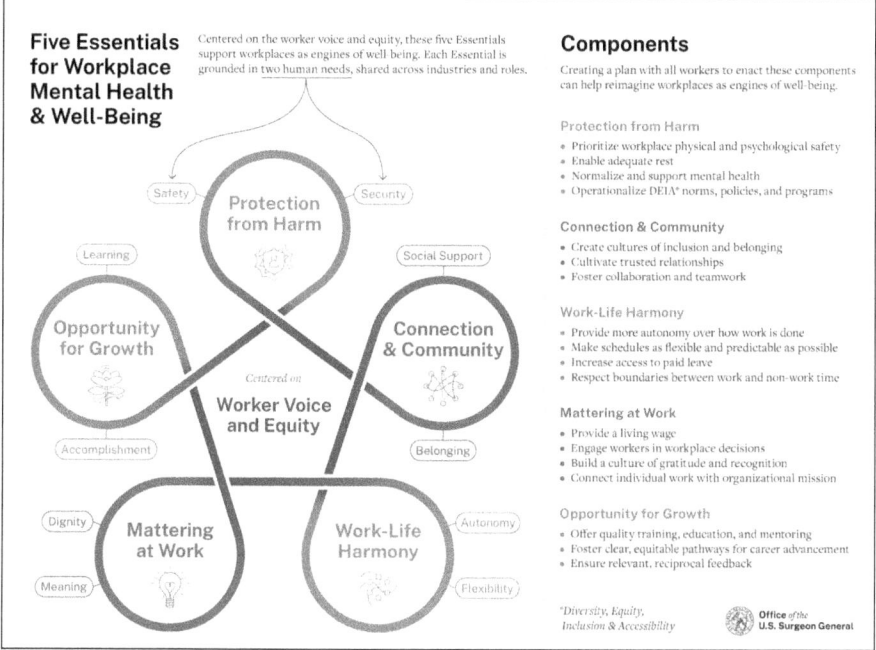

The five essentials for workplace mental health and well-being

Clearly, the conscious evolution of organizations drives many change initiatives, sourced from employees, the leaders, or the customers as the different stages come online. We will continue to see elements of orange and green, but more and more leaders are realizing that they need to shift to teal and indigo in order to gain and keep employees and customers.

As more and more humans express those next levels of violet and ultraviolet, we will see them make their way into human society and organizations decades from now.

21. The Environment and Climate Change

Our physical environment is another major driver of change. For eons, humans have worked with their surroundings, settling in areas that offer sufficient food and water sources. Land development has also accommodated the geography as we've built homes, businesses, and roads. Modern engineering has offered creative new solutions such as man-made islands and skyscrapers that seemingly defy gravity. We can travel to far-off locations via airplanes and submarines, and space travel will become the norm in the not-so-distant future.

Weather patterns also impact our activities and create change. For example, we move through the natural rhythms of the seasons. This regular pattern creates massive shifts in the agricultural and food industries, as well as the fashion and retail industries. Winter resort staffs get ready for skiers and snowboarders and summer resorts prepare for bikers, fishers, and swimmers. We also experience the common reactions to weather events, like seasonal snow removal or spring runoff. And of course, every natural disaster triggers a coordinated response from local officials.

But *how* we have successfully managed these shifts is twofold. First, they have been largely predictable in either their timing, location, or scale. Second, we have built strategies for responding to them, which we have improved through experience. For example, while tornadoes are not predictable, we know where they typically happen and have tools for monitoring them, warning people to prepare for their impact, and responding to the aftermath of their damage.

Unfortunately, the looming environmental shift will intensify natural disasters, creating new types of events that are much more damaging to industries and communities around the world. Organizations are *not* sufficiently prepared for what is coming.

As a scientist, I want to state that the future of climate change is very clear. While this discussion has been politicized for years, the reality is that the science is irrefutable. This is not just the opinion of a handful of people but rather the collective knowing among eight million active scientists in the world. Hundreds of thousands of scientists study the impact of climate change in a variety of fields. Further, 90 to 100 percent of publishing climate scientists agree that not only is climate change happening, but they have clear predictions of what our future looks like.

In interviewing several senior leaders for this book, I found that few executive teams are having discussions about the implications for their business, let alone making concrete plans to address them.

This chapter focuses on what is coming, much of which has already started and is reflected in headlines every year. For example, according to the National Oceanic and Atmospheric Administration (NOAA), 2024 brought an "historic number of billion-dollar disasters" with 27 disasters in the US alone. The total cost is nearly $182.7 billion in damages, lost inventory, buildings, staffing, and insurance, to name a few. Tragically, these disasters caused 568 fatalities.

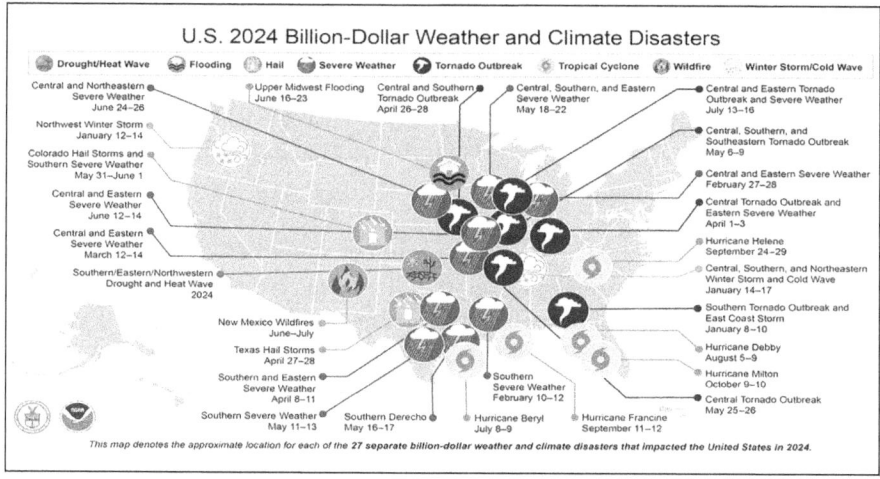

Billion-dollar weather and climate disasters in the US during 2024

Weather-based disasters are on the rise everywhere. Consider these recent devastating events:

- An intense cyclone hits Malawi in Africa, costing 1,000 lives and displacing 184,000 people (2023).
- Torrential rain and flooding strike Libya, killing 5,923 people with another 14,000 still missing and presumed dead (2023).
- A wildfire (sparked by heavy winds from a hurricane) razed the town of Lahaina on the Hawaiian island of Maui, costing 102 lives, and damaging the main source of income (tourism) for years to come (2023).
- Hurricane Helene caused widespread damage (~$90 billion) across Cuba, Mexico, and the US, with a death toll of 232 people (2024).
- Flash floods hit the European Union, causing widespread damage in Spain and killing 237 people (2024).
- Wildfires burned over 210 million acres across South America in Brazil, Bolivia, Chile, Colombia, Ecuador, and Peru (2024).
- An unprecedented blizzard along the Gulf Coast of the US caused over 75,000 power outages, halting travel, and costing over $500 million in damages and 13 deaths (2025).
- Cyclone Alfred hit Australia, causing severe beach erosion to the Gold Coast, which lost four million cubic tons of sand. The agriculture sector lost $17 million in crop damage and destruction of orchard trees (2025).

Many countries saw some of the worst disasters they have seen in decades and these events will become both more frequent and intense. In fact, scientists predict that extreme precipitation events will increase fourfold, and hurricanes will triple. As a result, the United Nations Climate Change Conference, called COP28, launched a "loss and damage" fund to provide financial assistance to developing countries for the costs of climate change.

Risks to Businesses

As we look at organizations, preparing for this new reality is imperative. At Columbia Business School, Dr. Bruce Usher studies financial investing and climate change. He identifies three environmental risks that cause businesses to fail when they are not adequately prepared: technological, policy, and physical.

Technological Risks

Certain products and ways of business will become obsolete, and companies will need to adapt or close their doors. Obviously, we can think of the shift away from fossil fuels and combustible engines leading to a world of vehicles powered by other sources like electricity or hydrogen.

Another example is the skiing industry. Ski resorts around the world are facing the reality that warming temperatures leave many without sufficient snow to operate for a season, threatening winter tourism in mountain regions. While many have turned to making artificial snow, this still requires temperatures below 0 degrees Celsius (32 Fahrenheit), and the number of those has been declining. In Montana and Colorado between 1980 and 2010, the average was 150 to 175 days. Estimates for 2020 to 2039 drop to 100 to 125 days, and as low as 75 days by 2080 to 2099.

If that seems too far off in the future to you, consider that in 1980, there were 81 operational ski areas in Montana and now there are only 16. This shift is directly impacting the Olympic Winter Games, reducing the number of sites that can host them. In fact, the International Olympic Committee estimates that only 15 countries on three continents will have "climate-reliable" venues for snow sports, due to climate change.

Policy-related Risks

Government agencies will pass new regulations in order to shift behavior by businesses and consumers alike, all of which will generate financial costs. For example, governments around the world are implementing new regulations for vehicle emissions. This directly impacts all aspects of car manufacturing from the design process to assembly on the factory floor, forcing major adjustments and costs.

Another example is the energy sector as governments are requiring higher percentages from renewable sources like wind and solar. This requires energy-based businesses to quickly adapt or risk closing down.

Physical Risks

The many physical risks from climate change include damage to business facilities and properties through events like extreme flooding and landslides, intense storms with high winds that exceed current building codes, and rising sea levels that will make entire regions inaccessible.

Further, costs include lawsuits and other financial liabilities such as higher insurance or costs of rebuilding or relocating. Consider this headline from the

Wall Street Journal: "PG&E: The First Climate-Change Bankruptcy, Probably Not the Last." Climate change drove a decade-long drought in California. In 2017, PG&E power lines triggered 17 major wildfires and destroyed nearly 200,000 acres. The damage spread over eight counties and killed 22 people, making it the most deadly and destructive fire season on record. PG&E faced $30 billion in liabilities leading it to seek bankruptcy.

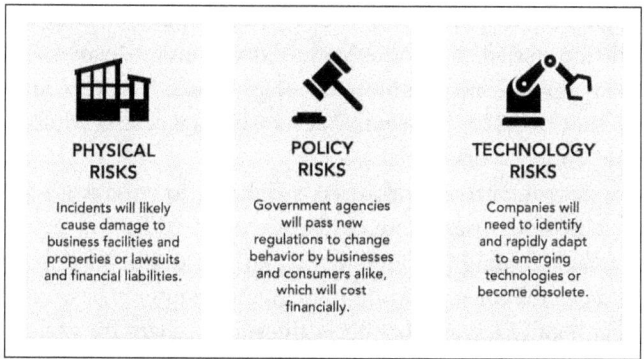

The three types of climate-related risks

In 2024, Texas experienced the largest wildfire in the state's history, burning over 1.1 million acres, which spread to Oklahoma. Utility company Xcel Energy has acknowledged that its facilities ignited the fire and will likely face similar legal and financial consequences. One headline reads, "The Great Plains now have 'wildfire years,' not seasons, as blazes start and spread earlier."

Tropical storms are also intensifying. Hurricane Otis defied all computer prediction models, rapidly growing from a tropical storm to a category 5, with sustained winds of 165 miles per hour and killing 27. Several modern high-rise buildings suffered unexpectedly severe damage, with walls blown out through the core of the buildings. This storm highlighted that current building codes may not be sufficient to withstand increasingly intense storms, suggesting the emphatic need for major refitting costs for businesses, which will be expensive.

Other ways climate change impacts businesses: Recently, China and India experienced extended heat waves, with "unsurvivable" temperatures. Not only did the daytime temperatures reach 47 degrees Celsius (116 Fahrenheit), the nighttime temperatures did not drop enough to provide the necessary reprieve.

In India, this created a cascading effect as people used more water in attempting to cool down, further depleting an already drought-ridden region. People used fans and air conditioners, initially pushing and then buckling the electrical power grids. Currently, only about 10 percent of buildings have air conditioners so this strain will likely grow in future. During this episode, thousands needed treatment for heat-related illnesses, straining already taxed medical facilities. Many died. In fact, 50 to 60 percent of total deaths in India in 2023 were heat-related mortalities.

In one rather alarming study from the University of Cambridge, researchers state, "Long-term projections indicate that Indian heatwaves could cross the survivability limit for a healthy human resting in the shade by 2050. They will impact the labor productivity, economic growth, and quality of life of around 310 to 480 million people. Estimates show a 15 percent decrease in outdoor working capacity during daylight due to extreme heat."

India is the most populated country on the planet, with 1.43 billion people. It represents nearly 18 percent of the world's population and is the world's largest workforce, according to the Society for Human Resource Management (SHRM). Many global corporations employ Indian workers and Ernst and Young states that by 2030, India will have 1 billion working adults—nearly one quarter of the world's workforce.

What happens when that workforce is fighting to survive a scorching heatwave? From a business perspective, heatwaves in India will have several significant impacts, including productivity, when it is too hot for people to work; utility costs, as companies attempt to regulate temperatures; insurance costs (property, health and life); and breaks in the supply chain for various industries. For example, COVID-19 surges in both China and India impacted manufacturing of goods in a range of industries, such as chip manufacturing, creating supply delays that played out for more than a year, causing disruptions in the car, computer, and many other industries. Some of which haven't returned to pre-pandemic stability.

India also represents a large percentage of the world's consumers, behind only the US and China. BMI reports that by 2027 India will be the world's third largest consumer market—which is also destined to be heavily impacted by heatwaves when people can't leave their homes to shop or get online due to power outages. Or have less money or time to shop due to heat-related illness, or even death. One week of high temperatures can cost millions of dollars in varying costs to businesses across a range of industries.

The Effects of Global Warming

As the planet warms, it causes a variety of shifts. Earth's atmosphere acts like a greenhouse, keeping the air around the planet within a certain range of life-sustaining temperatures. But now human activity is adding heat to the greenhouse faster than it can dissipate into space, much like when you roll up your car windows on a hot day. It is rising rapidly, and scientists recently started using the term "global boiling" to indicate the severity. In this section, I'll outline the seven major impacts of climate change.

Temperature is rising.
There is no doubt that the planet has warmed. Scientists have been keeping a range of records that confirm that the planet has warmed 1.1 degrees Celsius (2.1 Fahrenheit). Some people find it hard to believe that one to two degrees make a difference, but it only takes one degree to turn water into ice or steam.

What is most concerning is that, after 10,000 years of relative stability, the increase in temperature is accelerating, with the bulk occurring in the last 40 years and the past seven years have been the warmest. The World Meteorological Organization (WMO) officially confirmed that 2024 was the warmest year on record, by a huge margin, with every month from June to December logging new highs around the globe.

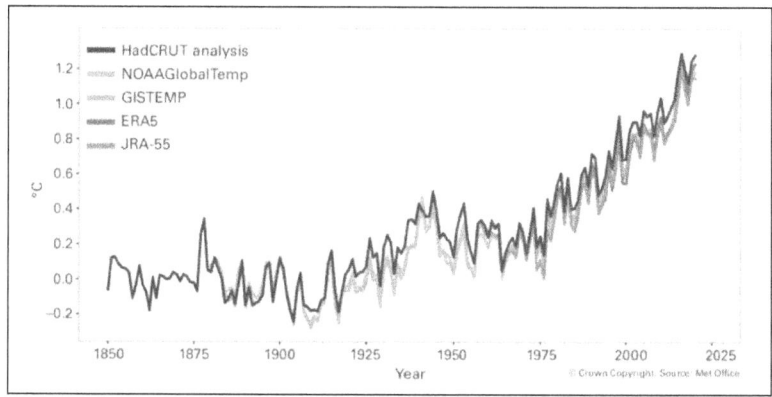

Five different measurement models show rapidly rising global temperature

According to ice core samples and tree ring analysis, the earth hasn't been this warm in 100,000 years. This means that in all of human history, no modern society has endured this level of heat. We are truly in unchartered territory.

This planetary warming is setting off a domino effect of several factors causing the climate to change and creating more dramatic evidence we can see and feel in our own communities. I highlight the major ones here so you can take the ramifications of each into consideration for your future plans.

Snow cover is decreasing.
Not surprisingly, as the planet warms, snow cover decreases. We have fewer and fewer days below the freezing point, which impacts snowfalls, as on warmer days it turns to rain before hitting the ground. Snow cover also melts faster, making it harder to build up the thick layer of snow needed for certain activities like skiing and snowboarding. We've already discussed the impact this is having on winter resorts and even the Olympic Games, but it also impacts flooding as a large amount of melting snow can release more water than rivers can handle.

It can also melt during the day but then freeze again overnight as temperatures drop, creating treacherous driving conditions that increase property damage, injuries, and even deaths. Even avalanches are impacted, as snow stacks and icy layers are more likely to fracture, causing tons of snow to plummet downhill. Recently, several ski resorts have experienced unexpected avalanches that injured or killed guests.

Scientists have discovered, as winters hit an average temperature of 17 degrees Fahrenheit (-8.3C), the timing speeds up, hurtling that area toward the "snow-loss cliff" where it will become snow-free. Consider this headline from a *Business Insider* article: "RIP Snow: American winters are getting so warm your kids may never get to build a snowman."

Ice sheets and glaciers are melting/shrinking.
Warmer temperatures also impact the earth's stores of ice. The large ice sheets in Greenland and Antarctica have historically played a role in keeping the earth the right temperature. Researchers use satellite photos and ice core samples, among many analytical tools, to measure the changes and found they are melting/shrinking at a concerning rate. Greenland's ice sheet has lost an average of 279 billion tons of ice per year (per year!) from 1993 to 2019. For Antarctica, the number is 148 billion tons per year. The Arctic Sea also holds ice and is declining at a similar rate. This massive conversion of ice to water is contributing to sea level rise.

What is particularly troubling is that as these ice sheets melt, they have the potential to dramatically change ocean currents. For example, Greenland's sheet could cause the Atlantic Meridional Overturning Circulation (AMOC) current to collapse, which would change weather worldwide. To a lesser extent, the Gulf Stream is also expected to be affected.

Glaciers are also melting/shrinking. Glaciers occur on land, in mountainous areas, and are a build-up of snow over time that creates a large, solid ice structure that gravity slowly moves downhill. Glacial ice samples show that they can range in age from 30,000 to 1 million years old. But they are disappearing simultaneously from the Alps, Andes, Alaska, Africa, Himalayas, and the Rockies. Glacial runoff contributes to further flooding in rivers and to sea level rise when that water reaches the ocean.

Sea level is rising.
Nearly three-quarters (71 percent) of the earth is covered by oceans, divided into the Pacific, Atlantic, Indian, and Antarctic. As all this ice melts, sea levels rise. Much like when you overfill your bathtub—except, unfortunately, we have no high-level drain to keep the sea from spilling over. In the last 100 years, the global sea level has risen eight inches (20 centimeters). And just like rising temperatures, the rate has accelerated, with the last 20 years producing twice as much sea level rise as the previous 100. NASA has built an interactive online map for projecting sea level rise. Explore the impact by visiting the website https://sealevel.nasa.gov/ipcc-ar6-sea-level-projection-tool.

Sea level rise has several implications for all of us. First, for those living near the coast, which is about 40 percent of the world's population, sea level is rising faster each year and is predicted to require the relocations of millions of people around the world. For example, the US government has published a 500-page report on the impact on businesses and communities in all the states bordering the Gulf of Mexico (Florida, Alabama, Mississippi, Louisiana, and Texas). The goal of this effort is to "analyze the unique challenges, needs, and opportunities associated with managing the relocation of people, infrastructure, and communities away from environmentally high-risk areas…in ways that are equitable, culturally appropriate, adaptive, and resilient to future regional climate conditions."

Second, storms can create a surge, immediately threatening homes, businesses, and lives. Winds build a tsunami-like push of ocean water inland, often raising water levels by up to 20 feet. Because water weighs about 1,700 pounds per cubic yard, the surge is strong enough to push large buildings off their foundations, with homes and cars floating back out to sea when the waters recede. Storm surges frequently damage roads, bridges, railways, sewers, and pipelines, creating long term challenges for the area.

Third, another often overlooked consequence of storm surges is that they ruin farmland. Pouring salt on agricultural land has long been used in war to prevent a community from growing food. So, the effects of storm surges exacerbate food shortages during times of upheaval, while contaminating groundwater, which impacts precious stores of fresh drinking water.

The major effects of global warming

Oceans are warming.
Scientists used terms like "unprecedented" and "astounding" when describing the sudden increase in ocean temperatures this year.

The ocean acts as a sponge, absorbing most of the heat (90 percent) trapped by our atmosphere. And it is the warmest it has been in the past 1,000 years, as confirmed by both the US NOAA and the World Meteorological Organization. Particularly, the top 100 meters (328 feet) of water warmed by 0.07 degrees Celsius in the last six months of 2024—now 0.61°C (1.1°F) above a 1981-2010 baseline. The ocean absorbed an additional 16 zettajoules of heat (compared to 2023) for a total of 1021—in contrast, humanity uses 0.5 zettajoule of energy per year to fuel the entire global economy.

Warming oceans harm fisheries, decreasing their populations. This directly impacts the people whose income comes from fishing (an estimated 650 to 800 million people worldwide).

Warming oceans fuel the strength of monsoons and spiraling tropical storms, which are called different names depending on over which ocean they form. Hurricanes form over the North Atlantic, central North Pacific, and eastern North Pacific, while typhoons develop over the Northwest Pacific, and cyclones develop over the South Pacific and Indian Oceans.

Warming oceans are also fueling unusual events like 100 percent relative humidity in China and South Asia. The air becomes saturated with moisture causing it to accumulate on walls and ceilings and then drip down to soak whatever is below it. Electronics short out, floors become dangerously slippery, and potato chips turn into mashed potatoes in the bag. In addition, super-fogs form, limiting visibility and increasing accidents. Increased humidity is also known to worsen allergies and make infectious diseases more transmissible.

Extreme weather events are increasing.
Recent years show how warming oceans increase the frequency and intensity of tropical storms, causing extensive damage as they make landfall. Because of recent storms, weather scientists are proposing to add a category 6 level to the long-standing five levels used for categorizing spiraling storms. Previously, category 5 was for storms exceeding 157 mph but will now be used for storms up to 191 mph and category 6 will be for storms exceeding 192 mph. To date, five storms have already hit that level in the last decade, including Hurricane Patricia, Typhoon Haiyan, and Typhoon Meranti. It's likely that more levels may be required in future years. This is known as "hazard intensification" and we'll see similar shifts for all kinds of weather events.

Tropical storms also bring storm surges, torrential rains, and flooding, all of which threaten property and people. Scientists estimate that damage from a monsoon in a crowded city, like Ho Chi Minh City, could dramatically increase from a cost of $300 million today to more than $1 billion by 2050.

As weather events intensify, it's likely we will need new standards for building codes, which will have implications for retrofitting existing buildings as well as insurance coverage, rates, and even availability. For example, in Florida, most home insurance companies have withdrawn coverage or are charging rates nearly four times higher than any other state.

In addition, extreme weather events like these are increasing in frequency and intensity, setting records each year around the world:
- High temperature days, including heat waves
- Droughts, causing water and food shortages and increasing wildfire risk
- Wildfires that destroy property and wildlife, and sometimes kill
- Smoke and super-fog, generated by wildfires, that can impact visibility and the air quality index for hundreds of miles
- Atmospheric rivers that bring torrential rains, including "rain bombs" that create record snowfall, flooding, and mudslides
- Polar vortexes that bring extremely cold air further south, creating dangerously cold temperatures both in regions accustomed to winter as

well as to those more tropical climates that are unprepared, buckling the power grid as people attempt to stay warm
- New headlines are added every day

Ocean acidification is increasing.
As the oceans warm while absorbing all that extra heat, it impacts the chemical makeup of the water, making the surface waters more acidic. In fact, the acidity has increased by about 30 percent, threatening the health of everything from coral and cold-water reefs to shellfish like crabs and shrimp to entire fisheries. Ocean acidification eats away the minerals that shellfish use to build their shells and skeletons, prompting the name "the osteoporosis of the sea." This impacts the food chain for fish, birds, and marine mammals.

It harms fisheries, impacting humans as one-fifth of the world's population derives 20 percent of its animal protein intake from fish. In addition, acidic conditions allow certain species of algae to bloom faster and produce more harmful toxins, potentially poisoning marine life and humans alike. Analysis by NOAA indicates that, at the current rate, the oceans will become 150 percent more acidic by the end of this century, achieving a level not seen in 20 million years.

Clearly, humans are not the only ones impacted by climate change, and it's happening on land too. In 2023, the Living Planet Index (LPI)—which monitors the world's populations of mammals, birds, fish, reptiles, and amphibians—reported an average decline of 69 percent in species populations since 1970. Think about that—more than two-thirds of Earth's species have disappeared in just fifty years!

Latin America shows the greatest regional decline (94 percent), while freshwater species populations have seen the greatest overall global decline (83 percent). Scientists at the UN Convention on Biological Diversity recently concluded that, "Every day, up to 150 species may go extinct. This means as many as 10 percent of species a decade." This has implications as animal species are used by humans for food sources, labor, and even medicines.

It's undeniable that our warming climate is driving all kinds of changes that we'll experience and to which we must adapt. Companies and governments around the world are currently working on helpful ways to reduce carbon emissions. But we need to move from reacting to individual events to creating a cohesive plan for meeting the reality barreling toward us. Global consulting firm McKinsey states,

> *"Physical climate risk and its socioeconomic impacts will affect everyone, directly or indirectly. While stakeholders and decision-makers are trying to respond to climate changes, there are three steps that we think they could consider: integrating climate risk into decision-making, accelerating the pace and scale of adaptation, and decarbonization at scale to prevent a further buildup of risks."*

Further, they argue that we will need to make decisions about "where to invest versus retreat" as we address each threat. For example, rising sea levels: one reaction is to invest, to build sea walls out in the water, while another option is to retreat, relocating people and buildings further inland. Both will require massive levels of resources, like money and energy, and will also require an extraordinary amount of coordination.

In terms of adaptation, every region is going to need to pursue a combination of investing strategies—such as building cooling shelters or innovating new food sources that are resistant to droughts and ocean acidification—as well as retreating strategies that will likely involve the migration of millions of people and animals finding stable ways to grow essential crops in new locations.

Given the level of climate change already underway, we need action now. Investors seem to have a clear view of our future and are pushing for radical change. Over 400 investors from around the world have come together to push governments and the United Nations to take more decisive action. Together, they control $32 trillion in assets and understand the threat that slow action will mean. They have signed the Global Investor Statement to Governments on Climate Change, where they lay out a demand for urgent action. One member states, "The reality is that the long-term nature of the challenge has, in our view, met a zombie-like response by many." They identify the potential for long-term and even catastrophic permanent damage to the world's economy.

But responding to climate change will also create opportunities. As the leader of one investment firm that manages $207 billion in assets describes it, "The transition to a low-carbon economy presents numerous opportunities to create value, and investors who ignore the changing world do so at their own peril."

In section VI, I'll provide some tools and strategies for senior leaders to use as they prepare for this inevitable future.

Change Journey 15
Industry: Investment
We are currently dealing with environment-driven change on multiple fronts. First, we built our headquarters in Boston and sea-level rise causes flooding several times per year to the point where we are relocating inland.

Second, we have offices in Chicago and Toronto where there are more intense winter storms than before. More of our employees are requesting to move, and we're having difficulty recruiting in those areas.

Third, one of our clients is a third-generation fishing business based in the Gulf of Mexico. They've been a leader for 50 years, but can no longer bring in the catches they once did. The CEO told me he feels completely unprepared for how to envision a future strategy based on a past that no longer exists.

22. Technology and Intelligence

There is no doubt that technology drives change. Since the creation of the first computer, we have been on a fast-moving bullet train of change. In fact, even bullet-train technology is speeding up, with new models in China and Japan reaching 280 mph or 450 kph.

If you drive through the commercial area of your town, you can see the impact of technology in those empty storefronts with "For Lease" signs on their doors. In addition to facilitating the rise of multinational chains that undercut the higher costs charged by small-scale operators, the final blow to brick-and-mortar stores was dealt by the onset of online shopping, which allowed consumers to buy without leaving their homes. Analysts expect this trend to continue.

Shopping is just one example. We are firmly in the middle of the fourth industrial revolution (4IR) that has pushed product innovation and organizational change in every industry. We can track major shifts through the preceding revolutions, bringing us to today, with the influence of the "internet of things" (IoT), cloud networks, and machine learning, to the explosion of artificial intelligence, and cyber-physical systems.

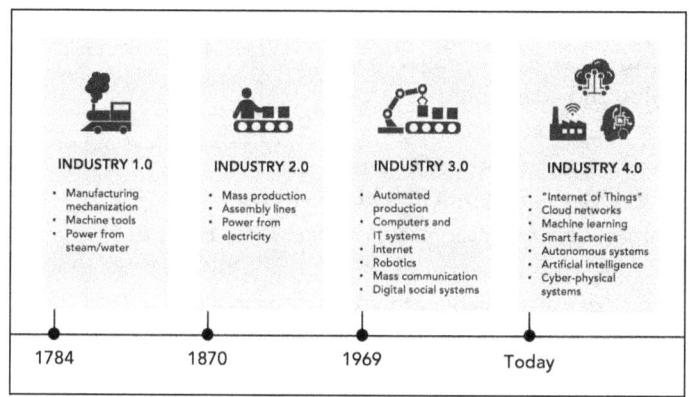

The four industrial revolutions

As Klaus Schwab, the Chair of the World Economic Forum has said, "In this fourth revolution, we are facing a range of new technologies that combine the physical, digital, and biological worlds. These new technologies will impact all disciplines, economies, and industries, and even challenge our ideas about what it means to be human."

Technology impacts every level of society from the individual to corporations and governments. Consider the changes you've experience in your own personal life. You likely have a smart phone in your pocket that has more computing power than the original large servers at NASA. And that phone can turn on the heat in your home from miles away, or deposit money in your bank account, or book your vacation flights and activities.

Also consider how often that phone changes: new versions of apps drop daily, and every new operating system pushes changes that can impact some of your well-grooved habits. So many aspects of our daily lives are now permanently tied to technology.

Now multiply that impact by every piece of technology at your job. From your computer to every system you use to do your daily work, like managing a project, communicating with your team, reaching your customers, and using your health benefits. Work systems are incredibly complex and a shift in one area, such as your ERP or your CRM can wreak havoc on other systems if they don't align perfectly.

No wonder IT personnel are often the highest paid with the strongest job security. Or at least they have been. More on that later in this chapter.

Technology at Work

Technology is a powerful catalyst for organizational change, influencing various aspects of business strategy and operations. The most common impacts:

1. Process automation
2. Data-driven decision-making
3. Digital transformation
4. Innovation in products and services
5. Enhanced communication and collaboration
6. Improved customer engagement
7. Agility and adaptability
8. Cost reduction
9. Risk mitigation and compliance
10. Employee empowerment and development

But incorporating technological advancements requires strategic leadership and a culture that embraces change. Each technology must align with organizational goals to drive sustainable growth and success.

The Speed of Change

The speed of change in technology continues to increase. For much of the past 60 years, this has been due to Moore's law, which states that the number of transistors on a microchip doubles about every two years, with a corresponding decrease in cost. Coined in 1965 by Intel co-founder Gordon Moore, Moore's law undergirds the success of the semiconductor industry that powers devices of all types and purposes. Today's transistors are microscopic, printed on small sheets of carbon and silicon, and are the highest global import/export value, and the fourth in volume.

Some have argued that Moore's law will reach its end before 2030, because while it's technically possible to keep adding more elements in smaller spaces, it becomes harder to cool the heat they generate. However, others feel that innovation is solving this problem in new ways, such as stacking chip structures into multi-layers, or using non-silicon materials, or new lithography techniques.

As technology speeds up, so does its adoption. For example, the image on p. 8 shows how, when the telephone was invented in 1876, it took 35 years for 25 percent of the US population to begin using it. The television hit that level in 26 years, the mobile phone 13 years, and the smart phone in 4. But then the tablet only took 2 years and the launch of ChatGPT, the AI large language search model, reached 25 percent adoption in less than a year!

This journey of adoption is at the heart of so many businesses and how they compete for market share. Sometimes the first on the scene takes the prize, but often a smaller competitor comes along later and builds a better product that disrupts the hierarchy. The ultimate competitive advantage is how fast these organizations can change internally and then get their customers to change too.

Take Skype and Zoom, for example. When the COVID-19 pandemic hit, Microsoft's Skype was already positioned as the go-to video service, which was suddenly in exponential demand. But they were quickly overtaken by Zoom that had focused more resources on better business features and call performance.

The pandemic drove rapid technology change around the world. Futurist Amy Webb states, "Thanks to the COVID-19 pandemic, 2020 saw a decade of digital transformation in the span of a few months." It fueled leaps forward in many related areas:
- Remote work
- Contactless interactions
- Collaborative tools
- Blockchain
- Artificial intelligence
- Cryptocurrencies
- Online learning
- And at least 500 more

For all these reasons, technology is one of the four core drivers of change in industries around the world.

Challenges with Technology

For all of technology's successes, its challenges can cause a company to falter or even fail. Consider this list of real examples and how they impact both the organization and its employees or customers.

The impact of small errors in code pushed out by cybersecurity firm CrowdStrike on July 19, 2024, causing the largest global IT outage in history. The incident rendered over 8.5 million Microsoft Windows devices/hosts inoperable, causing more than $5 billion in financial losses. The health care and banking sectors were hardest hit, with respective losses of $1.94 billion and $1.15 billion. Many airlines shut down for the day, and Delta Airlines is suing CrowdStrike, claiming that 7,000 canceled flights cost them more than $500 million.

According to the Financial Conduct Authority, which regulates the financial industry, states that, "issues linked to third parties such as technology suppliers, were the leading cause of 'operational incidents' in recent years" and have asked the institutions it oversees to plan for and demonstrate resilience to further crises like the one created by CrowdStrike.

Or how hackers continue to breach secure databases, releasing sensitive personal data from customers of companies like Capital One, Marriott, Heartland Payroll, eBay, Target, Equifax, LinkedIn, The Home Depot, and Microsoft.

Other small, but costly, technology errors occur every day as chatbots attempt to provide customer support. Consider the lawsuit against Air Canada, whose chatbot provided a passenger misinformation about discounted fares for bereavement travel. The passenger won the case, and the court found Air Canada guilty of "negligent misrepresentation." This and other cases are establishing that companies are legally responsible for their use of artificial intelligence.

There's a lot of discussion lately about AI generative models providing wrong answers (AKA "hallucinating"). For example, when asked to research a topic and provide a list of sources, ChatGPT will create a list of very real looking citations for studies—except that many are fake. There are several instances of lawyers using ChatGPT to prepare their legal briefs, only to discover that the cases were fabricated. They suffered sanctions, fines, and having their cases thrown out. Some were even fired from their firms.

AI is also now capable of producing realistic videos and audio messages that can be used for nefarious purposes. During the 2024 US presidential election, one organization created a realistic robocall audio message, supposedly from President Joe Biden, telling voters in New Hampshire to not vote in the primary and to "save" their vote for the November election. This is just one of over 1,000 incidents reported to the Artificial Intelligence Incident Database, which will surely grow as AI becomes more enmeshed in our lives. Similar examples of election interference have been reported around the world.

Realistic AI videos are also involved in significant crimes. Consider the Hong Kong finance worker who received an email from his CFO requesting that he transfer $25 million in funds. He was suspicious until he was invited to a video call where he saw his CFO and several other leaders confirm the request. The deepfake videos were so realistic that he made the transfer.

There is also the problem of facial recognition software, often used for law enforcement purposes. Except it only works correctly on white faces. Several people of color have been erroneously arrested and charged based on the faulty software. This instance is a perfect example of Conway's Law in action. Conway's law originated in computer programming or coding and articulates that the quality of a product reflects the quality of the team that builds it.

Detailed in the *The Guardian*'s article "How White Engineers Built Racist Code," the quality of this software directly reflects the fact that the majority of engineers are white men, and the facial recognition software they built is least accurate with people of darker skin tone, and especially women. In fact, engineering teams worldwide are overwhelmingly male, and often white or Asian.

This issue plays out in all kinds of technology, like products with motion-sensors, which tend to "not see" darker skin tones. Consider how ubiquitous motion-activated faucets, soap dispensers, and dryers are in public restrooms especially post-pandemic. Think about how frustrating it would be if they don't respond to you, and you must deal with this multiple times per day. Likewise, smart phone cameras are designed to best photograph lighter skin tones as are the filters designed to improve the images.

Computer algorithms often show racial bias as well, impacting everything from job applications and mortgage loans, to the way ads target consumers. In other words, "techno-racism" represents an ominous downside to technology that will only be fixed by hiring more diverse employees and setting up intentional assessments to mitigate unintentional bias.

Each of these examples demonstrates real dangers and liabilities technology has already created for organizations and individuals. Both intentional strategy and human intervention are required to counter technology's challenges and maximize its benefits.

In 2025, *Scientific American* published a special edition on AI. It's filled with articles by a range of experts offering their analysis and suggestions on the above issues, and many more. I highly recommend this science-based resource.

Replacing Jobs

As technology proliferates, employees grow increasingly concerned about being replaced. It's a valid concern, especially considering how many manufacturing jobs were reassigned from humans to robots during third industrial revolution.

Between 2011 and 2016, use of robotics in automotive manufacturing increased 200 percent in China, 52 percent in South Korea, 27 percent in Germany, and 14 percent in the US. The firm Oxford Economics predicts that by 2030 up to 20 million manufacturing jobs will be replaced by robots, mostly in low-skill and repetitive-action tasks. However, they also stress "that the productivity benefits from automation should boost growth, meaning as many jobs are created as lost."

Robots, machines that interact with physical objects, are best suited for manufacturing work. They can be programmed to do structured and autonomous or semi-autonomous tasks with consistent precision. Robots operate as programmed, without the need for historical data or ongoing learning. Further, robots can exceed the capabilities of their human counterparts in terms of carrying weight, speed of repetitions, working with minute detail, or working in hostile or dangerous environments. Robot usage has already revolutionized manufacturing lines, medical surgeries, and space exploration.

In comparison, artificial intelligence is best suited for complex decision-making and using data to create software or algorithms mimicking tasks that require human intelligence. AI requires computers and large data sets that it learns to improve outcomes and revise algorithms. Generative AI can create content like text, images, and audio.

One study found that 81 percent of executives have deployed or plan to deploy AI tools and technologies. Among those already deployed, 97 percent of executives report benefits such as increased productivity and efficiency, improved customer service, reduced repetitive tasks, fewer human errors, reduced business costs, and improved data analytics.

OpenAI created most of the popular AI models, including ChatGPT, Claude, Dalle, Ada, and Curie. All the major tech companies have their own: Meta has Llama, Google created Gemini, and Microsoft has CoPilot. Recently, a Chinese company released DeepSeek, achieving similar capabilities at much lower costs than the US companies. No doubt, many more competitors will launch soon—the future state of AI is unpredictable and rapidly evolving.

So far, development continues to lay bare the stark differences between machine learning and the ability to think. Thinking is a uniquely human trait, and will become more important as AI adoption continues to grow. Further, according to neuroscientist Dr. Anna Ivanova, even the human brain "is still an open question." Scientists are not clear on how the various brain regions create a coherent self, "let alone how a machine could mimic that."

AI needs a robotic system to interact with the physical world, which many companies are building. The market for humanoid AI robots is valued at more than $2 billion and growing quickly. There are currently more than 30 on the market, with more coming.

AI's ability to replace jobs is growing too, underscored by two recent examples: In one of the first instances of labor negotiations involving the impact of AI, both the Writers Guild of American (WGA) and the Screen Actors Guild-American Federation of Television and Radio Artists (SAG-AFTRA) went on strike to protect their jobs from potential threats. They sought to limit the use of AI-generated dialogue and scenes as well as AI-generated actors and voices sourced from an original person.

They realized that, without the right protections, an actor could be paid for one day of work and then an AI simulation could be used for the rest of the film or project. The strike went on for several months, until both groups were successful in getting their protections.

However, the threat is still present with new AI text-to-video platforms like Sora. After seeing a demonstration, Tyler Perry put an $800 million expansion of his film studios on hold, as the technology drastically changes what it means to capture footage and to create films. He stated, "Jobs are going to be lost."

Perhaps a more chilling picture is the loss of 70 percent of mid-level software development jobs in just 18 months, according to data from Indeed. A chart showing the sharp drop-off has gone viral, with both job seekers and recruiters commenting that it shows the real impact of AI.

J.T. O'Donnell, a recruiting industry executive, says that companies now only need a small number of high-level, advanced software developers at the top to oversee a stable of junior-level builders at low salaries. "The introduction of AI has made it possible to wipe out the whole middle level of jobs. And they're not coming back."

Job applicants are finding tech roles they had recently applied to being reposted at lower levels, and with 25 percent less pay, as AI fills the middle. However, not all workers will use AI, much less be replaced by it. The Pew Research Center identified how much different types of roles are exposed to AI.

- High-exposure roles include budget analysts, data entry, tax preparers, technical writers, and web developers.
- Medium-exposure roles include executives, veterinarians, interior designers, fundraisers, and sales managers.
- Low-exposure roles include childcare providers, dishwashers, hair stylists, firefighters, and plumbers.

It's important to remember, though, that the high and increasing fear of job loss activates the "survival" brain, because our paychecks are how we buy our basic necessities of food, water, and shelter. While organizations will need employees to embrace new technology like AI, they are going to instinctively and perhaps automatically resist it because it has the ability to threaten their livelihoods.

So leaders will need to be adept at identifying and messaging how AI might support their people, not replace them. Otherwise, AI adoption will be undermined by your workforce.

Lucas Petty, CEO of AI Daddy argues that when adopting AI in your business, the first phase is to focus on your people. He states, "The purpose of AI is to help people. You want to use AI to free up their time to do the tasks that only humans can do."

A study from the Massachusetts Institute of Technology (MIT) found that AI may actually benefit new or low-skilled workers. They looked at employees in a contact center who used a conversational AI assistant, driving a 14 percent increase in productivity, with the largest gains (35 percent) among the new and low-skilled workers. "These workers were effectively upskilled by the technology, rather than replaced," they concluded. Interestingly, there was no change in productivity for the highly skilled workers, indicating that AI may uplevel most of the workforce, bringing incredible gains to employees and an organization.

Lucas has designed five pillars for AI adoption: People, Process, Strategy, Tools, and Automation. While thousands of tools exist, your focus should be on strategically using AI to automate activities. He found that 70 percent of AI challenges relate to people and processes, 20 percent to technology issues, and 10 percent to algorithm-related obstacles.

People are central to the successful use and adoption of AI tools, which is why emotional intelligence (EQ) is growing in value in this modern world.

Artificial Meets Emotional Intelligence

As we prepare the workforce for the future, it's important to note that every increase in technology requires an equal increase in vital skills like critical thinking, emotional intelligence, and leadership.

McKinsey interviewed several corporate CEOs about their responsibility to shift mindsets and build their employees' capabilities to ensure successful transformation to the new digital age. Leadership will play a vital role in how well each organization weathers the tumultuous times of this new era.

In addition, McKinsey identified that while some jobs may be replaced by emerging technology, new jobs will arise that only humans can do. Deloitte expresses a similar view, stating, "Emotional intelligence, critical thinking, leadership, and complex problem-solving are innately human attributes—all are challenging for machines to emulate."

EQ is the ability to accurately gather emotional data and effectively use it to solve emotional challenges and build effective relationships with others. Dr. Daniel Goleman identifies four areas that make up EQ: self-awareness, self-control, awareness of others (including empathy), and building relationships.

According to Harvard Business Review, EQ is two times more predictive of performance than traditional intelligence or IQ. They found that EQ accounts for 80 to 90 percent of competencies that differentiate top performers. And the Center for Creative Leadership found that of careers that are derailed, 75 percent are for reasons related to emotional competencies, including inability to handle interpersonal problems, unsatisfactory team leadership during times of difficulty or conflict, or inability to adapt to change or elicit trust.

Brandon Hall likewise lists emotional intelligence as the number one competency of the digital age, and McKinsey predicts that demand for EQ skills will grow six times by 2030. The World Economic Form says that as technologies like AI proliferate, technical skills will need to be supplemented with strong social and collaboration skills, like emotional intelligence.

EQ, particularly self-regulation, helps people manage uncertainty and stress. Effective emotional control improves decision-making, resilience under pressure, and overall performance. Common productivity issues like procrastination and overcommitting often stem from unmanaged emotions, leading to burnout. EQ transforms productivity from merely doing more to achieving better outcomes.

We can also use technology to build better EQ skills. Mindfulness apps, online EQ training, and even wearable devices help people learn new behaviors.

These insights underscore the critical need for emotional intelligence in today's AI-enhanced workplaces. Employees and leaders who cultivate EQ are better prepared to navigate the complexities introduced by AI, supporting a healthy and productive work environment.

Fortunately, investment in EQ training pays off in many ways. Harvard found that a company that prioritizes emotional intelligence is 22 times more likely to perform higher than companies that do not. EQ training often yields a return on investment (ROI) as high as 1,000 percent, through increased productivity, innovation, retention, health and well-being, and revenue growth.

Critical Thinking

Companies all around the world are focusing on upskilling and reskilling their workforce to be ready now and into the future. Ron Carucci wrote an article published in *Forbes* titled "In the Age of AI, Critical Thinking Is More Needed Than Ever," and I couldn't agree more. Having taught critical thinking skills as a dean and faculty member at the University of California, I can attest that both individuals and organizations benefit.

Critical thinking is the process of analyzing available facts, evidence, observations, and arguments to make sound conclusions or informed choices. It involves recognizing underlying assumptions, providing justifications for ideas and actions, evaluating these justifications through comparisons with varying perspectives, assessing their rationality and potential consequences. Critical thinking exists on this continuum, which articulates different levels of intentionality and skill:

Unreflective > Challenged > Beginning > Practicing > Advanced > Master

At one end, the unreflective thinker doesn't reflect on their thinking and the effect it has on their lives. They do not consistently apply standards like accuracy, relevance, precision, and logic. As a result, they form opinions and make decisions based on prejudices and misconceptions. At the other end, the master thinker is totally in control of how they process information and make decisions. They exhibit superior practical knowledge and insight, always re-examining their assumptions for weaknesses, faulty logic, and bias. They spend a considerable amount of time analyzing their own responses and are strongly committed to being fair and gaining control over their own egocentrism.

There are five core skills in critical thinking:

1. **Observation:** The ability to notice and predict opportunities, problems, and solutions. Organizations can develop skill levels through competitive intelligence teams, scenario planning, and mindfulness training.

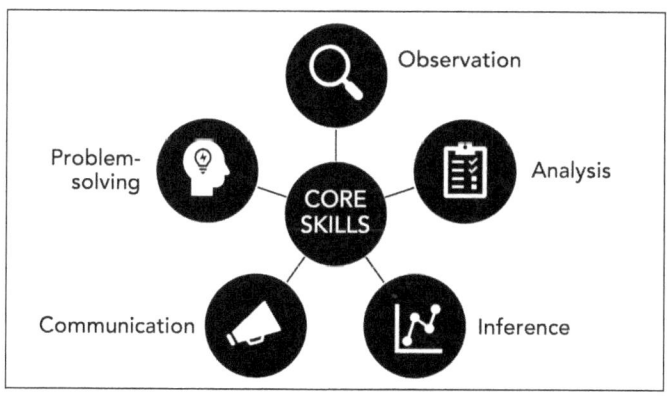

The five core skills of critical thinking

2. **Analysis:** The gathering, understanding, and interpreting of data and other information. Activities here include data analysis and interpretation training, formal data reviews, and strategies for evaluating sources in terms of validity and logical fallacies.

3. **Inference:** Drawing conclusions based on relevant data, information, and personal knowledge and experience. Skill-building exercises here include case study analysis, critical reading and discussion, and mind mapping.

4. **Communication:** Sharing and receiving information with others verbally, nonverbally, and in writing. Activities include role-playing scenarios, public speaking, and feedback sessions.

5. **Problem-solving:** The process of gathering analyzing and communicating information to identify and troubleshoot solutions. Beneficial activities are root-cause analysis, decision-making matrices, and simulation exercises.

It's clear that technology will continue to increasingly drive organizational change—but that despite its amazing potential, skilled humans are needed to properly design, develop, and deploy it. And its effective and ethical use depends on people receiving the right training, emotional intelligence, and critical-thinking skills.

Change Journey 16
Industry: Tech Startup
After successfully launching two prior businesses, I started a company with other cofounders at the dawn of the hype/excitement about the future of virtual reality (VR) technology. We felt there were many opportunities to bring VR to market for uses in entertainment, productivity, and training and development.

We raised $20 million in funding and built some of the most interesting and technically brilliant software that I had been a part of in my 30+ years of software development at both small and large companies (including Microsoft and Adobe).

We did have initial positive traction with some very important customers like Amazon, Microsoft, Valve, CNN, and Sony—important players that adopted our technology and engaged with us in what seemed to be a roadmap to drive growth in the VR space. We hoped this would lead to a growing business of building great products and delighting our customers. However, the hype cycle turned out to be just that—hype.

VR headsets have come a long way from their initial conceptualization in the 1960s but something about the medium defies broad and frequent use. Many millions of users tried VR but not enough continued with the frequency required for the market to grow. So, four years in, and with money still in the bank, we came to the incredibly difficult decision to essentially flush all our hard work down the toilet. And we were one of many companies that got stung by the low adoption rate of VR.

Because our software ran in the cloud, it cost us money each month to offer the service. We couldn't simply leave it out there for use by the customers we did have, or give it years for it to organically gather more users and eventually become self-sustaining. Venture capital–backed businesses must grow big and quickly, and we were simply not on that track. So, we closed the business and, while it was painful, it was the right choice. To date, VR has never really taken off for large commercial purposes.

Your Learning Journey

Take time to explore how the four drivers of change apply to your organization. Consider these questions:

- Which Greiner model phase does your organization fall into? Identify which functions are in which phases.
- What is the next crisis point you will encounter? How can you start preparing now so that you are ready?
- Using Laloux's model, which levels of consciousness does your organization exhibit? Identify how that shows up on a regular basis.
- Think about the senior leaders in your organization. Which consciousness do they each exhibit? How does their consciousness influence the organization?
- How has your business been impacted in the past by the environment and climate change?
- Looking ahead, what threats are most likely to negatively impact your business? What can you do now to prepare to mitigate them in the coming years?
- Review your past adoptions of technology. What went well and where did you struggle? Identify the strengths you can lean on and skills you need to improve moving forward.
- As you consider how to maximize the use of AI, download relevant tools and templates from AIDaddy.com. How can they help you create your strategy and action plan?

VI

DESIGNING + LEADING CHANGE: STRATEGIES FOR EXECUTIVES

"An organization's ability to learn, and translate that learning into action rapidly, is the ultimate competitive advantage."

Jack Welch,
Former CEO of General Electric

23. The Formula for Success

Today's leaders need to get change leadership right, with so many organizations living in a constant state of volatility, uncertainty, complexity, and ambiguity (VUCA). As we saw in the previous section, the four drivers of change shape many aspects of organizational growth and success. This section focuses on specific strategies and tools you can use to best lead your organization and drive successful change.

Costs of Change Failure

Many leaders fall into the old pattern of first identifying the need for change and then designing it in seclusion. Or, worse, making change for change's sake. As we have seen anecdotally in many of the Change Stories shared by industry insiders throughout this book, leaders may announce a change initiative but communication is often inconsistent or unclear. Their travelers then resist change, expressing a range of emotions as they go through the biological process of the change curve. Eventually, the change either fails (at rate of 50 to 70 percent) or people eventually adapt.

Recall that in chapter 1 we identified the three main types of failure with change: failure to launch, failure to sustain, or failure to scale. For example, one McKinsey study found that "less than one-third of respondents say their company's transformation has been successful at both improving organizational performance and sustaining those improvements over time."

As an executive, to help you focus on the shifts that will accelerate your own performance and that of your company, I recommend reviewing your past several change initiatives to analyze what type of change failure you experienced and its various associated costs.

	Cost	Output	Time	Quality	Energy
HARD COSTS	Unit costs Overhead costs Operating costs Variances Insurance/legal Penalties/fines Accident costs Sales expense	Units produced Tons manufactured Items assembled Reports processes Students graduated Grants awarded Tasks completed Accounts signed	Cycle time Response time Downtime Overtime Processing time Supervisory time Work stoppages	Errors Waste Rework Rejects Defects Shortages Failures Accidents	Water Fossil fuels Food Minerals Land Trees Pollution Waste
	Customer Service	**Creativity**	**Development**	**Culture**	
OTHER COSTS	Impression Service Loyalty Retention Complaints Returns	New ideas Innovation Risk taking Suggestions Collaboration Partnership Alliances	Job effectiveness Capability Performance Potential Promotions Requests for transfer	Turnover Complaints Grievances Absenteeism Tardiness Engagement Job satisfaction Employee brand	

Various costs affiliated with failed change

The first place to start are the actual hard costs—expenditures like unit costs and operating expenses. Then there are financial costs for output, time, quality, and energy. You may need to analyze a few different data sets to get a complete picture. You also need to review other potential costs in the areas of customer service, creativity and innovation, talent development, and organizational culture.

In chapter 1, we explored the costs of employee disengagement and turnover. I recommend you utilize those formulas to calculate your costs using real data from a specific function or your organization as a whole. Often, the costs are much higher than assumed and clearly demonstrate the value in building better change readiness and resilience. Doing a post-mortem on past failures will arm you with valuable data that will increase your likelihood of success moving forward.

Formula for Success

Global talent organization WTW found that only 43 percent of employees say their organization is good at managing change (down from nearly 60 percent in 2019). Only 25 percent report managing change as a major strength of their senior leaders.

But like any skill, change leadership can be learned and improved. Several studies indicate that the following formula drives consistent success when applied by executives: **D x V x F > R**.

D = **Dissatisfaction** with current state

V= **Vision** of a clear, preferred future

F= **First steps** to achieve the vision are mapped out

R = **Resistance** to change

When the product of Dissatisfaction, Vision, and First Steps are greater than the Resistance, you will get successful change. Originally created by David Gleicher, the formula was articulated by Richard Beckhard and Reuben Harris to help leaders understand how to overcome people's natural resistance to change: by being intentional about articulating a clear vision of the future and laying out the first steps to get there.

As Simon Sinek says, "Start with why." The why may be very clear to you but you need to share it. You're asking people to go on a journey, perhaps a long and challenging one. They need to know where they are going and why you think it will make a difference. Articulate the goal you are trying to achieve or the danger you are trying to avoid.

Remember, if you don't share the why, your people will create their own narrative, and it will always be the worst-case scenario.

There also must be sufficient dissatisfaction to motivate people forward—the travelers' dissatisfaction, not the leaders'. If you want to increase people's motivation, then the change must solve some of their pain points. And it must be authentically framed as meaningful to them. What are the benefits to the travelers for embracing this change? If they cannot answer "What's in it for me?" you will meet higher resistance. One common mistake made by executives is only focusing on the reasons they see for needed change without evaluating and acknowledging the level of dissatisfaction that currently exists for the people who will have to go through the new disruption.

We watched an example of this unfold in real time with Southwest Airlines, an organization that benefited for decades from a fiercely loyal customer base that loved its different model for low-cost travel that distinguished it from their peers. So when they decided to roll back two of its defining features—free checked bags and open seating—social media channels were quickly flooded by angry customers, who no longer saw a reason to stick with Southwest now that had become like every other airline.

Unfortunately, the executives at Southwest also failed to prepare their employees for this change, leaving them to handle frustrated customers without any information or strategy. Within a few days, CEO Bob Jordan, responded with his own video stating the "why" for the change, solely focused on the need to make more profits for the company and shareholders.

As digital transformation consultant Ema Roloff observed, "There was not a single thing in there that had to do with the customer and their experience." She went on to say Jordan's video offered nothing to help customers see a benefit for them if they support the change. These budget-minded travelers found it especially offensive that the reason was to further increase the profits when the company had a net profit of $465 million in 2024 and the CEO earns an annual salary of $9.3 million.

It's no surprise, then, that the travelers of this journey chose to quit and switch to other airlines, not because they got a better offer but because they felt betrayed. Time will tell what the ultimate damage is for this mismanaged change, but it clearly shows how important it is to correctly address the dissatisfaction and vision elements of the formula.

As leaders, this means that you need to articulate the goals and benefits you identify for the change in terms that matter to your travelers. The best way to do this is to seek their perspectives and recommendations. One study by Workhuman (formerly Globoforce) found that when employees agree that their voice matters, they are four times more likely to be excited about change.

Peter Senge, from the MIT Sloan School of Management, articulates a five-level model of involvement that leaders can offer their people. Each level creates increasing engagement and actively reduces resistance to change:

- **Tell:** This is the lowest level of involvement because you tell your people what they are doing to do.
- **Sell:** This next level still tells people what they are going to do but now you add the reasons you think it's a good idea—the why.
- **Test:** In this middle level, you share what you plan to do but also seek their input and ideas for improving your plan.
- **Consult:** This level creates more involvement because you share parameters but let your people decide what to do within them.
- **Cocreate:** In this highest level, you start with a blank slate and let the employees lead the process and create guiding principles along the way.

Including travelers/employees sends a strong signal that you value their input, which increases trust and engagement. But it accomplishes more than that, as another WTW study showed. Researchers reviewed organizations going through change and identified "change masters," those exceptionally adept at navigating change. These organizations surpassed their peers in anticipating market needs, navigating global dynamics, instilling confidence in the change, and getting the pace of change "right in their employees' eyes." They achieved 264 percent greater revenue growth, 33 percent greater return on assets, and 68 percent great return on capital.

Notably, these change masters involve employees in decision-making and prioritize a positive employee experience as part of their culture. As a result, they achieve higher ratings from their employees versus those who work in average change organizations. Consider these results:

- 90 percent of employees reported that their leadership had a clear vision for the future, maintaining a relentless focus on communicating why the change is happening and what the organization is trying to achieve (vs. 73 percent)
- Almost 90 percent of employees expressed satisfaction with their involvement in decisions that affect their work, denoting a stronger trust level in the company and its leadership.
- 84 percent of employees felt that decisions were made in a timely manner (vs. 68 percent)

The final part of the formula for success is to map out the first steps to achieve the vision. Remember, change can illicit fear and uncertainty so it helps when people can see the path forward. In fact, it's important to hold on announcing the change until you can include information about all the elements of the formula, including first steps. We'll cover this more in the following chapters.

Some organizations benefit from establishing an infrastructure for change. McKinsey found that change programs with clear roles, responsibilities, and governance were almost six-and-a-half times more likely to succeed, reporting, "The vast majority of successful programs include four such elements: an executive steering committee (ESC), a change-management office (CMO), executive sponsors (ESs), and initiative owners (IOs) and their teams."

The formula for success will help you achieve your goals with change and will also increase employee engagement, reduce attrition, and drive revenue growth. Use the data above to help you spend adequate time analyzing your upcoming change initiatives. Put them through the formula and identify where you have gaps to fill. Each element should become part of your messaging and communications plan, as well as your project management process.

The 6-Phase Model of Change

As we synthesize elements from previous chapters on the brain science of resistance and the formula for success, it's clear that a new process is needed to guide executives/expedition designers. Following this six-phase model of change improves the change readiness and resilience of your organization.

Phase 1: Identify the Need for Change
During this phase, you bring the right people to the table to work together to accurately define the problem as it relates to your context. You look at the organization's vision, stage of growth, market, and various pressures to consider the type of change that is needed. You also assess the inevitable resistance and how much trust exists between the leaders and the employees.

Phase 2: Build the Lead Team
You bring together the right people to form a collaborative team, involving those most impacted by the change, champions of the change, as well as those most likely to resist. Together, the team reviews the information from phase 1 along with other relevant data and crafts a few potential solutions.

Phase 3: Evaluate Potential Solutions
The lead team analyzes and evaluates pros and cons of each potential solution including potential consequences through a futures wheel or seven generations process. They create an Input Team and invite members to provide subject matter expertise and critical review of the options. They also pilot test options and ultimately decide on the change to be implemented and sketch out the execution plan.

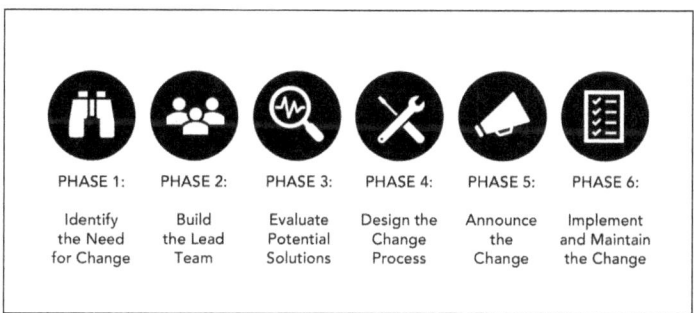

The six-phase model of change

Phase 4: Design the Change Process
In this phase, you invite more key people to participate in discussions, expanding your circle of buy-in for the change and execution plan. The team is trained on messaging and crafts a compelling vision for the change. In addition, they're trained on how to facilitate the announcement, and help others transition through the rollout.

Phase 5: Announce the Change
In this phase, you roll out the change plan to the rest of the organization. The lead team plays an active role in facilitating the transition process. Feedback is authentically requested, considered, and addressed while the natural resistance is managed with emotional intelligence.

Phase 6: Implement and Maintain the Change
The change is launched and implemented. Drawing on empathy and patience, the lead team helps its travelers through the awkward process of breaking old habits and forming new ones. The group actively assesses progress, responding quickly to challenges, and adjusting the plan as needed. You measure progress and frequently celebrate wins, while continuing to build in and bolster systems and practices that keep the change from backsliding.

In the next chapters, we'll dive into tools and strategies for each of the phases. We'll also explore why knowing when to quit is a vital skill and special circumstances surrounding mergers and acquisitions (M&A).

Change Journey 17
Industry: Higher Education
Our college went through a change of leadership, moving from nearly two decades of an all-female team to a group of all-male executives. The female leaders had believed in mentoring and empowering their people while the new executives seemed Machiavellian in their approach.

Needless to say, it was a big change for myself and many of the other leaders. The new leadership team quickly began replacing the current heads of departments. But it seemed that their criteria was finding those who would blindly follow their directions. Professional standards were compromised as they installed people with less experience or expertise than their predecessors. Worse, announcements for these replacements were done in academic meetings and on our campus chat system!

After one year and three months of this new management, the school appears calm but what lies underneath the change are ripples of confusion, insecurities, and anxieties. Heads of colleges and offices cannot speak honestly or refute the opinions of our new executives for fear that their positions will be at stake.

I have decided to give up my position, but I still have a few months before I finally leave my post. Despite the betrayal of the staff and the distrust that has infiltrated our organization, I work hard to efficiently mentor my team, and manage our student programs and services. I struggle to do what is right, but it zaps my energy every day.

24. Phases 1–2: Decide and Lead

As an executive, your focus is the long-term success of your organization. This means that you're often looking to the future and anticipating potential opportunities, protecting from disruptors, and preparing for unexpected dangers not yet visible. These all inform your organization's present state and how it must shift to align with what you see coming. There are several strategies you can use to empower your success.

Phase 1: Identify the Need for Change

First, you must identify the need for change. This ranges from reacting to an immediate crisis that needs to be resolved in the next 10 hours to starting preparations for something that will be vital in 10 years.

Change leadership requires an organized approach to help you discern which of the everyday whirlwind of issues to address and problems to solve deserve attention. Determine the criteria that matter most for your business and its strategic goals. Distinguish between immediate issues that you need to react to from longer-term goals where you can intentionally drive a proactive response. Both are important and each needs to be scaffolded by a structured process.

Quick and reactive change

The pandemic is a perfect example of a quick and reactive change. It was a stressful wake-up call for many leaders, who found themselves unprepared to pivot their business and workforce almost overnight. The good news is that we can leverage that experience and build on it to help you prepare for quick and reactive changes in the future.

Consider the likely sources of short-term crises for your organization and industry. Perhaps it's a massive software failure like CrowdStrike. Or the sudden canceling of government contracts via an executive order. Or a grounded ship in the Suez Canal that halts your vital supplies. These will all drive quick and reactive change initiatives that might make or break your organization's future. Simultaneously, draft a clear plan for responding to the natural disasters most likely to impact your organization, employees, vendors, and customers. It's not a question of if anymore, but when and how bad.

For these quick and reactive changes, create a process in advance that you can activated when needed. Identify those who will play a role and articulate their responsibilities. Create a decision tree that will guide you when time is short, and pressure is high. Often, this kind of crisis would benefit from seeking the input from the travelers but there is likely no time. However, if you include them in creating the process, it will go a long way to ensuring success. Research examples of best practices and adopt as many as you can.

In addition, prepare communications plans and messaging with relevant local emergency resources, that can be adjusted to fit the situation. By building your response in advance, you will greatly increase your likelihood of success.

Medium and pressing change
The majority of change initiatives unfold in the present and near future. As they arise, you'll have time to research solutions and launch a well-thought-out plan. You still need a structured process but now you will have the luxury of time and calm. Design processes that can be applied for a range of changes, to maximize efficiency and allow space for incremental improvements as you learn what works and what doesn't.

Some medium-term changes will focus on a function or department, such as sales or engineering. Others will have implications across the organization, such as budget planning and policies for employees.

Use the formula for success described in chapter 23. Since time affords you the opportunity, it's important to involve your travelers in these kinds of changes, which will greatly reduce their resistance. Include them in deciding and cocreating the change, using lead and input teams. Listen to their feedback and build healthy respect and psychological safety into your culture.

Invest in preparing your managers to lead change effectively. According to Gartner, change management is one of the top five priorities for HR leaders. However, 82 percent say their managers aren't equipped to lead change and, even if they are, 77 percent say their employees are change fatigued.

Have you provided your managers with clear communications and expectations? Do they know how to message the change and address possible complaints or concerns? They would greatly benefit from leadership development classes and change-readiness training. Every investment in guides will pay off, as they have a direct impact on how well your employees embrace or resist change.

Also consider how you prepare the travelers for the change. Think ahead to the "new normal" when the change is in place and what words and actions your travelers will need. Leverage learning to help them develop habits in advance so that the change sticks. Remember, it takes 40 to 50 repetitions to form a habit, which is why many change initiatives fail, simply because people default to their old behaviors (especially under stress).

Be sure to include your learning team in the trailblazing group, as they play a vital role in preparing your leaders, managers, and employees.

Long-term and strategic change
For your organization's long-term vision, you'll need to separate your time leading the day-to-day operations from time to plan and innovate for the future. Many executives do a great job leading short- and medium-term changes but their excellence in those areas sometimes shortchanges their ability to think strategically.

It's helpful to engage the input of your board, as well as subject matter experts, to help you look well into the future. It also requires taking a broader view of your industry to identify potential opportunities and threats.

Executive teams should set aside dedicated time to envision potential futures five, ten, and twenty years from now. As in the shorter ranges, this time of long-range visioning and planning should also have a structured process that involves various stakeholders including customers, employees, vendors, and other communities that may be impacted by your business.

Some executives borrow a Native American tradition drawn from the Iroquois or Haudenosaunee Confederacy, and dating back to the 1400s, of thinking forward seven generations. It articulates a commitment to making decisions by considering the impact it will have seven generations into the future, or about 200 years. It requires leaders to make decisions that not only benefit themselves, but those not yet born, ensuring a sustainable world for them. It also includes remembering and honoring the seven generations that came before you and the decisions they made to make your current existence possible.

Underscoring the importance of this principle, Dr. Michael Skinner has studied the long-term impacts of pesticides and found that exposure in one rat negatively impacts the fertility of the next four generations. Despite having no direct exposure, the damage from those chemicals lived on in subsequent four generations, passed down from their great-grandmother.

Research on "forever chemicals" shows a similar impact in humans. Since the 1950s, they've been used in everything from industrial machines to skin products but now are linked to several cancers and impaired immunity. They take hundreds or even thousands of years to degrade, and are currently found in drinking water, soil, and even human tissue. Now that we know the results of such short-term thinking, embrace the seven generations principle to help your organization make better and more ethical choices for the future.

An important part of leading change is getting the right support from within your organization. Support exists on a continuum, from active resistance to active support. People often move forward on this continuum as they move through the emotions of the change curve described in chapter 4.

Active Resistor	Passive Resistor	Neutral	Passive Supporter	Active Supporter
Actively resists the change, behaviorally or verbally; not afraid to speak out/act out in response	Says the "right" things; but does not change their behavior and may covertly interfere	No firm opinion about the change; may think it doesn't affect them or perhaps is reserving judgment	Does the "right" thing but doesn't vocalize their support or encourage others	Actively supports the change through words and behaviors; encourages others

The continuum of change support

Identify the resistors early so you can involve them in the process, as they need more time to move through the change curve than others. Monitor the neutral and passive supporters to ensure they are shifting over time and involve the active supports early so they can help shift others.

Phase 2: Build the Lead Team

The next important phase in your process is building the lead team, which is responsible for designing and leading the change. This group will meet regularly and oversee the entire change initiative from conception to finish. Research shows that teams of four to seven people are the most effective in terms of communication and accountability.

Ideally, you want to put together a combination of roles (designers, trailblazers, guides, and travelers) and personal qualities or characteristics. There may be overlaps between them, so play with the combination until it feels right. You want at least one person who was part of phase 1, where you identified and defined the problem. You also need at least one to two representatives from the group or groups who will be most impacted by the change (the travelers).

Invite at least one active supporter or champion who believes that this change is important and can see the positive outcome it will bring. It's also helpful to have at least one neutral member, who will be the least impacted by, or the least resistant to, the change.

In terms of qualities, choose people who exhibit emotional intelligence. Successful team members need self-awareness, self-control when under stress, empathy, and the ability to build rapport and positive relationships. Ideally, you want people who have empathy for and patience with the inevitable resistance that will arise, as well as the ability to be calm and firm.

This group will also need to know how to assess data, make decisions, communicate, and ultimately guide project implementation. If you're lucky, you have lots of good people to choose from. If pickings for these qualities are slim, you can develop your lead team with some training and coaching. (Even an all-star team will benefit from some training.)

Once you identify people, invite them to join the lead team. Notify them of the scope of the project and how long you estimate it will take. They need to be able to devote the right amount of focus and energy for the entire duration of the design and implementation process. If they cannot do that, then move them into another role.

Encourage them to establish ground rules for working together to build psychological safety and trust, and productive ways to resolve inevitable conflict.

The input team
Once the lead team is up and running, they will eventually build the input team who provides expertise insight, and feedback at various stages of the design and rollout. This team should include key guides and travelers as well as influential supporters and resistors who step in for a specific window of time or activity.

The input team serves as advisors to the lead team. They may participate for one meeting or continue for a portion of the process. It bears repeating that the two most important groups to involve early on are the travelers who will be most impacted by the change and the strongest resistors. These are often the same people, but not always.

Your travelers are those people who will have to change their behavior to implement your vision, whether employees, customers, or vendors. Their input is immensely valuable as no one has their vital perspective.

Active resistors are vocal about their concerns and/or influential. A common mistake is to avoid this group—usually because of concerns they will be difficult to work with. And that may be true, but if you don't work with them now, they are likely to sabotage your efforts later. Of all the groups you need to get on the change curve early, it's this one.

And don't forget your champions! You want to include those active supports who believe that change is needed and can envision the positive outcomes. Here are a variety of ways to involve members of the input team:

- **Subject matter experts:** Their expertise will guide your choices. Include someone from HR because the change will ultimately impact people and it may affect key process like compensation, job descriptions, and policies. The same goes for IT—they need to be included early since everything touches technology in some way. There may be other key functions you need to involve as well, like finance or engineering.

- **Evaluators:** If you are considering a few options, invite key people to help evaluate the pros and cons of each. For example, let's say you're choosing between two different buildings to lease. Seek feedback from the people who will be moved to those buildings. Whenever you can give people choice, it helps with the emotional transition of change. But never give a false sense of choice, which can actively damage trust.

- **Early adopters:** Invite key people to participate as early adopters or pilot testers, to get important feedback on what is working and what needs to shift. A lot of problems can be addressed when you take the time to test the change initiative before launching it on a large scale.

- **Trainers:** Involve people to serve in a trainer capacity during the implementation phase. They become knowledgeable on the change and assist people in their departments or functions with the implementation.

These two first phases go a long way to setting your organization up for success. In the next chapters, we will dig into the remaining phases and strategies you can use to boost your success.

Change Journey 18
Industry: Financial/Insurance
I worked as a Claim Manager and Director of Sales Operations at a national mortgage insurance company. During a tumultuous financial period for the industry, the executive team decided to restructure our company, dividing it into two parts—one for dismantling and one for sale. A new CEO

was appointed and upon reviewing the company's assets, believed the split decision had been thoroughly vetted. Consequently, another leader was brought in and executed the final stages of the split, which involved substantial layoffs (over 500 employees, constituting half the company) and unconventional customer-facing decisions.

Subsequently, the new CEO realized that the plan had not been thoroughly vetted and after a comprehensive review, he opted to reunite the company, designating us as a "core asset" due to our position as the largest mortgage insurer in a struggling industry. This in and of itself was critical because he was willing to change course. However, the challenge now was the aftermath of the massive layoffs. This effort was led by two talented leaders who rebuilt the organization. They invested time in identifying trustworthy individuals who were genuinely aligned with the changes at hand. However, it wasn't merely about having "yes people" on board; they sought team members who could provide constructive pushback and valuable feedback.

The reconstruction phase was not without its challenges, and it wasn't flawlessly executed. Nevertheless, they succeeded by identifying and leveraging key talents within the company, eliminating longstanding leaders who resisted change, and bringing in new leadership to fill critical gaps. Communication played a pivotal role, with town halls and transparent communication strategies. Investments were made in technology to support business operations and sales teams, and efforts were made to rebuild customer relationships.

They did other things like bring in employee resource groups and DEI that never existed before. The CEO was a strong supporter of transgender rights and he added gender affirmation surgery as a health benefit. That benefit was life-changing for a dear friend of mine. It went so far beyond the business to the people.

Importantly, there was a commitment to transparency, devoid of any disingenuous tactics or gaslighting that often occurs with significant changes. We never heard the "we are a family" speech to entice us to commit to them while never committing to us.

An outside consultant was instrumental in creating a safe environment for candid discussions. The gathered insights weren't used for punitive measures; instead, there was a focus on planning and redirecting efforts.

In essence, the key factor was these leaders' ability to identify and empower individuals they could trust, fostering an environment where open communication and constructive criticism were valued. The result of our efforts was substantial growth, propelling us to become the largest mortgage insurance company in the US, successfully rebounding from the aftermath of the crisis. Ultimately, the company achieved a notable milestone by being acquired in a multibillion-dollar deal.

25. Phases 3-4: Evaluate and Design

After you have created the lead team, it's time to move to the next phases in the model.

Phase 3: Evaluate Potential Solutions

The lead team analyzes and evaluates pros and cons of each potential solution, including potential consequences through a futures wheel or seven generations process. Members of the input team will provide subject matter expertise and critical review of the options, as well as pilot testing options. The goal is to finalize the parameters of change to be implemented and sketch out the execution plan.

Tim Brown, author of *Change by Design*, argues that a good solution lives at the intersection of three key factors:

- **Feasibility:** What is functionally possible given your context. It needs to work with your existing structure and resources, give or take a few minor tweaks. For example, if someone suggests doubling your staff to make it work, it's probably not really feasible. The question here is "Can we do it?"
- **Viability:** How likely the solution is to be sustainable within your context. A change that you can only sustain for a few months is not really going to solve your problem in the long run, unless you have a second change initiative that takes over after an initial burst of energy. The question here is "Can we keep it up?"
- **Desirability:** How much people, such as employees or customers, will embrace the change. Taking natural resistance and the change curve into account, the question here is "Can we get people on board?"

As you explore various options, put them through the tests of feasibility, viability, and desirability, perhaps rating them on a scale so that you can more easily compare.

Also consider the scope and pace of the change. A new software system is one level of scope, whereas a reorganization that shifts roles, reporting relationships, and even office locations is another. Do you plan to roll out the change quickly or over a long period of time? This will be largely contextual. Some groups can handle a lot of change and some can't. What you don't want to do is cause unnecessary distress and harm trust by pacing a series of changes, so that your travelers barely recover from one before you launch the next.

Consider the duration of the change and how much effort it will take above and beyond people's regular workload. People can sustain intense bursts of energy for a short time but they are not sustainable, which threatens chances of success.

Think through how success will be measured for the change and apply it to each possible solution. What are the markers of progress to know we are solving the problem? When and how will these be measured? Next, assess how the internal workings of your organization will support each possible solution. Are the right systems and policies in place? How does each option align with your current culture?

Now it's time to consider the domino-effect of consequences, and one tool I love introducing to executives is the futures wheel.

Create a Futures Wheel
Considering the potential future consequences of any decision is valuable, and especially so when considering change. One tool I love introducing executives to is the Futures Wheel. It's a structured way to work through several layers of potential consequences. When used correctly, it can help ensure that you are planning appropriately and protect you from unintended but potentially devastating outcomes.

The futures wheel starts with the change in the middle—for example, cutting the budget by 20 percent. The next row out are the first-order consequences—these may be positive, neutral, or negative, but all flow as a direct impact of the change. For a budget cut, first-order consequences might include a hiring freeze, a pause on investing in IT, or offering leadership training.

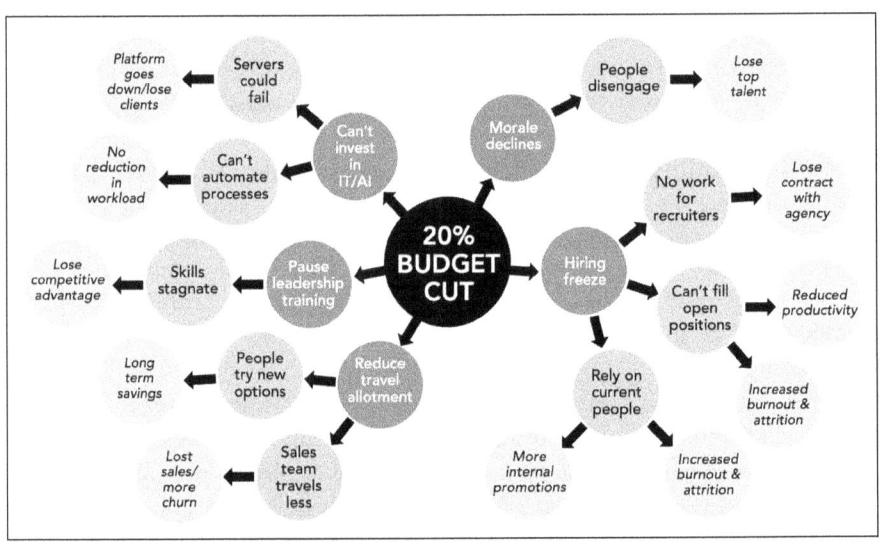

Example of a futures wheel for a budget cut

The second-order consequences are the next row out. For example, a consequence of a hiring freeze might be that a key role cannot be filled, or a recruiter doesn't have enough work. A second-order consequence of not investing in IT is that a server that was due to be replaced might fail.

Next, list the third-order consequences which arise from the second-order ones. If you cannot fill a key role, you might increase burnout on the team which could lead to resignations. If a server fails, it might take down a critical system that hosts financial records or customer data, which might ultimately cost you customers.

Of course, consequences may also be positive—a budget cut might save the company from filing bankruptcy, saving jobs.

Future wheels are best when multiple people provide input, especially if you involve people from different levels in the organization. The view from the executive suite is very different than what the people on the front lines see.

Build your futures wheel using a blank wall and sticky notes or a white board. There are also a few online tools that allow for collaboration across times zones and regions.

Once you build a futures wheel, talk through the benefits and costs of each consequence. Every choice has an impact, but your goal is to make informed and intentional decisions about the tradeoffs while preventing an unexpected or damaging outcome. After all, a 20 percent savings won't matter if you end up in a multimillion-dollar lawsuit.

Futures wheels may be used for assessing all kinds of changes with products, people, processes, and policies. For example, if you decide to expand your offerings to the European Union, you'll face first-order consequences like increased regulations, navigating cultural and language differences, and unfamiliar distribution systems.

Use futures wheels to improve your ability to predict and analyze change initiatives. Invite people to provide input and listen—really listen—to their ideas, questions, concerns, and critiques. Make it psychologically safe to kick the tires, so to speak, to ensure nothing important is missed.

As you invite members of the input team to participate in this process, use their feedback and reactions to generate more topics for your evaluation process. Play the devil's advocate and envision best- and worst-case scenarios, narrowing the field to the best options.

Ideally, you want to end with two to three viable solutions—options that will address the problem and pass the above tests.

Surfacing Concerns

Once you have some potential solutions, it's time to go looking for resistance. While your team certainly can make the final decision, you have a wonderful opportunity here to include others, creating more buy-in for the process.

By giving various stakeholders the chance to provide input or even vote on the options, you will gain valuable insight and allow important concerns to surface. This is where you might hold focus groups with more key stakeholders, including resistors. Or you might conduct an anonymous survey, seeking input across the entire organization.

Start with transparency. Share the team's work to date, discussing the brainstorming and evaluating processes. Discuss who has been involved so far, so people see the range of input you have sought. And announce the options you have landed on and why. Be clear that you are seeking their input because you value their thoughts and experiences and, that your goal is to design the best option possible. Your solicitation must be authentic, though. If you don't really mean it, you will damage trust.

This will be your third round of information sharing, so you should be nudging people along the change curve at each of the six phases. At this point, there are two categories of concerns that tend to arise.

The first is employee priorities. Dr. David Rock's research has identified five common primary priorities employees tend to have when confronted with change—Status, Certainty, Autonomy, Relationships, and Fairness—known as the SCARF model. (Read more on p. 75.)

The second category are the concerns people have about the change process itself. Typically, they have different types of concerns that tend to show up in a certain order and align with the various parts of the change curve, namely:

- **Intention**—People need to understand the why of change, or the business case driving it. Change is uncomfortable so people want to feel sure it is truly necessary before they embrace it.

- **Impact**—People have questions about how the change impacts them directly, asking "What's in it for me?" We're driven to first focus on what we might lose. Worst-case-scenario thinking is part of our biological wiring for survival. People want to know if they will have the time, energy, and resources to manage the change.

- **Implementation**—These are the details of how and when the change will be implemented. Concerns here are often about time and access. People want to know what support they'll receive and what happens if things don't go smoothly.

- **Outcome**—People want to know the effect the change will have. You'll hear questions like, "Will it really make a difference?" or "It is worth all this effort?" This is the relevance and payoff of the change, and you'll want to share the metrics you're using to measure success. Their comments also give you valuable information for crafting the vision.

- **Collaboration**—People want to know who is involved and how they will work together. They ask questions like, "How will information get shared?" and "Who will be responsible for _____?" Some people need to know who is on board before they commit, and there's usually a tipping point in terms of either influential people or numbers.

- **Maintenance**—How problems will be addressed and improvements made. These types of questions or comments indicate that people are envisioning the new future and embracing the change in their mind.

This process is very important to the reputation of your team. If you deliver what you promise, you will build more trust for future change initiatives. If you don't, you'll have a more challenging run. So pay careful attention to what you hear from the stakeholders.

Phase 4: Design the Change Process

In this phase, you'll use the data you gathered to hone your final choices and make adjustments based on the feedback people provide. Use what you have learned to craft a compelling vision for change, articulating the why, perceived benefits to the travelers and organization, how you will execute the plan, and a detailed timeline.

In the next phase, you will make the announcement and launch your communications plan to cascade the information throughout the organization but, for now, you will be getting ready.

These are the critical elements of the change plan:

- **Purpose:** The why behind the change and how it will benefit the organization and travelers.

- **Scope:** The discrete steps and actions the project includes and what falls outside of the project scope.

- **Stakeholders:** Who will be impacted by the change and who will play a role in its successful rollout.

- **Key performance indicators:** How success will be measured. Includes a baseline for the current state and which metrics need to move and by how much.

- **Risk assessment:** Potential risks and mitigation strategies.

- **Timeline:** Specific milestones and deadlines for the change.

- **Project execution:** The details who will oversee the task of implementing the change and who needs to sign off at each critical stage.

- **Resources:** The budget, personnel, tools, etc., needed to successfully complete the change

- **Communication plan:** How messages will be sent to keep stakeholders informed and shared up and downstream.

- **Training:** Plan for training and support to help people adapt to the change and build the right habits.

Create a document that details everything clearly and concisely. Regularly review and update your change-management plan. Elements will be used in the next two phases of the change process.

26. Phases 5–6: Announce and Implement

These final two phases are action-packed and can move quickly. Your preparation in the earlier phases will set you up for success but diligence is critical during these last phases.

Phase 5: Announce the Change

In this phase, the change is announced to the rest of the organization. The lead team plays an active role in facilitating the transition process. Feedback is authentically requested, considered, and addressed while the natural resistance is managed with emotional intelligence.

Cascading communication

Once you are ready to communicate the change, create a solid communications plan. This will ensure that you send accurate and timely information to everyone in the organization, thus reducing the start of rumors and misinformation.

Once you are ready to communicate the change, create a solid communications plan. This will ensure that you send accurate and timely information to everyone impacted, thus reducing the start of rumors and misinformation.

It also ensures that your messaging gets to the right people at the right time. WTW discovered that there is a steep fall off with change communications, with only 68 percent of leaders "getting the message" about change. So that's already a significant problem because that should be close to 100 percent. Since leaders are not clear about what changes are happening and why, it's not surprise that only 53 percent of managers know. It further trickles down to only 40 percent of employees, which means 60 percent are in the dark! It's like they are out wandering around on a trail but don't know where they are going and when they will get there. How can they possibly bring their good ideas, strengths, or motivation if they are that unclear?

As an executive, it's your responsibility to fix the cascade of communication. Let's consider now messages about change flow through an organization: An executive communicates to their direct reports who are senior leaders overseeing their own functions—for example, a CEO meeting with the C-suite of the chief revenue officer (CRO) and chief marketing officer (CMO). In an ideal world, those senior leaders then communicate to their direct reports, who are directors or managers. But what happens if, at that first meeting, one of them is confused or doesn't see it as a priority? What if they leave on a business trip and don't meet with their direct reports? That stops the communication in its tracks and a segment of the business under that leader goes dark.

Even if the first cascade goes smoothly, more problems can arise at the manager level. What if a manager wasn't at the meeting where the communication happened? Or what if they don't agree with the plan or like their leader? Or what if they don't hold one-on-one meetings with their employees? Then the communication goes dark for another segment of the business.

And what happens if these two functions, sales and marketing, are expected to collaborate on key business priorities? What if the CRO thinks and talks in tasks and details while the CMO focuses on outcomes and big picture? How will that impact these teams as they try to align their actions to collaborate? It's likely that teams on both sides are missing critical information that impacts their success.

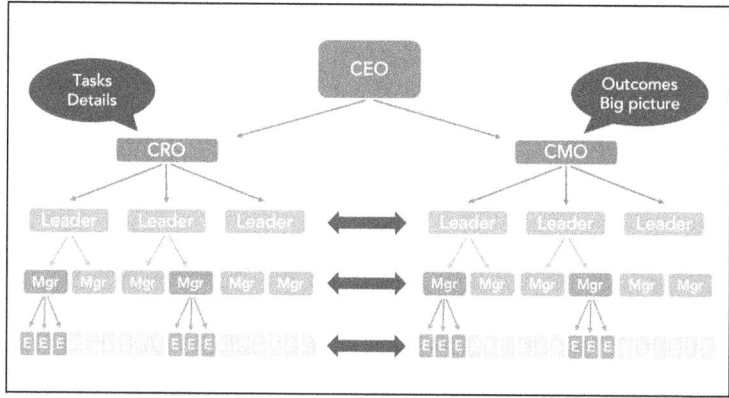

Bottlenecks or blocks in the cascade of information

These proven strategies will ensure a successful cascade:

1. **Actively address blocks in the cascade of information.** Be clear in your expectations for how and when your leaders are to communicate the information. Periodically track the flow and address repeat offenders so they understand the importance of their role.

2. **Use multiple channels to go around bottlenecks.** There are many options for getting the word out like all-hands meetings, video announcements, emails, team or project meetings, instant messaging systems, texts, posters, mailed letters or cards, and even signs posted on bathroom stalls. Use whatever method/s best align with the message you need to convey.

3. **Customize your messages for various audiences.** Different groups in your organization—senior leaders, managers, frontline employees, customers, vendors, suppliers, board members, shareholders, and community partners—need different information, so tailor messaging accordingly. Identify each group's concerns and priorities so you clearly articulate the why of the change in terms that matter to them.

4. **Follow-through and follow-up.** Your communications plan is a vital part of how you build rapport and trust. Make sure that you continue to communicate, creating several relevant touchpoints. Be especially mindful of following up on any questions or concerns people raise and delivering on any promises you make.

Facilitate the transition

The moment you announce the change, you'll immediately begin facilitating others. Remember, the announcement is the event that disrupts many people's status quo and launches the change curve in the organization. Remember your own journey through the change curve: like you, they need information and time. Even if you do everything perfectly, there will be grumbling—it's human nature and it's unavoidable.

So, brace yourself and be ready with empathy and patience. You don't have to solve all the problems. Just listen. You can do a lot to reduce resistance simply by making others feel heard. If you're defensive or focus on selling the vision too hard, you'll miss a critical opportunity to build more rapport.

Use this as a time to collect their concerns and questions. Take notes on their suggestions and complaints. Listening doesn't mean that you validate everything they say or that you are going to give up on the change. You can say things like: "I hear that you are really concerned about the timeline. What are your worries?" or "It sounds like you think you need more resources. Can you be more specific?" End with, "Thank you for sharing that with me. I'll take this back to the team and get back with you."

Change is a bit of a negotiation with the travelers—you are expressing what you need to happen, but you also need them to get onboard. They will often tell you what they need or at least, what will reduce their resistance.

One important caveat here: don't rush to make any changes. Learn to distinguish resistance to change from legitimate concerns.

This is the first part of the change curve. You can expect other challenges before things turn around. Some concerns will naturally dissipate with time and information. But those that endure warrant your sincere attention. If you can authentically respond to their concerns, with some choices or adjustments, it goes a long way to reducing resistance and building trust.

Give people clear information about the timeline. They need time to mentally say goodbye to the old ways of doing things and get ready for the new. A clear timeline helps everyone know what to expect in terms of pace, and the milestones along the way.

During this phase, you'll also be facilitating yourself. I find this is the most difficult part of the process for most leaders. You've been doing all this hard work, taking great care to make the best choices possible for the organization and your people. It's natural to want your efforts to be seen and appreciated. But it's not going happen. At least, not right away.

Be sure to take care of yourselves and each other. While the wider group may not appreciate how hard you have worked, you can certainly acknowledge each other. Stay connected as a group, talk about how it's going, and celebrate your successes.

A big part of this transition is preparing people for new habits. Many change initiatives may be supported by intentional and specific training. Training helps people make the mental and emotional shifts crucial to the success of both technical and transitional components of change. So, schedule it at a time when it will provide a boost to people's motivation.

Delivering difficult news

Some changes are going to be perceived as negative no matter what you do. If you find that you have to deliver bad news, consider these additional strategies.

First, don't try to soften the blow of bad news by spreading it out. If you know that you need to cut the budget by 20 percent, don't first tell them to cut it by 10 percent and then in six months, tell them that you are cutting another 10 percent. This hobbles your chances of successful change by launching your people on to the change curve twice and severely damaging trust. They will wonder what's coming next and start anticipating more bad news. They may begin reading all kinds of doomsday signs into things. (Remember, when humans are under stress, they are wired to look for the worst-case scenario.) This can cause employees to disengage or leave as they start seeking more stable and predictable environments. A lot of companies have lost some of their best talent because they misunderstand people's need for constancy.

Second, some changes, like layoffs or acquisitions, have legal implications, as do changes that affect groups represented by labor unions. These types of changes must often be conducted precisely in terms of timing, communication, and documentation. It's vital that you seek appropriate legal counsel and adhere to their recommendations.

Finally, Announcing bad news is often very hard on the leaders who have to do it but don't expect your people to make you feel better. I don't personally know any leader who has enjoyed implementing change that they know will hurt others. But it's the reality of every organization that, sometimes, tough choices must be made. When you're a leader, you're expected to deal with these challenges professionally and appropriately. You may feel bad at having to implement the change but people have a right to their feelings of upset. It's not a reflection of their respect for you that they're frustrated, sad, or angry. Try not to take it personally.

But DO take care of yourself during these challenging times. Make sure you seek the support of your family and friends as well as the other leaders involved with the change.

Phase 6: Implement and Maintain the Change

The change is launched and implemented. The lead team draws on empathy and patience as the awkward process of breaking old habits and forming new ones unfolds. The group actively assesses progress, responding quickly to challenges and implementing appropriate adjustments to the plan. Progress is measured, and wins are frequently celebrated. And you build in systems and practices that keep the change from backsliding.

This last phase focuses on executing the change plan and measuring progress. Track your metrics and make adjustments as needed. Use your guides and active supporters to keep people motivated through the milestones.

Recognize effort and progress as you go. Small acts of acknowledgment go a long way to helping your people feel like the effort is worth it.

If problems arise, address them transparently and quickly. Change never unfolds perfectly but you can provide valuable guidance and empathy that keeps people focused and motivated.

Change Journey 19
Industry: Video Technology

My company had just pivoted away from what we thought was a lucrative business venture. We had built an amazing team and gained some early successes, but not enough to be viable.

We were sitting on a meaningful amount of working capital ($3 million), more than many startups every dream of having access to. We had a great stack of technology that perhaps could be repurposed to a new use. We had a great team of 20 folks with diverse skills in engineering, marketing, customer service/sales, and general operations in place (bookkeeping, legal, etc.) as well as an office space. These felt like a base from which we could "pivot" and try something completely different without having to start from scratch.

I worked with the team to organize and hatch a plan to restart with a new product direction and a rebranded company. We were intentional and focused and didn't take for granted that this was going to be HARD. Not only did we have to create an entirely new product and start over, but we also were going to have to do serious work on our culture and mission to make sure everyone was aligned to the new vision.

We did a ton of developmental projects as a group where we workshopped all kinds of team dynamics in our attempt to get everyone aligned and fully committed to the new version. It seemed like we were succeeding. But in retrospect, there were some red flags.

When we originally hired everyone on the team, they were excited for the vision of the first company and product. While we tried to make the pivot, many people's hearts just were not in it. Perhaps it would have been better to kick everyone off the ship, give them 90 days, and invite them back onto the new ship at their honest fresh discretion.

Another tell-tale sign that we didn't really succeed in aligning the new team: my other three co-founders did not stick around for the new journey. And when I asked some of the remaining team to act as cofounders (for example, taking pay cuts and receiving more stock), none were interested or willing to take that same risk. I took that at the time to be a financial or economic practicality, but perhaps it was much more—a signal that nobody believed in the new company the way I should have expected or required.

Another bad signal: sequentially all but a few folks quit to go do "what they really wanted to be doing." For me, this company was my everything—the only thing in the world I wanted to do. For everyone else in the team, it was the thing that they found themselves doing after the first dream had died, and it was convenient to continue with the people they liked, the same health care plan, and the momentum of the existing job.

This was all the more true when COVID hit. Everyone was shell-shocked and the world stopped for that year. Our team rallied around each other—they cared about each other and we were a good "team." But I misread that unity as being about the business. As people left, I had to rebuild the leadership team with new faces. They came in excited and committed—and sadly in ways that the people they were leading perhaps were not.

This isn't a story about failure (although there is plenty of failure herein). It is my honest reflection that:

1. Intentional focus on mission/culture/team dynamics is critical and deserves 10 to 15 percent of the team's energy and attention ALWAYS, not just during crises.
2. Big pivots are super hard, and a lot can be done to help get people onboard and committed to new objectives.
3. It is also worth noting that there should be brutal honesty in evaluating whether everyone actually is and can be part of tectonic changes when they come. Sometimes, it is healthy to embrace that change is too great, and a good opportunity for folks to say "I'm not down for this change—I want out".

As a leader, I learned a very valuable lesson in team alignment and commitment, and would approach the next such pivot with greater curiosity and empathy for helping team members decide they were _not_ OK with the new direction. An open and honest discussion with the team would have served everyone better. If we were not going to succeed in the new direction, we did nobody a service keeping people on payroll while they figured out their new jobs. It would have been economically advantageous for us to offer everyone generous severance to spur the change and recommitment of new team members.

27. Know When to Quit

All this focus on driving successful change can make us forget that knowing when to quit is another crucial skill executives need. Sometimes the best course of action is to pull the plug on a struggling change initiative, rather than putting in more effort and resources.

Culturally, we glorify those with grit over those who quit. But quitting is sometimes the smart—even heroic—choice. Let's delve into the skill of quitting so that you can apply it appropriately in your organization.

The Science of Quitting

To get better at quitting, the first thing to realize is that humans are biologically predisposed to persevere, sometimes to our detriment. We are psychologically biased to keep going, sometimes to the peril of the project or people. Throughout this chapter, I share seven strategies I have identified that counterbalance these dangerous biases.

Consider the fateful year of 1996 on Mount Everest, when eight people lost their lives. There were several expedition groups on the mountain that year. Two of the most experienced leaders, Rob Hall and Scott Fischer, were advising their own clients, stating that the turnaround deadline was 1:00 p.m. They said it was vital to set turnaround criteria before starting out because once people are moving they are less likely to revisit that decision. They knew that eight times more people die on the way down from Everest than on the way up because they wait too long and compromise their safe return.

Strategy #1: Set your quitting criteria before you start.

During the May 10th push to the summit, several experienced climbers got stuck behind slower, less-experienced groups. Even though they had the strength and skill to summit and had paid tens of thousands of dollars to achieve this goal, they turned around at the deadline. They knew they were actually paid to get them home safely, which they achieved.

The tragedy that occurred that year happened because both Rob and Scott violated their own cardinal rule: they kept going well past their turnaround time, and as a result, eight people died, including themselves. Several books and documentaries have told this story and the footage is heartbreaking. Rob's wife was pregnant and when it was clear that he was trapped at the top, they relayed his call to her over the radios. Everyone on the mountain heard them choose a name for their baby and say their painful goodbyes.

So, what happened, when this tragedy was avoidable? First, Rob and Scott fell victim to several psychological biases that skew our perception and judgment, ones they even knew about! We'll explore them in the next section.

Second, the unexpected blizzard conditions, oxygen deprivation, and exhaustion impacted their ability to think clearly and act logically. Third, our culture glorifies stories of perseverance and grit. No books or movies tell the story of the other leaders who brought their clients safely down Mount Everest that day.

As a result, we all have blind spots around the skill of quitting and perhaps even an aversion to it. Most of us grew up with negative messages around people who quit, and so we likely avoid looking for examples to learn from, or seeing the ability to quit as a skill.

The Neuroscience of Reward

Three neurotransmitters that play a vital role in how we set and achieve goals. First, we have dopamine, which is the "wanting" neurochemical. It's what makes us desire things, seek them out, and gives us the motivation to explore and be curious. Dopamine drives our motivation to act.

Next, we have the opioid neurotransmitter, which is the "liking" feeling we get. It's responsible for pleasure, reward, and our sense of enjoyment. It drives the satisfaction we feel for acting.

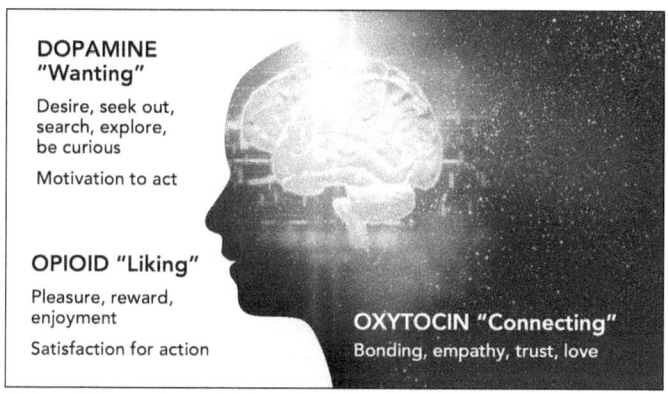

The three neurotransmitters of reward

Finally, we have oxytocin, which is the "connecting" neurotransmitter. This chemical is responsible for bonding, empathy, and our feelings of trust and love. It gets released through skin-on-skin contact like high fives, fist bumps, and hugs, so is often a key player when people strive and achieve together.

These chemicals are powerful and can contribute to us ignoring the blind spots the psychological biases create.

Psychological Biases

Let's explore the five main psychological biases that can negatively impact our ability to quit at the right time.

Sunk-cost effect

This is a systematic cognitive error in which people consider the money, time, effort or any other resources they have previously sunk into an endeavor when making decisions about whether to continue and spend more. It causes people to stick to situations they ought to be quitting.

We see this in play out on Mount Everest nearly every season. Climbers have spent months training, weeks acclimating at the base camp, and tens of thousands of dollars. Turning around when you can see the summit means losing all that investment.

Another example of the sunk-cost effect is the high-speed train in California, designed to connect San Diego to San Francisco. In 2008, voters approved $9 billion in bonds with an expected cost of $100 billion. Years of effort and billions of more dollars later, this project is nowhere near completion. The latest estimate predicts that a 171-mile section in central California might be finished by 2033, and the entire line might not be finished until 2050, with costs projected to exceed $300 billion. It might have been better to shut down the project early on.

Strategy #2: Intentionally counterbalance our biases.

Loss aversion

As we learned in chapter 10, humans are wired to avoid repeating failure, via the habenula. Studies show that the emotional impact of a loss is greater than the corresponding impact of an equivalent gain. In fact, losing feels about two times as bad to us as winning feels good.

As a result, loss aversion makes us want to keep going because it's the only way to avoid realizing the loss. You can see this at any casino in the world. People will keep playing when they are deep in their losses because they only realize that loss when they cash in their chips. Until they walk away, they can maintain the illusion that they can still win it back and more.

The same is true for business. Loss aversion is at the core of many poor business decisions because executives focus on realizing the investment with a win, to the point where they continue accruing more losses. Nobel prize winner Dr. Daniel Kahneman, who studies these biases, and particularly loss aversion, articulates that quitting on time usually feels like quitting too early, especially when you're in the losses.

Escalation of commitment

When we are in the losses, we are not only more likely to stick to a losing course of action but also double down and invest *more* to turn it around. One example is Harold Staw, the CEO of a successful chain of California retail stores in the 1950s. He oversaw a period of enormous profit and expansion into Texas. But then the business started faltering and instead of cutting his losses, he invested his family's wealth in trying to save the unsavable. His son, Barry Staw, published an article in *Organizational Behavior & Human Performance*, highlighting his father's struggle with the escalation of commitment.

Strategy #3: Every goal should have at least one "unless."

Monkeys and pedestals
Astro Teller, leader of the X innovation hub, has articulated a hypothetical situation to help people know where to allocate their resources. He says that if you were assigned to train a monkey to recite Shakespeare while standing on a pedestal, the first thing you should do is train the monkey. That's the most difficult part of the project and if you cannot accomplish it, you should find that out as soon as possible and quit while you're ahead.

But, he argues, most people run to build the pedestal first, because it's easy and it's the part of the problem they know how to solve. Building pedestal is a waste of both time and resources if the ultimate goal cannot be achieved.

We can see this play out with California's speed train project. The difficult part of creating this line is that there are mountains at both ends in San Francisco and San Diego. Instead of tackling that first, they keep building track in the flat land of central California because it's doable—but there was never really a need for high-speed transportation in this rural agricultural area. Worse, they still don't have a viable plan for solving those two monkeys. But each governor continues to push the project forward because pulling the plug would confirm that the project was a failure.

I've seen this same situation play out in all kinds of organizations. Change is launched and instead of focusing on the hardest parts, people focus on the smaller tasks or easier aspects of the project. This creates the illusion that you're making progress towards your goal, but in reality, the initiative may be doomed even though the reality won't hit until you're well into the losses.

Strategy #4: Tackle the monkeys first and build pedestals last.

Optimism bias
Humans are biologically optimistic. We tend to consistently overestimate our likelihood of experiencing positive events and underestimate our likelihood of experiencing negative ones. The reality is that 90 percent of innovation projects fail and a large portion of change initiatives fail too.

To underscore this reality, Dr. Arnold Cooper at Purdue University conducted a study of entrepreneurs. Results show that these startup founders estimated their chance of succeeding as 81 percent but felt other similar ventures only had a 59 percent change of succeeding. Further, the majority (80 percent) estimated their change of success as greater than 70 percent, and one-third believed it was 100 percent. That is the optimism bias at work, and while it can spur the confidence to take risks, it often blinds people to the very real issues or roadblocks they need to prepare for.

Another sign of optimism bias is when people start touting "good news" in the middle of what is obviously a struggling or failing project. Again, the California bullet train is a great example. Their website now boasts a list of the 13,000 jobs the project has created.

Or consider the creation of the US Department of Government Efficiency (DOGE). In its first few weeks, its website touted a long list of supposed savings, only to have them removed shortly thereafter, as it didn't reflect a balanced picture. For example, it included contracts that were already set to expire before the new administration assumed power.

As a leader, become skilled at accurately assessing the likelihood of failure. Ask yourself questions like: What is our confidence level in this project? Will we be right 90 percent of the time? If the project estimates meet our criteria, how often will the estimates be wrong by 25 percent? 50 percent? 100 percent?

Strategy #5: Accurately estimate your likelihood of failure.

Status quo bias
The status quo bias says humans are more tolerant of bad outcomes that come from sticking with what we're already doing than bad outcomes that come from switching to something new. As a result, people overwhelmingly stick with the status quo option, even when that option is associated with a lower expected value. We know from earlier chapters that humans resist change, and this is that principle in action. The discomfort of change or fear of the unknown is often more powerful than continuing on a known path, even a failing one.

Annie Duke, author of *Quit: The Power of Knowing When to Walk Away*, puts it this way: "Sticking with a course of action is the only way to find out for sure how it will turn out. Quitting requires being okay with not knowing what might have been."

In her book, Duke shares the example of Stewart Butterfield, an entrepreneur who had started an online game called Game Neverending. The game failed but one of the features allowed players to upload and tag photos. He was able to spin that off into the photo sharing site Flickr, which he sold to Yahoo for $25 million in 2005.

Riding that wave of success, Stewart leaned into creating Glitch, an online game he'd been dreaming about for decades. He secured $17.5million in venture capital and launched in 2011, immediately gaining a devoted following of paid monthly subscribers.

However, to make the game profitable, Glitch had to attract 95 to 100 new users playing the free version just to convert one person to a monthly subscription. So, they invested in a large marketing and sales campaign to grow the funnel and subscriber base. And it worked! They saw a 7 percent growth per week, the greatest they had achieved to date.

But Butterfield realized this status quo would not pay off in the long run. They would need to maintain that level of growth for 31 weeks to break even. To succeed, they would need to gain hundreds of thousands of paying users, which meant they had to attract tens of millions of people to try the free version. It was a losing proposition, one that would burn through their capital.

Imagine his team's surprise when, after achieving the best growth to date, he pulled the plug and gave the $6 million they still had in the bank back to the investors. As Duke states, "For everyone else, it felt like quitting too soon." But Butterfield refused to stick with the status quo because he could see the long-term cost and bad outcome.

This story has a happy ending. Just like before, Butterfield had built a compelling feature into his game. It was a live messaging component he had named "Searchable Log of All Conversations and Knowledge." He took that piece and spun it off into SLACK, which he sold to Salesforce in 2020 for $27.7 billion!

Sticking with the status quo is not necessarily a bad move as long as you're cognizant of it. It might make sense to let things continue for a bit to gather more information, but if you do, be ruthless with reviewing your quitting criteria and the data that might be contributing to over-optimism.

Strategy #6: Acknowledge when you're choosing the status quo.

Endowment effect

The final psychological bias is a cognitive illusion that when we own something, we value it more than an identical item we do not own. If you have ever hosted or been to a garage sale, you can see this play out in front of your eyes. The seller sets the price based on what they paid for the item and the fond memories they have of it, overinflating it's actual worth. The buyer, on the other hand, sees the item more realistically and views it through the lens of what they are willing to pay for it.

Ironically, people will often demand more to give up an object than they would be willing to pay to acquire it. Any estate sale or auction host will tell you that they've seen this happen again and again, often costing the person what income they could have received.

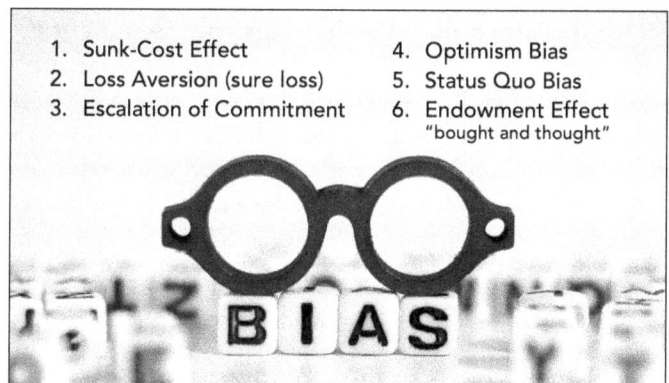

Psychological biases that impact quitting decisions

How does this relate to change? It's a bit like the sunk cost effect. We tend to overvalue work we have done or investments we have made, impacting the value we think something is worth. This plays out with mergers and acquisition negotiations as well as business evaluations for loans and investments.

We also become endowed to our ideas, thoughts, and beliefs—they become part of us. As Annie Duke states, "When it comes to quitting, the most painful thing to do is quit who you are. Our ideas, beliefs, and actions are part of our identity."

The endowment effect is active with the things we create and build. Novelists and filmmakers notoriously must engage in a process called "kill your darlings"—a ruthless process for cutting out scenes and characters you love for the good of the overall story arc or screentime.

I have experienced this myself. When I write a book or build a keynote presentation or training, I find it challenging to cut content that I have spent hours crafting and polishing. I will attempt my own version of killing my darlings (in truth, I move them into another folder in case I can salvage them for another opportunity), and I also engage professional editors who are more objective.

Music artists face the same struggle, which is why they lean on professional producers. Taylor Swift is rumored to have hundreds of songs in "the vault"—tracks packed away, never to see the light of day, as the final choices were made to create a sonically and thematically cohesive album. Strategically, she has motivated fans to buy newly released versions of previous albums by including several tracks from the vault to guarantee a new listening experience.

The endowment effect means that we must be careful with the things we "bought and thought." If you build something you are certain is buildable, you create a twofold problem. You put in time, money and effort, which creates a sunk-cost issue. And you endow the thing you have built, viewing it as "special" in a way others do not, which makes it even harder to abandon course.

Strategy #7: Be extra mindful with things you "bought or thought."

All of these psychological biases color our vision, preventing us from seeing things clearly. As an executive, you want to actively counterbalance their effects. Consider how you can lean on key people to challenge ideas and assumptions. Build processes that have strong checks and balances. Analyze past decisions to discover which biases you tend to experience and look for times when quitting paid off. Establish criteria that will help you make the right decisions. Continue to strengthen your skill of quitting at the right time.

Change Journey 20
Industry: Pharmaceuticals

Despite drafting communications plans for change initiatives throughout much of my career, including crisis simulations and media training, this particular project was a struggle.

The company wanted to glean insights from new healthcare data sources while simultaneously streamlining the clinical trials process. That latter task alone typically takes years, considerable resolve, and millions of dollars. This sprawling (in both mission and scope) change initiative sought to harmonize and synthesize outdated skill sets and technology into a lean/agile platform to process and clean Big Data from the products. One challenge was that the different siloed groups of subject-matter experts did not exchange viewpoints frequently or deeply enough to mesh consistently.

Despite many "Center of Excellence" attempts to inject accountability and ownership into a regular cadence of meetings and open-mic conferences, these lessons mostly did not "stick." This led to resource squeezes, external-expert churn, and occasionally, blame-shifting and finger-pointing.

Another challenge was lack of consistent, in-the-trenches leadership, especially at the sponsorship level. Executive sponsors would reiterate their expectations and demands at quarterly steering-committee meetings, but soon after, conflicts would once again ensue. It felt like classic "set up to fail" syndrome. Few had the time, interest, or attention span to dive deep enough to see or gauge the net effects of their function's activities (or lack thereof) on the initiative's overall progress (e.g., order management cycle).

When I left the organization, the initiative was still underway, seven years and counting. I do not know if it was ever cut back in scope or halted, but it felt like a sunk-cost fallacy made team members feel as if turning back was no longer an option.

28. Mergers and Acquisitions

Mergers and acquisitions (M&A) represent a unique type of change. Every year, many organizations and their employees experience this intense change journey that when mismanaged, can undermine the value the deal is trying to capture. This chapter focuses on special challenges and opportunities that executives face when navigating M&A deals. I interviewed several leaders who played a central role in some of the biggest deals of the past few years with Nestlé, Microsoft, Amazon, Starbucks, McDonnell Douglas Aerospace, Cisco, and T-Mobile. I am pleased to share their wisdom in this chapter.

While the term "M&A" is ubiquitous in business, it combines different types of business deals.

- A **merger** is when two companies of near-equal size and strength combine to form a single new entity where they share control and resources. They cease to exist separately and operate under a new name or structure. Only about 27 percent of deals are mergers.
- An **acquisition** is when one company purchases another and takes over its operations, assets, and liabilities. Whether a friendly or hostile takeover, the purchasing company assumes control. The acquired company may still operate under its original name/brand, or it may be absorbed into the purchaser or even shuttered altogether. The majority (73 percent) of deals are acquisitions.

M&A deals fluctuated over the past 10 years, with activity reaching its lowest level during 2023 but increasing 15 percent ($3.4 trillion) in 2024. While a welcome change, it is still half of the $6.1 trillion in deals that occurred 2021, this decade's peak of activity. The biggest sectors were technology (19 percent), healthcare (10 percent), and finance (9 percent). Globally, North America represented half (50 percent) of the M&A activity, while EMEA represented 25 percent, and APAC 22 percent.

The Institute for Mergers, Acquisitions, and Alliances tracks all activity, organizing deals into the major sectors of: consumer products and services, software and IT, media and entertainment, healthcare, pharmaceutical and biotechnology, energy and power, chemicals, and artificial intelligence.

Mergers are rare but some of the biggest merger deals in the past decade include the following:

- In 2020, United Technologies and Raytheon merged in a $121 billion deal, becoming Raytheon Technologies. They were able to maximize each other's customer bases and technologies to become the second highest earning defense company in the US.
- Two significant mergers reshaped the global chemical industry. In 2017, Dow Chemical and Dupont merged in a deal valued at $130 billion, becoming DowDupont. In 2019, ChemChina and Sinochem merged to create the world's largest chemical conglomerate, operating in over 150

countries with a workforce of more than 220,000 employees. The deal was valued at $245 billion.
- Petroleum and energy companies Exxon and Mobil merged in 1997 to become ExxonMobil, which continues to grow its portfolio and performance through further acquisitions, including its recent purchase of Pioneer Natural Resources for $64.5 billion. This gives ExxonMobil the largest acreage in the Permian Basin, with twice as many low-cost net drilling locations than their closest competitor.

Acquisitions are far more common. These are some of the biggest deals in recent years:
- Cisco acquired Splunk for $28 billion in cash in 2023. This deal represented Cisco's largest acquisition of the more than 200 acquisitions they have done to date. Acquiring Splunk creates a significant expansion for Cisco into cybersecurity and data observability.
- Mars is set to acquire Kellanova for $35.9 billion, pending regulatory approval. This deal allows the candy giant to move into the snack market with Kellanova's portfolio of Pringles, Cheeze-Its, and Pop-Tarts.
- Verizon is acquiring Frontier Communications for $19.6 billion in 2026. This will increase Verizon's fiber network coverage and delivery of broadband services.

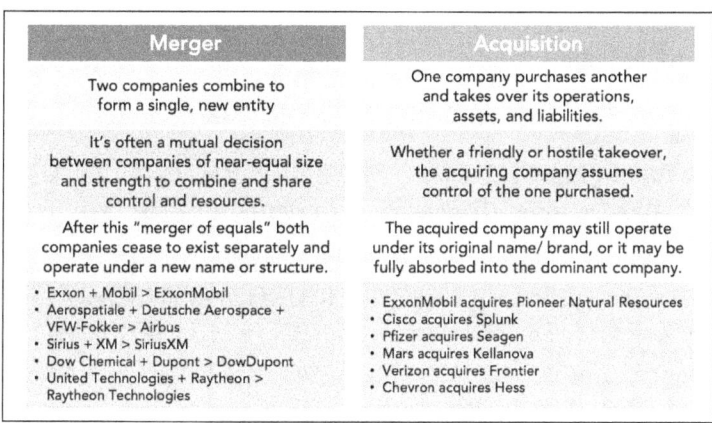

Comparison of mergers and acquisitions

Goals for Mergers & Acquisitions

Companies engage in M&As to accomplish specific strategic goals to enhance their competitive position and drive growth. These goals vary by deal, but the top goals are:

1. **Market share expansion:** By merging with or acquiring another company, businesses can quickly increase their market share by entering new markets, expanding geographically, reaching new customer segments, and gaining access to a broader customer base.

2. **Access to new technologies or expertise:** Acquiring companies with innovative technologies or specialized expertise allows firms to stay competitive by gaining skilled employees and management teams, thereby enhancing their human capital and organizational capabilities.

3. **Achieving synergies:** M&A can lead to synergies where the combined value exceeds the sum of its parts, often through cost reductions and revenue enhancements.

4. **Diversification:** Companies pursue M&A to diversify their product lines, services, or market presence, thus reducing risk and dependence on a single market or product.

5. **Vertical integration:** Acquiring suppliers or distributors helps companies control more stages of their supply chain, leading to increased efficiencies and reduced costs.

6. **Financial benefits:** M&A can provide financial advantages such as improved cash flow, increased financial capacity, tax benefits, and economies of scale. Combining operations can lead to cost savings through increased production efficiency, bulk purchasing, and streamlined processes.

7. **Eliminating competition:** Merging with or acquiring competitors can reduce market competition, allowing the company to increase pricing power and market dominance.

The experts I interviewed say this about what M&A success looks like.

"The business outcome is achieved but more importantly, all the stakeholders involved, like employees and customers end up better than before."

"The smoothest integrations happen when the teams are familiar with one another and decisions about talent are made early. When I was part of Microsoft, we'd go to the potential acquisition and immerse ourselves for weeks. We'd interview their talent and participate in lots of meetings to learn about their products, operations, and customers. It made a huge difference."

"I define success in terms of the people. When M&As go well, your employer brand improves, and people are knocking down the door to work there. This leads to more suitors and M&A opportunities in the future."

"Remember that the people in the company to be acquired didn't choose the experience. You have a limited time to share the culture and why this deal will be good for them. The more you invest in them, make them feel wanted, and remove ambiguity by respecting their expertise with appropriate titles and compensation, the best the integration will go and you'll keep the people who made that company successful in the first place."

Learn from Failed Deals

However, not all M&A deals are successful. In fact, multiple studies suggest that between 50 and 90 percent of M&A transactions fail to achieve their expected value. For mid-sized companies, the failure rate tends to be on the higher end, primarily due to inadequate planning and expertise.

A study by Grant Thornton found that only 14 percent of executives felt their M&A deals exceeded initial expectations for income or rate of return. And mega-deals seem to be the worst. An analysis of 60 large transactions since 2020 revealed that 75 percent of the acquiring companies underperformed in relation to their industry's benchmarks.

One of the most famous examples occurred in 2000 when America Online and Time Warner merged in a $350 billion deal, attempting to capitalize on the convergence of internet and mass media. Unfortunately, the dot-com bubble burst and further strategic missteps caused a financial loss of $99 billion, the largest ever reported to that date. Within nine years, AOL was spun off into a separate entity and sold to Verizon for $4.4 billion.

Legal challenges may also cause failures. Capital One is attempting to acquire Discover Financial for $35.3 billion in an all-stock deal, which would make it the largest issuer of credit cards in the US. However, a class-action lawsuit and potential investigation by the Federal Trade Commission (FTC) may block the deal. And a court blocked the $25 billion merger between grocery giants Kroger and Albertsons over antitrust concerns. Now Albertsons is suing Kroger for breaching the merger agreement.

No industry is immune from these challenges. In what is thought to be one of the worst deals in biopharma, Bayer's $63 billion acquisition of Monsanto was tainted by lawsuits alleging that Monsanto's products caused cancer. Billions of dollars in settlements have made this deal very expensive for Bayer.

The leaders I interviewed had this to say about failures:

> *"Deals with founders can be challenging. Their identity is so embedded in the vision of the product that if the deal negatively impacts their ability to birth that passion into the world, it won't happen. There needs to be proper support of their vision in the integration plan."*

> *"Our executives were so overly focused on culture alignment that they did not do enough due diligence around business metrics. While the business we acquired seemed strong financially, their year-over-year growth had dropped from 20 to 12 percent. The deal ended up costing us in many ways."*

> *"Often, leaders fall in love with a company and the idea of buying them. But if they don't get clear about how it will unfold, and how we'll set them up for success, it can fall apart. Often, budgets later shift, and the effort isn't properly resourced, which undermines the success of the deal."*

> *"When you're buying another company, the value is in the people who made it successful. It's important to survey them every few weeks and keep an eye out for dips in morale or an uptick in attrition. If you lose the most important people, you'll lose the value you were after. And worse, word gets out that you're not good with M&A and other companies won't consider deals with you."*

These are the three biggest causes of M&A deal failures:
- regulatory challenges
- strategic misalignments
- clashes between the organizational cultures

Best Practices for Success

To avoid these challenges and potential failures, executives should focus on a disciplined, transparent, and integrative approach—before, during, and after the deal. Here are ten best practices and strategies that can help:

1. Conduct a deep strategic-fit analysis.
Before the deal, clearly define the deal rationale: Is it about scale, entering a new market, acquiring technology, talent, or IP? All stakeholders must agree. Next, test alignment across dimensions like market goals, operations, product strategy, risk appetite, and long-term vision. Finally, engage in realistic scenario planning. Consider "what ifs" around future industry shifts or performance misses.

2. Do your cultural due diligence.
Cultural integration is often one of the most underestimated challenges in mergers and acquisitions. Misaligned cultures can lead to employee turnover, low morale, poor collaboration, and ultimately failure to realize deal value. During the pre-deal phase, assess cultural values and norms. Use surveys, focus groups, and leadership interviews to understand how decisions are made, how teams operate, and what employees value. Explore critical elements like employee engagement, decision hierarchy, preferences regarding speed versus stability, etc. Surface potential red flags and friction points, for example one company is very hierarchical with top-down influence where the other is highly autonomous and collaborative. Realistically evaluate how you will overcome the red flags and friction points, as cultural clashes have undermined many M&As.

3. Involve and align leadership early on.
Involve both companies' leaders early in the process, as misalignment or mistrust at the top often spreads throughout an organization. Establish a joint steering committee to focus on decision-making cadence, trust-building, and shared goals. This group will continue to play a critical role throughout and beyond the deal's implementation, especially with the rest of these best practices.

4. Align on metrics and key performance indicators (KPIs).

Develop joint success metrics tied to the deal rationale, such as revenue synergies, product roadmaps, supply efficiencies, and customer bases. Track leading indicators like customer satisfaction, adoption rates, and employee engagement alongside lagging metrics like sales, churn, productivity, and employee or customer attrition. Include important cultural KPIs alongside financial ones in integration steering committees. Use pulse surveys, retention data, and sentiment analysis to monitor cultural progress.

5. Create a shared integration playbook.

The most successful M&A companies use playbooks. Yours should outline elements like your deal priorities, roadmap of synergy capture, brand and go-to-market strategy, and cultural integration. Design the integration in phases and build in flexibility to adjust if certain assumptions don't hold post-deal. Establish a dedicated integration team with decision-making authority and empower them to surface misalignments quickly and course-correct as needed. It's vital to include cross-functional leaders from both organizations, and not just those in finance or operations. See some examples on the next page.

Ten best practices for M&A deals

6. Properly value the people you're acquiring.

The value you are buying, whether it's technology, a product, or a customer base, comes from the employees who built it. And if they ultimately leave, you'll lose the very thing you were trying to capture. Ensure that you accurately identify the key people at every level in the organization, not just senior leadership. Honor their expertise with appropriate titles and compensation, being mindful of the psychological impact of perceived demotions or reduced influence. Be sure that leaders from both companies end up in similar roles with influence that reflects their contributions. Avoid putting the acquired company's employees under people at the purchasing company—reporting to supervisors with less experience or expertise signals a lack of trust and respect that will inevitably hasten their departure, to find a place where they will feel valued.

7. Appoint culture champions from both sides.

Select respected, credible employees from both organizations to serve as culture ambassadors. Their role is to create a cultural vision for the combined entity that includes input from both leadership teams and anticipates and addresses cultural misalignments. These champions can help bridge gaps, encourage open dialogue, and support change at the grassroots level.

Instead of imposing one company's culture, co-create new norms that reflect the strengths of both. Use facilitated workshops or offsites to develop a joint culture charter or guiding principles. Keep the best elements from each company, such as one's innovation process and the other's customer service rituals, blending them together and avoiding a "winner-loser" mindset. Align incentives and KPIs to reinforce the new culture and measure progress to ensure success.

8. Communicate transparently and often.

Communicate the "why" behind the deal to employees, investors, and customers, with specific messaging for each group about the benefits to them. Be clear about what will change and what won't, how success will be measured, and the timeline. Use several channels and formats to create multiple opportunities for people to hear important information and provide frequent updates throughout the integration process. Intentionally and directly address fears and unknowns—particularly around layoffs, reporting lines, and day-to-day norms. Don't overlook the middle managers as they are the connective tissue between strategy and execution. Equip them with tools, messaging, and training to lead their teams through change. Good communications plans have a roadmap and toolkit that details all the messaging for every phase of the deal.

9. Execute the plan in phases.

Don't try to merge everything at once. Use a phased approach that respects the pace of change for each team. Some areas may benefit from quick alignment; others may need a slower, more consultative approach. Consider where you can gain some quick wins first. Approach high-risk areas or issues with deliberate planning, involving those who will be most affected. Preserve autonomy where needed—sometimes called "light-touch integration." It's vital to support employee transitions in both organizations throughout the process. Provide platforms for employees to ask questions, give feedback, and share their concerns. Offer training in emotional intelligence, resilience, and change management. Acknowledge and reward successes.

10. Monitor progress to ensure success.

Once the deal closes, your work continues. Realizing the value of the deal may take months or even years and the dedicated integration plays a vital role throughout the process. Post-close, continue to review strategic goals and metrics every quarter. Conduct post-deal reviews of key elements or groups. Adjust the integration roadmap if the external environment or internal capabilities shift. Acknowledge and reward teams or individuals who demonstrate integration success. Share stories of collaboration, innovation, and new cultural rituals that are emerging. Analyze the integration to harvest lessons learned and use them to update your strategy and playbook for the next deal.

Build an M&A Playbook

Organizations that engage in M&A deals frequently create a structured approach to effectively execute these deals, building playbooks they use again and again. While not publicly available in full due to their proprietary nature, I can share some highlights from three companies known for the best practices.

Example: Cisco

Cisco is known for seamless integration and best-in-class integration, especially in tech. Their key playbook elements include:
- Dedicated M&A integration team: A standing team of specialists runs integration like a product launch.
- Day 1 planning: Clear communication plan and operational continuity.
- Cultural assimilation workshops: Cisco interviews key personnel pre-acquisition to assess cultural compatibility.
- Tech stack mapping: Every product and backend tool is assessed for integration, replacement, or sunset.
- Post-merger metrics: Track customer retention, employee satisfaction, product roadmap delivery.
- Key strength: Planning for systematic repeatability and emphasize people and product synergy.

Example: Johnson & Johnson

Johnson & Johnson is known for their healthcare and regulatory alignment model. Their playbook is geared toward integrating regulated healthcare companies, where safety, compliance, and product continuity are vital. Their key playbook elements include:
- Pre-deal risk audit: Focus on FDA status, IP disputes, and clinical trial pipeline risk.
- Compliance-first integration: Legal, QA, and regulatory teams are embedded from day one.
- Customer continuity teams: They focus on patient and provider experience to reduce churn.
- Portfolio optimization: Post-acquisition, they review overlap and divest or shut down redundant assets.
- Retention programs: They prioritize targeted retention bonuses for key talent like scientists, researchers, and commercial leaders.
- Key strength: Embedding risk mitigation and regulatory diligence in every phase.

Example: Danaher Business System (DBS)
Danaher is a serial acquirer with a legendary system for scaling operational excellence post-acquisition using their proprietary "DBS" model. Key playbook elements include:
- Value stream mapping: Before and after the deal, they map workflows to identify waste and improvement opportunities.
- Kaizen & lean integration: Kaizen is a Japanese philosophy focused on continuous improvement. Within 90 days, they launch improvement events across core functions like sales, operations, and supply chain.
- Decentralized management: They empower acquired companies with tools and metrics, not micro-control.
- Leadership rotation: Danaher rotates execs into acquired firms to align vision and culture.
- Performance dashboards: Weekly tracking of KPIs with rapid escalation paths.
- Key strength: Operational uplift becomes the value driver—not just cost-cutting.

M&A deals are a regular part of business and require special treatment as a particularly challenging type of change journey. Using these best practices and tools will ensure that you set up the deals for success and realize their maximum value and potential for future growth.

Your Learning Journey

Take time to explore how you can utilize the various strategies for executives. Consider these questions:
- Use the formula for success to analyze an upcoming change journey. What issues do you need to address to increase your success?
- Apply the six-phase model of change to an upcoming change journey. Identify key elements like your lead and input teams, a futures wheel, and your communications plan to ensure successful cascades of your messaging.
- Assess your quitting skills. Reflect on the six psychological biases and identify which you have experienced in the past. What new strategies can you implement now to reduce their impact in the future?
- How often does your organization engage in mergers and acquisitions? Apply the 10 best practices to help you create your M&A playbook.

THE PATH AHEAD: FINAL THOUGHTS ON CHANGE

"In times of change. learners inherit the earth; while the rest find themselves equipped to deal with a world that no longer exists."

Eric Hoffer, philosopher and author,
Reflections on the Human Condition

29. Final Thoughts on Change

No doubt about it: change is the one constant we can count on. It will be part of our professional and personal lives until the moment we take our last breath. And because change in our modern day has become both intense and relentless, our human biology is being pushed to its limits. By leveraging knowledge from neuroscience, biology, and organizational psychology, you can now approach change in a new way, understanding our natural resistance and finding ways to help each other thrive through the chaos and confusion.

The Change Quest® model gives us a framework that's based in human biology. This graphic illustrates the model, showing the different types of change journeys as mountains in the distance. We have the travelers who vary in their motivation from running toward it to actively resisting it. Then, we have the tents for the different communities involved in change—the travelers, guides, trailblazers, and expedition designers. Each group has different tools and strategies to help them play their specific role in making change successful.

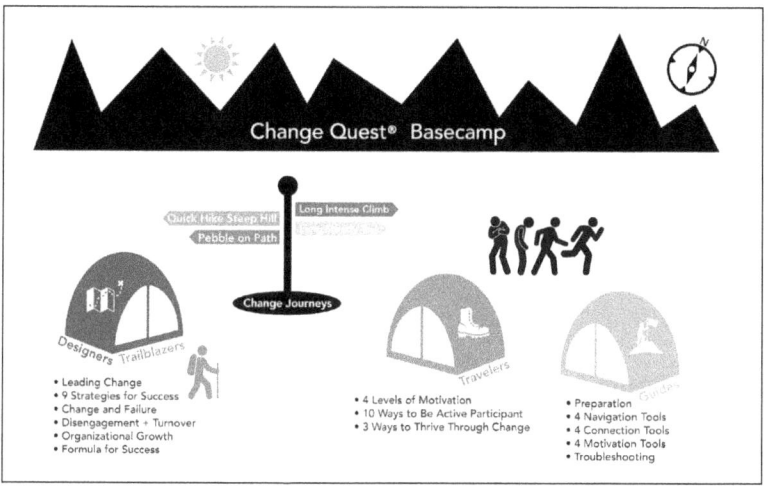

Basecamp for the Change Quest® model

This model offers many benefits. First, it will help you respond more effectively when you're on the receiving end of change, both personally and professionally. Second, it gives everyone a shared language and approach to change, which accelerates your ability to effectively design, lead, and respond. Third, using science-based tools and strategies will effectively enhances your organization's change readiness, agility, and resilience, which can be a powerful competitive advantage in today's markets.

As you use the Change Quest model and tools, you will develop new habits that directly support your success. You can also share them, to further amplify this effect and profoundly impact the success of those you lead and influence. To bring this training to your organization, visit BrainAwareTraining.com.

Like any skill, practice will increase your competence. Luckily, in today's world, you will have ample opportunities to work with change.

Consider using this material in your personal life as well. My husband and I use the model at home with our family. Every year, we share our map of change journeys and our motivation for each one. This has allowed us to better support each other, and also make better decisions around vacations, house projects, and down time.

I'll close by saying that we can all benefit from knowing how to harness our biology to maximize our potential. Continue to tend to your own growth and development. You have a lot of unrealized ability within you—we all do. Part of our journey as humans is learning how to step up to that potential and help others do the same. Cultural anthropologist Margaret Mead said it best:

> *"Never doubt that a small group of thoughtful, committed, citizens can change the world. Indeed, it is the only thing that ever has."*

Thank you for taking this learning journey with me.
Warmly,

Synthesize Your Learning Journey into Action

As we conclude, look over your notes from the various learning journeys in this book. You should now have a robust understanding of change and how to best navigate its challenges. Take a moment to finalize your notes and create an action plan that will unfold over the next few weeks and months.

- What are your three biggest takeaways from this book?
- What are some actions you can take in the next 30, 60, and 90 days that will help you thrive as a traveler on a change journey?
- If you are in the role of designer, trailblazer or guide for others, what are some actions you can take in the next 30, 60, and 90 days that will help make a better experience for your travelers?
- Consider how you might share some of what you have learned with colleagues and leaders in your organization. For additional resources and training materials to help you with this, visit BrainAwareTraining.com.

REFERENCES + RECOMMENDATIONS

INTRODUCTION
Llopis, G. (2012, Nov. 5). Five most effective ways to sell change. *Forbes.* https://www.forbes.com/sites/glennllopis/2012/11/05/5-most-effective-ways-to-sell-change/
Andreatta, B. (2025). Change Quest® training program. Santa Barbara, CA: 7th Mind, Inc.

I: UNDERSTANDING CHANGE
Megginson, L. (1963). Lessons from Europe for American business. *Southwestern Social Science Quarterly, 44*(1), 3-13.

Chapter 1
Gupta, D. (2024, Dec. 13). 8 change management failures to learn from. *The Whatfix Blog.* https://whatfix.com/blog/5-change-management-strategy-failures-to-learn-from/
Christian, A. (2023, Dec. 22). Five cautionary tales of business leadership in 2023. *BBC News.* https://www.bbc.com/worklife/article/20231218-five-cautionary-tales-of-business-leadership-in-2023
Dennison, K. (2024, Dec. 12). An update on return to office policies as we enter 2025. *Forbes.* https://www.forbes.com/sites/karadennison/2024/12/12/an-update-on-return-to-office-policies-as-we-enter-2025/
Elliott, B. (2024, Nov. 12). Return-to-office mandates: How to lose your best performers. *Management Review.* https://sloanreview.mit.edu/article/return-to-office-mandates-how-to-lose-your-best-performers/
Maurer, R. (2024, Dec. 17). RTO mandates lead to higher turnover, recruiting challenges. *SHRM.* https://www.shrm.org/topics-tools/news/employee-relations/rto-mandates-lead-to-higher-turnover--recruiting-challenges
Nohria, N., & Beer, M. (2000, May-June). Cracking the code of change. *Harvard Business Review.*
Smith, M. (2002). Success rates for different types of organizational change. *Performance Improvement, 41*(1), 26-45.
Leonard, D., & Coltea, C. (2013, May 24). Most change initiatives fail—but they don't have to. *Gallup Business Journal.*
Gleeson, B. (2017, July 25). One reason why most change management fails. *Forbes.* https://www.forbes.com/sites/brentgleeson/2017/07/25/1-reason-why-most-change-management-efforts-fail/#2c083a34546b
Herman, B. (2012, Sep. 24). 70% of hospital strategic initiatives fail: How hospitals can avoid those failures. *Becker's Hospital Review.*
Keller, C. & Viltz-Emerson, D. (2023, May 10). The business case for change management when driving organization transformation. *WTW.* https://www.wtwco.com/en-us/insights/2023/05/the-business-case-for-change-management-when-driving-organization-transformation
Melhorn, S. F. (2025, Feb. 11). Understanding America's labor shortage. *US Chamber of Commerce.* https://www.uschamber.com/workforce/understanding-americas-labor-shortage
World Economic Forum. (2025, Jan. 7). *The future of jobs report 2025.* https://www.weforum.org/reports/the-future-of-jobs-report-2025/
US Bureau of Labor Statistics (2025, June). https://www.bls.gov/cps/
Globoforce.com. (2015). *Employee Recognition Report.*
Gallup. (2025). *State of the global workplace.* https://www.gallup.com/workplace/349484/state-of-the-global-workplace.aspx
Gallup. (2017). *State of the American workplace.* https://www.gallup.com/workplace/238085/state-american-workplace-report-2017.aspx
Wiger, B. & Pendell, R. (2025, Feb. 11). 7 workplace challenges for 2025. *Gallup.* https://www.gallup.com/workplace/654329/workplace-challenges-2025.aspx
Society for Human Resource Management. (n.d.). *Placing dollar cost on turnover.* https://www.shrm.org/resourcesandtools/hr-topics/behavioral-competencies/critical-evaluation/pages/placing-dollar-costs-on-turnover.aspx
Bonusly (n.d.). *Cost of employee turnover calculator.* https://bonusly.com/cost-of-employee-turnover-calculator

Chapter 2
Thormundsson, B. (2024, Sep. 10). *Rate of adoption of recent technologies in the US 2027-2025 by technology.* https://www.statista.com/statistics/1407132/adoption-recent-technologies-us/
Desjardins, J. (2018, Feb. 14). The rising speed of technological adoption. *Visual capitalist.* https://www.visualcapitalist.com/rising-speed-technological-adoption/
DeGusta, M. (2012, May 9). Are smart phones spreading faster than any technology in human history? *MIT Technology Review.* https://www.technologyreview.com/s/427787/are-smart-phones-spreading-faster-than-any-technology-in-human-history/
Bersin, J. (2016, May). Global human capital trends 2016. *Deloitte University Press.* https://www2.deloitte.com/content/dam/Deloitte/global/Documents/HumanCapital/gx-dup-global-human-capital-trends-2016.pdf
Better Business Learning Pty, Ltd. (2016). The 12 common types of organizational change. https://changeactivation.com/downloads/12-common-types-of-organizational-change/

Chapter 3
Bridges, W., & Bridges, S. (2009). *Managing transitions: Making the most of change.* Cambridge, MA: Da Capo Lifelong Books.

Chapter 4
Kubler-Ross, E. (1969). *On death and dying: What the dying have to teach doctors, nurses, clergy, and their own families.* New York, NY: Simon & Schuster.
Perlman, D., & Takacs, G. (1990, April). The 10 stages of change: To cope with change effectively, organizations must consciously and constructively deal with the human emotions associated with it. *Nursing Management, 21*(4), 33-38.
Schneider, D., & Goldwasser, C. (1998). Be a model leader of change. *Management Review, 87*(3).
Andreatta, B. (2013). *Leading change* [Video file]. Carpinteria, CA: LinkedIn Learning.
Musselwhite, C. (2007, June 1). Leading change: Creating an organization that lives change. *Inc.* https://www.inc.com/resources/leadership/articles/20070601/musselwhite.html
Kotter, J. (1996). *Leading change.* Cambridge, MA: Harvard Business Review Press.
Hiatt, J. (2006). *ADKAR: A model for change in business, government, and our community.* Fort Collins, CO: Prosci Research.

Chapter 5
Hatami, H., Maor, D., & Simon, P. (2023, June 15). All change: The new era of perpetual organizational upheaval. *McKinsey & Company.* https://www.mckinsey.com/capabilities/people-and-organizational-performance/our-insights/all-change-the-new-era-of-perpetual-organizational-upheaval

Baker, M. (2020, Oct. 14). Gartner cautions HR leaders the risk of change fatigue has doubled. *Gartner.* https://www.gartner.com/en/newsroom/press-releases/2020-10-14-gartner-cautions-hr-leaders-that-the-risk-of-change-fatigue-among-employees-has-doubled-in-2020-this-year

Gartner Research (2024, Aug. 14). Strategies to build readiness for transformational change. *Gartner.* https://www.gartner.com/en/confirmation/human-resources/research/strategies-to-build-readiness-for-transformational-change

Cox, C.B., Gallegos, E., Pool, G.J., Gilley, K.M. & Haight, N. (2022). Mapping the nomological network of change fatigue: identifying predictors, mediators and consequences. *Journal of Organizational Change Management, 35*(4), 718-733. https://doi.org/10.1108/JOCM-12-2021-0369

Sameh Abd Elhay, E. & El-Gilany, A.-H. (2022, Mar.). Nursing staff's change fatigue, psychological resilience, and job satisfaction at Mansoura University Hospital. *Egyptian Journal of Health Care, 13*(1), 1825–1839. https://doiorg/10.21608/ejhc.2022.246429

Scholey, E. & Apps, M. (2022, Aug. 22). Fatigue: Tough days at work change your prefrontal metabolites. *Current Biology (32),* 874-896.

Fitzell, J. (2015, June 26). Change fatigue. *Professionals Australia.* http://www.professionalsaustralia.org.au/blog/change-fatigue/

Morain, C. O. & Aykens, P. (2023, May 9). Employees are losing patience with change initiatives. *Harvard Business Review.* https://hbr.org/2023/05/employees-are-losing-patience-with-change-initiatives

Staff (2015, Sep. 10). Change fatigue more problematic than senior leaders may think. *HR Review.* https://www.hrreview.co.uk/hr-news/strategy-news/change-fatigue-problematic-senior-leaders-may-think/59102

Carter-Ferry, N. (2024, Aug. 18). Combating change fatigue: Signs, symptoms, and coping. *Indeed.* https://www.indeed.com/career-advice/news/combating-change-fatigue

Powers, L. (2024, Nov. 1). How to recognize change fatigue in your people. *Prosci.* https://www.prosci.com/blog/how-to-recognize-change-fatigue-in-your-people

Turner, J. (2022, Oct. 4). What are HR's top priorities and trends for 2023. *Gartner.* https://www.gartner.com/en/articles/what-will-hr-focus-on-in-2023.

Morain, C. O. & Aykens, P. (2023, May 9). Employees are losing patience with change initiatives. *Harvard Business Review.* https://hbr.org/2023/05/employees-are-losing-patience-with-change-initiatives

Turner, D. (2016, Mar. 7). Six actions to reduce and prevent change fatigue. *Turner Change Management, Inc.*

Duck, J. (2001). *Change monster: The human forces that fuel or foil corporate transformation and change.* New York, NY: Crown Business.

Gibbons, P. (2019). *The science of organizational change: How leaders set strategy, change behavior and create an agile culture.* Las Vegas, NV: Phronesis Media.

Staff. (2019, May 28). Burn-out an "occupational phenomenon": International classification of diseases. *World Health Organization.* https://www.who.int/news/item/28-05-2019-burn-out-an-occupational-phenomenon-international-classification-of-diseases

Staff. (2021, Jan. 1). A timeline of Covid-19 developments in 2020. *AJMC.* https://www.ajmc.com/view/a-timeline-of-covid19-developments-in-2020

Bradshaw, R. & Editorial Team. (2025, Jan. 27). Startling remote work burnout statistics. *Apollo Technical.* https://www.apollotechnical.com/remote-work-burnout-statistics/

Hastwell, C. (2020, May 15). Understanding employee burnout: Key causes, symptoms, and prevention strategies. *Great Place to Work.* https://www.greatplacetowork.com/resources/blog/employee-burnout-causes-symptoms-strategies

Nagoski, E. & Nagoski, A. (2020). *Burnout: The secret to unlocking the stress cycle.* New York, NY: Ballantine Books.

Smith, M. (2025, Jan. 20). Burnout: symptoms, treatment, and coping strategy tips. *HelpGuide.* https://www.helpguide.org/mental-health/stress/burnout-prevention-and-recovery

II: THE BRAIN SCIENCE OF CHANGE + RESISTANCE

Angelou, M. (2013, May 19). Episode 416 of *Super Soul Sunday.* https://www.oprah.com/own-super-soul-sunday/the-best-advice-maya-angelou-has-ever-given-and-received-video_1

Chapter 6
Andreatta, B. (2019). *Wired to grow: Harness the power of brain science to learn and master any skill (2e).* Santa Barbara, CA: 7th Mind Publishing.

Maslow, A. (1943). A theory of human motivation. *Psychological Review, 50*(4), 370-396.

Chapter 7
Wright, A. (1997). Amygdala—general considerations. *Neuroscience Online.* https://nba.uth.tmc.edu/neuroscience/s4/chapter06.html

Belson, K. (Producer), DeMicco, K. (Director), Hartwell, J. (Producer) & Sanders, C. (Director). (2013). *The Croods* [Motion picture]. United States: Dream Works Animation.

Gallagher, M. & Chiba, A. (1996) The amygdala and emotion. *Current Opinion in Neurobiology, 6*(2), 221-227.

Henny Penny. (n.d.). In *Wikipedia.* https://en.wikipedia.org/wiki/Henny_Penny

Chapter 8
Moser, M., & Moser, E. (2016). Where am I? Where am I going? *Scientific American, 313*(1), 26-33.

Igarashi, K. (2023, Feb.) Entorhinal cortex dysfunction in Alzheimer's disease. *Trends in neurosciences, 46*(2), 124-136.

Tavares, R., et.al. (2015). A map for social navigation in the human brain. *Neuron, 87*(1).

Kahneman, D. (2013). *Thinking, fast and slow.* New York, NY: Farrar, Straus and Giroux.

Chapter 9
Duhigg, C. (2012). *The power of habit: Why we do what we do in life and business.* New York, NY: Random House.

Lally, P., van Jaarsveld, C., Potts, H., & Wardle, J. (2010, Oct.). How are habits formed: Modelling habit formation in the real world. *European Journal of Social Psychology, 40*(6), 998-1009.

Phelps, E. (2004). Human emotion and memory: Interactions of the amygdala and hippocampal complex. *Current Opinion in Neurobiology, 14*(2), 198-202.

Gardner, B., Lally, P., & Wardle, J. (2012, Dec.). Making health habitual: The psychology of 'habit-formation' and general practice. *The British Journal of General Practice, 62*(605), 664–666.

Del Giudice, M., Manera, V., & Keysers, C. (2009, Mar.). Programmed to learn? The ontogeny of mirror neurons. *Developmental Science, 12*(2), 350-363.

Favila, N., Gurney, K., & Overton, P. (2024). Role of the basal ganglia in innate and learned behavioural sequences. *Reviews in the Neurosciences, 35*(1), 35-55.

Bos, C. (2013, Aug. 29). Rick Rescorla—Saved 2,687 lives on September 11. *Awesome Stories.* https://www.awesomestories.com/asset/view/Rick-Rescorla-Saved-2-687-Lives-on-September-11

Rick Rescorla. (n.d.). In *Wikipedia*. https://en.wikipedia.org/wiki/Rick_Rescorla
Andreatta, B. (2015, Sep. 8). Six tips for working with the brain to create real behavior change. *Talent Development,* 48-53.
Clear, J. (2018). *Atomic habits: An easy and proven way to build good habits and break bad ones.* New York, NY: Avery.
Spears, J. (2025). *Atomic habits workbook: Your step-by-step guide to building good habits and breaking bad ones.* Morrisville, NC: Lulu Press.
Lapwood, A. (2024). Videos on *TikTok* and *Youtube* (@AnnaLapwoodOrgan).

Chapter 10
Dai, Q. et. al. (2024, Nov.). Psychological resilience is positively correlated with Habenula volume. Journal of Affective Disorders, 365, 178-184.
Hikosaka, O. (2010, July). The habenula: From stress evasion to value-based decision-making. *Nature Reviews Neuroscience, 11*(7), 503-513.
Ullsperger, M. & Von Cramon, D. (2003). Error monitoring using external feedback: Specific roles of the habenular complex. *Journal of Neuroscience, 23*(10), 4308-4314.
Mannekote Thippaiah, S., et al. (2025). The clinical impact of habenular dysfunction on depression and suicidality. *Current Behavioral Neuroscience Reports, 12*(4). https://doi.org/10.1007/s40473-024-00295-6
Seligman, M. (1972). Learned helplessness. *Annual Review of Medicine, 23*(1), 407-412.
Peterson, C., Maier, S., & Seligman, M. (1995). *Learned helplessness: A theory for the age of personal control.* Oxford, UK: Oxford University Press.
Brown, B. (2012). *Daring greatly: How the courage to be vulnerable transforms the way we live, love, parent and lead.* New York, NY: Gotham.

Chapter 11
Nohria, N. & Beer, M. (2000, May-June). Cracking the code of change. *Harvard Business Review.*
Kotter, J. (2007, Jan.). Leading change: Why transformation efforts fail. *Harvard Business Review.*
Heath, C. & Heath, D. (2010). *Switch: How to change things when change is hard.* New York, NY: Crown Business.
Andreatta, B. & Reinert, J. (Hosts). (2025–present). *Brain Aware podcast with Anthony Onesto* [Audio podcast]. Brain Aware Training. www.brainawaretraining.com/podcast/Season1

III: A NEW MODEL FOR CHANGE + TRANSITION
Bernard Shaw, G. (n.d.). *BrainyQuote.com.* https://www.brainyquote.com/quotes/george_bernard_shaw_386923

Chapter 12
Andreatta, B. (2024, May 21). *The neuroscience of change.* Presentation at the Association for Talent Development (ATD) International Conference and Exposition. New Orleans, LA.
Andreatta, B. (2025). *Change Quest®* training program. Santa Barbara, CA: 7th Mind, Inc.

Chapter 13
Andreatta, B. (2025). *Change Quest®* training program. Santa Barbara, CA: 7th Mind, Inc.
Krakauer, J. (1997). *Into thin air: A personal account of the Mount Everest disaster.* New York, NY: Villard Books.
Boukreev, A. & DeWalt, G. (1997). *The climb: Tragic ambitions on Everest.* New York, NY: St. Martin's Press.
Senge, P. (1994). *Fifth discipline fieldbook: Strategies and tools for building a learning organization.* New York, NY: Crown Business.
Tangel, A. & Sindreu, J. (2024, Oct. 25). What went so wrong with Boeing? *The Wall Street Journal.* https://www.wsj.com/business/boeing-max-starliner-dreamliner-ortberg-468f3000
Terlep, S. (2025, Mar. 6). Boeing seeks plan b after fire destroys key supplier's plant. *The Wall Street Journal.* https://www.wsj.com/business/airlines/boeing-seeks-plan-b-after-fire-destroys-key-suppliers-plant-3db01683
Boeing 737 max groundings. (2025, Mar. 5). In *Wikipedia.* https://en.wikipedia.org/wiki/Boeing_737_MAX_groundings
T-Mobile. (2024, Feb. 1). T-Mobile awarded #1 in customer care by J.D. Power in 13th consecutive win. https://www.t-mobile.com/news/un-carrier/2024jd-power-customer-care
Timsit, A. (2023, Feb. 21). A four-day workweek pilot was so successful most firms say they won't go back. *Washington Post.* https://www.washingtonpost.com/wellness/2023/02/21/four-day-work-week-results-uk/
Kawaja, T. (2024, Dec. 1). Why Publicis is winning. *AdExchanger.* https://www.adexchanger.com/data-driven-thinking/why-publicis-is-winning/
Wahba, P. (2024, Oct. 4). Philips new CEO is overhauling company culture and adding a role to the C-suite. *Fortune.* https://fortune.com/2024/10/03/philips-cpap-recall-ceo-roy-jakobs/
Nakashima, L. H. (2023, Sept. 27). Magalu's remarkable digital transformation: A game-changer in Brazilian retail. *LinkedIn.* https://www.linkedin.com/pulse/magalus-remarkable-digital-transformation-brazilian-retail-nakashima/
Hobart, B. (2023, Aug. 7). Magalu: Inside Brazil's omnichannel powerhouse. *The Diff.* https://www.thediff.co/archive/magalu-inside-brazils-omnichannel/

Chapter 14
Andreatta, B. (2025). *Change Quest®* training program. Santa Barbara, CA: 7th Mind, Inc.
Staff (2022, Feb. 21). Pandemic hobbies. *Pitney Bowes.* https://www.pitneybowes.com/us/blog/pandemic-hobbies.html
Hess, A. (2021, Mar. 26). Online learning boomed during the pandemic. *CNBC.* https://www.cnbc.com/2021/03/26/online-learning-boomed-during-the-pandemic-but-soon-students-return-to-school.html
Spinney, L. (2017, Sep. 27). How the 1918 flu pandemic revolutionized public health. *Smithsonian magazine.* https://www.smithsonianmag.com/history/how-1918-flu-pandemic-revolutionized-public-health-180965025/
Andreatta, B. (2024). *Wired to become: The brain science of finding your purpose, creating meaningful work, and achieving your potential.* Santa Barbara, CA: 7th Mind Publishing.
Cich, J. (2022, July 8). *PTSD vs. PTSI: Considerations for professional wellness.* Concordia University. https://www.csp.edu/publication/ptsd-vs-ptsi-considerations-for-professional-wellness/
World Health Organization (2022, Mar. 2). *Covid-19 pandemic triggers 25% increase in prevalence of anxiety and depression worldwide.* https://www.who.int/news/item/02-03-2022-covid-19-pandemic-triggers-25-increase-in-prevalence-of-anxiety-and-depression-worldwide
Kaufman, S. B. (2020, April 20). Post-traumatic growth: Finding meaning and creativity in adversity. *Scientific American Blog Network.* https://blogs.scientificamerican.com/beautiful-minds/post-traumatic-growth-finding-meaning-and-creativity-in-adversity/
Olson, K., Shanafelt, T., & Southwick, S. (2020, October 8). Pandemic-driven posttraumatic growth for organizations and individuals. *JAMA Network.* https://jamanetwork.com/journals/jama/fullarticle/2771807

Weir, K. (2020). (rep.). Life after COVID-19: Making space for growth. *American Psychological Association*. https://www.apa.org/monitor/2020/06/covid-life-after

Kaufman, S. B. (2020, April 20). Post-traumatic growth: Finding meaning and creativity in adversity. *Scientific American Blog Network*. https://blogs.scientificamerican.com/beautiful-minds/post-traumatic-growth-finding-meaning-and-creativity-in-adversity/

Tedeschi, R.G. (2020, July). Growth after trauma. *Harvard Business Review*. https://hbr.org/2020/07/growth-after-trauma

Tedeschi, R., & Calhoun, L. (2004). Posttraumatic growth: conceptual foundations and empirical evidence. *Semantic Scholar*. https://www.semanticscholar.org/paper/Posttraumatic-Growth%3A-Conceptual-Foundations-and-Tedeschi-Calhoun/9948d303099caa7915eb23da1df89602f70a0f1d?p2df

Olson K., Shanafelt T., Southwick S. (2020). Pandemic-Driven Posttraumatic Growth for Organizations and Individuals. *Journal of the American Medical Association*. 324(18):1829–1830. doi:10.1001/jama.2020.20275

IV: THRIVING THROUGH CHANGE: STRATEGIES FOR SUCCESS

Tubman, H. (n.d.) Great dreams campaign. *Tubman.org*. https://www.tubman.org/great-dreams-campaign.html

Chapter 15

Andreatta, B. (2025). *Change Quest®* training program. Santa Barbara, CA: 7th Mind, Inc.

Rock, D. (2008, Jan.). SCARF: A brain-based model for collaborating with and influencing others. *NeuroLeadership Journal*.

Bosman, M. (2012, July 24). Neuroleadership: Lead in a way that will engage people's minds. *Strategic Leadership Institute*. https://strategicleaders.wordpress.com/2012/07/24/neuroleadership-lead-in-a-way-that-will-engage-peoples-minds/

National Heart, Lung & Blood Institute. (2012, Feb. 12). Facts about problem sleepiness. *National Institutes of Health*. https://www.nhlbi.nih.gov/files/docs/public/sleep/pslp_fs.pdf

Lyman, L. (2016). *Brain science for principals: What school leaders need to know*. Lanham, MD: Rowman & Littlefield.

Andreatta, B. (2019). *Wired to grow: Harness the power of brain science to learn and master any skill (2e)*. Santa Barbara, CA: 7th Mind Publishing.

Dalton-Smith, S. (2019). *Sacred rest: Recover your life, renew your energy, restore your sanity*. Murray, KY: FaithWords.

Hölzel, B., et. al. (2011). Mindfulness practice leads to increases in regional brain gray matter density. *Psychiatry Research, 191*(1), 36-43.

Ricard, M., Lutz, A., & Davidson, R. (2014). Neuroscience reveals the secrets of meditation's benefits. *Scientific American, 311*(5), 38-45.

Goleman, D. & Davidson, R. (2017). *Altered traits: Science reveals how meditation changes your mind, brain, and body*. New York, NY: Avery.

McGreevey, S. (2011, Jan. 21). Eight weeks to a better brain. *Harvard Gazette*. https://news.harvard.edu/gazette/story/2011/01/eight-weeks-to-a-better-brain/

Brown, S. (2010). *Play: How it shapes the brain, opens the imagination, and invigorates the soul*. New York, NY: Avery.

Hoehn, C. (2014). Play it away: a workaholics cure for anxiety. CharlieHoehn.com.

Sutton-Smith, B. (n.d.) *Good Reads*. https://www.goodreads.com/quotes/680282-the-opposite-of-play-is-not-work-the-opposite-of-play

Seligman, M. (2011). *Flourish: A visionary new understanding of happiness and well-being*. New York, NY: Free Press.

Chapter 16

Andreatta, B. (2025). *Change Quest®* training program. Santa Barbara, CA: 7th Mind, Inc.

Charmine, C. (2012). *Positive intelligence*. Austin, TX: Greenleaf Press.

Chapter 17

Sinek, S. (2009). *Start with why: How great leaders inspire everyone to take action*. New York, NY: Portfolio.

Duhigg, C. (2012). *The power of habit: Why we do what we do in life and business*. New York, NY: Random House.

Website (n.d.). AppreciationAtWork.com

Chapman, G. & White, P. (2019). *The five languages of appreciation in the workplace*. Chicago, IL: Northfield Publishing.

Goldberg, E. (2022, Mar. 4). Why your boss wants to know your love language. *New York Times*. https://www.nytimes.com/2022/03/04/business/employee-satisfaction-remote-work.html

Staff. (2025, Jan. 13). 8 best VR training companies to look for in 2025. *Lumeto*. https://lumeto.com/blog/best-vr-training-companies

Pink, D. (2011). *Drive: The surprising truth about what motivates us*. New York, NY: Riverhead Books.

Hurst, A. (2019). *The purpose economy: How your desire for impact, personal growth and community is changing the world (3e)*. Boise, ID: Elevate.

Mackey, J., & Sisodia, R. (2014). *Conscious capitalism: Liberating the heroic spirit of business*. Cambridge, MA: Harvard Business Review Press.

Sisodia, R. & Gelb, M. (2019). *The Healing Organization: Awakening the conscience of business to help save the world*. Nashville, TN: HarperCollins Leadership.

Hurst, A., & Resch, N. (2022). *Workforce purpose index 2022*. Imperative. https://www.imperative.com/workforce-purpose-index

Dweck, C. (2008). *Mindset: The new psychology of success*. New York, NY: Random House.

Globoforce. (2015). *2015 Employee recognition report*. https://www.workhuman.com/

Rath, T. & Clifton, D. (2004). *How full is your bucket?* Washington, DC: Gallup Press.

Workleap. (n.d.) *Employee engagement benchmark report*. https://workleap.com/resources/employee-engagement-benchmark-report

Workleap. (n.d.) *State of employee experience: The road ahead*. https://workleap.com/resources/the-state-of-employee-experience

Gallup. (2025, Feb. 11). *The importance of employee recognition: Low cost, high impact*. https://www.gallup.com/workplace/236441/employee-recognition-low-cost-high-impact.aspx

Chesney, C., Covey, S., & Huling, J. (2012). *The four disciplines of execution: Achieving your wildly important goals*. New York, NY: FreePress.

Goleman, D. (1995). *Emotional intelligence: Why it can matter more than IQ*. New York, NY: Bantam.

Brown, B. (2013). Empathy [Video File]. *RSA Animates*. www.thersa.org/discover/videos/rsa-shorts/2013/12/Brene-Brown-on-Empathy

Wiseman, T. (1996). A concept analysis of empathy. *Journal of Advanced Nursing, 23*(6).

Duhigg, C. (2013). The power of habit: How target knows you better than you do [Video File] *Columbia Business School*. www.youtube.com/watch?v=0G_beU-SmLw

Edmondson, A. (2012). *Teaming: How organizations learn, innovate, and compete in the knowledge economy*. San Francisco, CA: Jossey-Bass.

Edmondson, A. (1999). Psychological safety and learning behavior in work teams. *Administrative Science Quarterly, 44*(2), 350-383.

Duhigg, C. (2016, February 28). What Google learned from its quest to build the perfect team. *New York Times*. https://www.nytimes.com/2016/02/28/magazine/what-google-learned-from-its-quest-to-build-the-perfect-team.html

Brown B. (2012). Listening to Shame [Video File]. *TED Talk*. www.ted.com/talks/brene_brown_listening_to_shame

Brown, B. (2010). The power of vulnerability [Video File]. *TEDx Houston*. www.ted.com/talks/brene_brown_on_vulnerability

Website (n.d.). Re:Work by Google (rework.withgoogle.com).

Eisenberger, N.I. (2012). The neural bases of social pain: Evidence for shared representations with physical pain. *Psychosomatic Medicine, 74*(2), 126-135.

Editorial Board. (2024, Aug. 13). The anatomy of a corporate turnaround. *Financial Times*. https://www.ft.com/content/aebfb0d6-33ed-40f0-9193-20a183aef9e7

Stewart, A. (n.d.). Country club no more: Inside Microsoft's move to cull staff on performance. *Business Insider*. https://www.businessinsider.com/microsoft-performance-management-low-performers-country-club-2025

Chapter 18

Andreatta, B. (2025). *Change Quest®* training program. Santa Barbara, CA: 7th Mind, Inc.

Stokel-Walker, C. (2020, May 12). How Skype lost its crown to Zoom. *Wired*. https://www.wired.com/story/skype-coronavirus-pandemic/

Rizzolatti, G., & Craighero, L. (2004). The mirror-neuron system. *Annual Review of Neuroscience, 27*, 169-192.

Winerman, L. (2005). The mind's mirror. *American Psychological Association, 36*(9), 48.

Iacoboni, M. (2009). *Mirroring people: The science of empathy and how we connect with others*. New York, NY: Picador/Macmillan.

V: THE FOUR DRIVERS OF CHANGE

Frankl, V. (1963). *Man's search for meaning: An introduction to logotherapy*. Boston, MA: Beacon Press.

Chapter 19

Ramis, H. (Director), & Albert, T. (Producer). (1993). *Groundhog Day* [Motion picture]. US: Columbia Pictures.

Greiner, L. E. (1972, Aug.). Evolution and revolution as organizations grow. developing an effective organization. *Harvard Business Review*, 165–174.

Greiner, L. (1998, May). Evolution and revolution as organizations grow. *Harvard Business Review*.

Andreatta, B. (2018). *Organizational learning and development* [Video file]. Carpinteria, CA: LinkedIn Learning.

Larry E. Greiner. (2024, Feb. 5). In *Wikipedia*. https://en.wikipedia.org/w/index.php?title=Larry_E._Greiner&oldid=1203913447

Mainiero, L. & Tromley, C. (n.d.). *Developing managerial skills in organizational behavior: exercises, cases, and readings* 322–329.

Greiner, L. E. & Schein, V. E. (1989). *Power and organization development: mobilizing power to implement change*. Reading, MA: Addison-Wesley.

Greiner, L. (1970, Jan. 1). Actionable knowledge in action in *The Palgrave Handbook of Organizational Change Thinkers*. https://link.springer.com/referenceworkentry/10.1007/978-3-319-49820-1_41-2

Family business review. (2024, Jan. 15). In *Wikipedia*. https://en.wikipedia.org/wiki/Family_Business_Review

Sullivan, T. (2021, Sep. 17). Blitzscaling. Harvard Business Review. https://hbr.org/2016/04/blitzscaling

Hoffman, R. (2021, Sep. 8). Reid Hoffman shares the secrets of getting to scale. *Inc*. https://www.inc.com/reid-hoffman/masters-scale-blitzscaling-linkedin-book.html

Hoffman, R. (2023, Sep. 8). LinkedIn co-founder Reid Hoffman shares the secrets of getting to scale. *Inc*. https://www.inc.com/reid-hoffman/masters-scale-blitzscaling-linkedin-book.html

Harnish, V. (2022). *Scaling up: How a few companies make it… and why the rest don't*. Charleston, SC: Forbes Books.

Chapter 20

Laloux, F. (2014). *Reinventing organizations: A guide to creating organizations inspired by the next stage of human consciousness*. Millis, MA: Nelson Parker.

Gober, M. (2018). *An end to upside down thinking: Dispelling the myth that the brain produces consciousness, and the implications for everyday life*. Cardiff, CA: Waterside Productions.

Pollan, M. (2018). *How to change your mind: what the new science of psychedelics teaches us about consciousness, dying, addiction, depression, and transcendence*. New York, NY: Penguin Press.

Burch, K. (2023, Sep. 24). I changed my views studying near-death experiences; consciousness isn't as we think. *Business Insider*. https://www.businessinsider.com/studied-near-death-experiences-our-explanation-of-consciousness-is-wrong-2023-9

Mackey, J., & Sisodia, R. (2013). *Conscious capitalism: Liberating the heroic spirit of business*. Cambridge, MA: Harvard Business Review.

Kofman, F. (2006). *Conscious business: How to build value through values*. Louisville, CO: Sounds True Publishing.

Sisodia, R., Wolfe, D., & Sheth, J. (2014). *Firms of endearment: How world class companies profit from passion and purpose (2e)*. London, UK: Pearson.

Sisodia, R. & Gelb, M. (2019). *The Healing Organization: Awakening the conscience of business to help save the world*. Nashville, TN: HarperCollins Leadership.

Robertson, B. (2015). *Holacracy: The new management system for a rapidly changing world*. New York, NY: Henry Holt & Co.

Hoff, M. (2023, Sep. 24). The 25 big companies with the best cultures. *Business Insider*. https://www.businessinsider.com/best-company-culture-comparably-2022-12#13-chewy-13

Marcene, B. (2023, Nov. 20). 5 companies known for their stellar company culture. *America's Small Business Network*. https://www.asbn.com/manage-your-business/culture/5-companies-known-for-their-stellar-company-culture/

Patel, S. (2023, April 26). 10 excellent company culture examples for inspiration. *Entrepreneur*. https://www.entrepreneur.com/growing-a-business/10-examples-of-companies-with-fantastic-cultures/249174

US Surgeon General (n.d.). *Workplace mental health & well-being: Current priorities of the US Surgeon General*. https://www.hhs.gov/surgeongeneral/priorities/workplace-well-being/index.html

Gast, A., Illanes, P., Probst, N., Schaninger, B., & Simpson, B. (2020, April 22). *Purpose: Shifting from why to how*. McKinsey & Company. https://www.mckinsey.com/capabilities/people-and-organizational-performance/our-insights/purpose-shifting-from-why-to-how

Chapter 21

NASA. (n.d.). *Do scientists agree on climate change?* https://climate.nasa.gov/faq/17/do-scientists-agree-on-climate-change/

Fellows, U. of H. E. (2024, Feb. 20). Fact checking the claim of 97% consensus on Anthropogenic climate change. *Forbes*. https://www.forbes.com/sites/uhenergy/2016/12/14/fact-checking-the-97-consensus-on-anthropogenic-climate-change/?sh=b670a6c11576

Navarre, B. (2023, Dec. 28). Here are 10 of the deadliest natural disasters in 2023. *US News*. https://www.usnews.com/news/best-countries/slideshows/here-are-10-of-the-deadliest-natural-disasters-in-2023

NOAA National Centers for Environmental Information (NCEI). *US billion-dollar weather and climate disasters* (2025). https://www.ncei.noaa.gov/access/billions/

Cann, C. (2024, Mar. 9). Xcel Energy "acknowledges" role in sparking largest wildfire in Texas history. *USA Today*. https://www.usatoday.com/story/news/nation/2024/03/07/texas-smokehouse-creek-fire-xcel/72879012007/

Pope, A. (2024, Mar. 18). The Great Plains now have "wildfire years," not seasons, as blazes start and spread earlier. *KCUR*. https://www.kcur.org/2024-03-15/the-great-plains-now-have-wildfire-years-not-seasons-as-blazes-start-and-spread-earlier

Kekesi, A., Huffman, G., Lang, S., & Schuler, L. (2024, Jan. 14). NASA Scientific Visualization studio. *NASA*. https://svs.gsfc.nasa.gov/5181/

Mogul, R. (2023, June 26). Humans approaching limits of "survivability" as sweltering heatwaves engulf parts of Asia. *CNN*. https://www.cnn.com/2023/06/26/india/india-heatwave-extreme-weather-rain-intl-hnk/index.html

Pandey, K. (2023, July 26). Data gaps in heatwave deaths widen as India battles record-smashing temperatures. *Down To Earth*. https://www.downtoearth.org.in/news/climate-change/data-gaps-in-heatwave-deaths-widen-as-india-battles-record-smashing-temperatures-90839

Anand, S. (2023, Dec. 21). India: What you need to know about the world's largest workforce. *SHRM*. https://www.shrm.org/topics-tools/news/india-need-to-know-worlds-largest-workforce

Jacob, C. (2023, Sep. 7). India's consumer market set to become the world's third largest by 2027, behind the U.S. and China. *CNBC*. https://www.cnbc.com/2023/09/07/india-consumer-market-to-be-the-worlds-third-largest-by-2027-report-.htm

Secon, H. (2020, Feb. 21). Photos of abandoned ski lifts and snowless slopes reveal the toll that rising temperatures are taking on winter resorts. *Business Insider*. https://www.businessinsider.com/ski-resorts-face-no-snow-empty-mountains-lost-customers-photos-2020-2

Dunbar, G. (2023, Nov. 29). IOC lines up French Alps to host 2030 Winter Olympics and Salt Lake City for 2034 edition. *AP News*. https://apnews.com/article/olympics-winter-salt-lake-2030-2034-ioc-e7da1e36b747395f2417b5e8c1d33088

NASA. (n.d.). Evidence. *NASA*. https://climate.nasa.gov/evidence/

National Geographic Education. (n.d.). Global warming. *National Geographic*. https://education.nationalgeographic.org/resource/global-warming/

WMO (2024, Jan. 11). 2023 smashes global temperature record. *World Meteorological Organization*. https://wmo.int/media/news/wmo-confirms-2023-smashes-global-temperature-record

Boudreau, C. (2024, Jan. 11). The world hasn't been this warm in 100,000 years. *Business Insider*. https://www.businessinsider.com/world-hottest-year-ever-history-climate-crisis-2024-1

Becker, R. (2024, Jan. 12). Will avalanches in California worsen with climate change? *CalMatters*. https://calmatters.org/environment/2024/01/avalanches-california-climate-change/

Herr, A. (2024, Feb. 19). The snowy winters of your childhood are gone for good. *Business Insider*. https://www.businessinsider.com/death-of-snow-america-midwest-warm-winter-skiing-climate-change-2024-2

USGS (n.d.) What is a glacier? US Geological Society. https://www.usgs.gov/faqs/what-glacier

Borenstein, S. (n.d.). Atlantic ocean currents may be on the verge of collapse, a new study shows. *Business Insider*. https://www.businessinsider.com/atlantic-ocean-currents-collapse-shut-down-new-study-2024-2

Cohen, J. E., Sachs, J., Gallup, J., Mellinger, A., & Small, C. (1997, Nov. 14). Estimates of coastal populations. *Science*. https://www.science.org/doi/10.1126/science.278.5341.1209c

Carrington, D. (2024, Jan. 11). "Astounding" ocean temperatures in 2023 intensified extreme weather, data shows. *The Guardian*. https://www.theguardian.com/environment/2024/jan/11/ocean-warming-temperatures-2023-extreme-weather-data

National Geographic (n.d.). Hurricanes, cyclones, and typhoons explained. *National Geographic*. https://education.nationalgeographic.org/resource/hurricanes-cyclones-and-typhoons-explained/

Dance, S. (2024, Feb. 5). Hurricanes are getting so intense, scientists propose a category 6. *Washington Post*. https://www.washingtonpost.com/weather/2024/02/05/hurricanes-category6/

Orwig, J. (2024, Feb. 6). Scientists say hurricanes are growing so powerful that we need to add a category 6. *Business Insider*. https://www.businessinsider.com/hurricane-category-6-wind-speed-prediction-2024-2

National Academies Press (2024). Community-driven relocation recommendations for the U.S. Gulf Coast Region and beyond. *National Academies Press*.

NOAA. (2020, March 25). Storm surge. *US Climate Resilience Toolkit*. https://toolkit.climate.gov/topics/coastal/storm-surge

Hersher, R. (2024, Feb. 6). Scientists explore whether to add a "category 6" designation for Hurricanes. *NPR*. https://www.npr.org/2024/02/06/1229440080/scientists-explore-whether-to-add-a-category-6-designation-for-hurricanes#.

SCMP. (2024, Mar. 5). Hongkongers battling slippery floors as humidity hits 100%. *Young Post*. https://www.scmp.com/yp/discover/news/hong-kong/article/3254335/hongkongers-battle-slippery-floors-humidity-hits-100-observatory-says-monsoon-will-soon-cool-air

Hernandez, T. (2024, Feb. 15). Florida's property insurance crisis: how did we get here and how do lawmakers fix it? *WPBF*. https://www.wpbf.com/article/floridas-property-insurance-crisis-how-did-we-get-here-and-how-do-lawmakers-fix-it/46801457

Foerster, J. (2023, Dec. 21). 5 unprecedented weather events of 2023 poised to be the new normal. *Forbes*. https://www.forbes.com/sites/jimfoerster/2023/12/18/five-unprecedented-weather-events-of-2023/?sh=7d567e037bea

NOAA Fisheries. (n.d.). *Understanding ocean acidification*. https://www.fisheries.noaa.gov/insight/understanding-ocean-acidification

Nace, T. (2024, Feb. 20). With $32 trillion in assets, investors demand immediate action on climate change. *Forbes*. https://www.forbes.com/sites/trevornace/2018/12/11/with-32-trillion-in-assets-investors-demand-immediate-action-on-climate-change/?sh=1fd487cd2b48

Smith, A. B. (2025, Jan. 10). An active year of U.S. billion-dollar weather and climate disasters. *NOAA Climate*. https://www.climate.gov/news-features/blogs/beyond-data/2024-active-year-us-billion-dollar-weather-and-climate-disasters

Kennedy, J., Blunden, J., Alvar-Beltrán, J., & Kappelle, M. (2021). 2020 Global state of climate. *World Meteorological Organization*. https://www.researchgate.net/publication/350979227_2020_Global_State_of_Climate

McScience. (2023, June 30). Acids and bases: KS3. *McScience CIC*. https://mcscience.co.uk/ks3/acids-and-bases/#acid

Derna dam collapses. (2025, Mar. 12). In *Wikipedia*. https://en.wikipedia.org/wiki/Derna_dam_collapses

Igini, M. (2025, Jan. 13). North and South America saw "exceptional" wildfire season. *Earth.org*. https://earth.org/north-and-south-america-endured-exceptional-wildfire-season-in-2024/

Phillips, T. & Blair, L. (2024, Oct. 2). "The Earth is crying out for help". *The Guardian*. https://www.theguardian.com/global-development/2024/oct/02/south-america-wildfire-smoke-deforestation-drought

Collins, N. (2025, Jan. 29). Historic January 2025 snowstorm in the southern US. *Climate*. https://www.climate.gov/news-features/event-tracker/historic-january-2025-snowstorm-southern-us

Suardy, D. (2024, Nov. 20). Flash floods in Spain: Joining forces for rapid recovery. *European Civil Protection and Humanitarian Aid Operations*. https://civil-protection-humanitarian-aid.ec.europa.eu/news-stories/stories/flash-floods-spain-joining-forces-rapid-recovery_en

City of Gold Coast. (n.d.). Beaches restoration program (Cyclone Alfred). https://www.goldcoast.qld.gov.au/Services/Projects-works/Beaches-restoration-program-Cyclone-Alfred

World Meteorological Organization (2025, Mar. 19). *State of the global climate 2024 report.* https://wmo.int/publication-series/state-of-global-climate-2024

Chapter 22

Tayir, H. (2024, Dec. 31). China breaks its own record for "the world's fastest highspeed train." *CNN.* https://www.cnn.com/travel/china-cr450-bullet-train-prototype-intl-hnk/index.html

Walrath-Holdridge, M. (2025, Feb. 14). Could 2025 bring a new "retail reality"? *USA Today.* https://www.usatoday.com/story/money/2025/02/14/retail-stores-closing-2025-joann-jcpenney/78528342007.

Nilson, P. (2024, July 25). The 10 fastest high-speed trains in the world. *Railway Technology.* https://www.railway-technology.com/features/the-10-fastest-high-speed-trains-in-the-world/?cf-view

Khalid, A. (2021, Mar. 17). The 6 emerging tech trends that you need to know about now. *Inc.* https://www.inc.com/amrita-khalid/tech-trends-forecast-future-amy-webb.html

Tardi, C. (2024, April 2). What is Moore's law and is it still true? *Investopedia.* https://www.investopedia.com/terms/m/mooreslaw.asp

Brier, P. (2023, Dec. 15). Moore's law isn't dead, it is changing. *Capgemini.* https://www.capgemini.com/insights/expert-perspectives/moores-law-isnt-dead-it-is-changing/

Fung, B. (2024, July 24). We finally know what caused the global tech outage and how much it cost. *CNN Business.* https://www.cnn.com/2024/07/24/tech/crowdstrike-outage-cost-cause/index.html

Hurley, J. (2024, Oct. 31). Get ready for your own crowdstrike, city regulator tells firms. *The Times.* https://www.thetimes.com/business-money/companies/article/get-ready-for-your-own-crowdstrike-city-regulator-tells-firms-tp0t57pst

Garcia, M. (2024, Feb. 20). What Air Canada lost in "remarkable" lying AI chatbot case. *Forbes.* https://www.forbes.com/sites/marisagarcia/2024/02/19/what-air-canada-lost-in-remarkable-lying-ai-chatbot-case/

Alkaissi, H., & McFarlane, S. (2023). Artificial Hallucinations in ChatGPT. *Cureus,* 15(2), e35179. https://doi.org/10.7759/cureus.35179

McMichael, J. (2023, Jan. 20). Artificial intelligence and the research paper: A librarian's perspective. *SMU Libraries.* https://blog.smu.edu/smulibraries/2023/01/20/artificial-intelligence-and-the-research-paper-a-librarians-perspective/

Block, D. et al. (2023, Nov. 16). These lawyers used ChatGPT to save time. They got fired and fined. *Washington Post.* https://www.washingtonpost.com/technology/2023/11/16/chatgpt-lawyer-fired-ai/

Chin, K. (2024, Dec. 30). Biggest data breaches in US history. *UpGuard.* https://www.upguard.com/blog/biggest-data-breaches-us

Steck, E. & Kaczynski, A. (2024, Jan. 22). Fake Joe Biden robocall urges New Hampshire voters not to vote in Tuesday's Democratic primary. *CNN Politics.* https://www.cnn.com/2024/01/22/politics/fake-joe-biden-robocall/index.html

Website: AI Incident Database (n.d.). About. https://incidentdatabase.ai/about/

Chen, H. & Magramo, K. (2024, Feb. 4). Finance worker pays out $25 million after video call with deepfake 'chief financial officer.' *CNN.* https://www.cnn.com/2024/02/04/asia/deepfake-cfo-scam-hong-kong-intl-hnk/index.html

Gilson, N. (2021, Dec. 28). Conway's Law: The little-known principle that influences your work more than you think. *Atlassian.* https://www.atlassian.com/blog/teamwork/what-is-conways-law-acmi

Breland, A. (2017, Dec. 4). How white engineers built racist code – and why it's dangerous for black people. *The Guardian.* https://www.theguardian.com/technology/2017/dec/04/racist-facial-recognition-white-coders-black-people-police

Karimi, F. (2021, May 9). People of color have a new enemy: Techno-racism. *CNN.* https://www.cnn.com/2021/05/09/us/techno-racism-explainer-trnd/index.html

Ren, X., & Heacock, H. (2022). Sensitivity of infrared sensor faucet on different skin colours and how it can potentially affect equity in public health. *BCIT Environmental Public Health Journal.* 10.47339/ephj.2022.216.

Admin. (2025, Feb. 19). 4 examples of racism in technology and what we can do about it. *TGW Studio.* https://www.tgwstudio.com/4-examples-of-racism-in-technology-and-what-we-can-do-about-it/

Scientific American Special Edition (2025, Spring). AI: How the machine-learning revolution is transforming science and everyday life. *Scientific American.*

Pluralsight. (2024). *AI skills report.* https://www.pluralsight.com/resource-center/ai-skills-report-2024

Sinto America (n.d.). *The key differences between robotics and AI.* https://sintoamerica.com/the-key-differences-between-robotics-and-ai

Khillar, S. (2019, July 5). Difference between robots and artificial intelligence. *Difference Between.* https://www.differencebetween.net/technology/difference-between-robots-and-artificial-intelligence/

Cellan-Jones, Rory. (2019, June 26) Robots 'to replace up to 20 million factory jobs' by 2030. *BBC.* https://www.bbc.com/news/business-48760799

Kaduri, B. & Stansfield, T. (2024, Oct. 8). 10 most popular AI models of 2024. *Orca Security.* https://orca.security/resources/blog/top-10-most-popular-ai-models-2024/

Ng, Kelly. (2025, Feb. 5). Robots 'to replace up to 20 million factory jobs' by 2030. *BBC.* https://www.bbc.com/news/articles/c5yv5976z9po

Biba, J. (2025, Mar. 10). Top 27 humanoid robots in use right now. *Built In.* https://builtin.com/robotics/humanoid-robots

Fried, I. & Dickey, M.R. (2023, May 3). AI stars in Hollywood labor negotiations. *Axios.* https://www.axios.com/local/san-francisco/2023/05/03/artificial-intelligence-labor-hollywood

Wilkinson, A. & Stewart, E. (2023, Sep. 25). The Hollywood writers' strike is over and they won big. *Vox.* https://www.vox.com/culture/2023/9/24/23888673/wga-strike-end-sag-aftra-contract

Anguiano, D. (2023, Dec. 6). SAG-Aftra union ratifies strike-ending contract with Hollywood studios. *The Guardian.* https://www.theguardian.com/culture/2023/dec/05/sag-aftra-union-ratifies-contract-hollywood-studios

Kilkenny, K. (2024, Feb. 23). Tyler Perry puts $800m studio expansion on hold. *The Hollywood Reporter.* https://www.hollywoodreporter.com/business/business-news/tyler-perry-ai-alarm-1235833276/

Indeed (2025, March 13). Software development job postings on Indeed in the US. *Federal Reserve Bank of St. Louis.* https://fred.stlouisfed.org/series/IHLIDXUSTPSOFTDEVE

Donnell, J.T. (2025, Mar.). This chilling statistic explains how the job market is changing forever. [Video]. *TikTok.* https://www.tiktok.com/@j.t.odonnell/video/7478772725641661726?_r=1&_t=ZP-8ubmCHJnV8h

Shields, W. (2025, Mar. 24). Artificial intelligence develops life-saving cancer treatment in record time. *LinkedIn.* https://www.linkedin.com/pulse/artificial-intelligence-develops-life-saving-cancer-record-shields/

Wong, M. (2024, Mar. 13). AI could help translate alien languages. *The Atlantic.* https://www.theatlantic.com/newsletters/archive/2024/03/ai-may-allow-us-to-talk-to-whales/677644/

Luchtenberg, D. (2022, Jan. 7). The fourth industrial revolution will be people powered. *McKinsey & Company.* https://www.mckinsey.com/capabilities/operations/our-insights/the-fourth-industrial-revolution-will-be-people-powered

AI Institute. (n.d). Generative AI and the future of work. *Deloitte.* https://www2.deloitte.com/us/en/pages/consulting/articles/generative-ai-and-the-future-of-work.html

Landry, L. (2019, April 3). Why emotional intelligence is important in leadership. *Harvard Business Online.* https://online.hbs.edu/blog/post/emotional-intelligence-in-leadership

Cooke, M. (2020). Upskilling employees in the evolving remote-work environment. *Brandon Hall Group*. https://brandonhall.com/brandon-hall-group-research-highlights-july-13-17-2020/

Bughin, J., et al. (2018, May 23). Skill shift: Automation and the future of the workforce. *McKinsey & Company*. https://www.mckinsey.com/featured-insights/future-of-work/skill-shift-automation-and-the-future-of-the-workforce

World Economic Forum. (2020). *The future of jobs report*. https://www3.weforum.org/docs/WEF_Future_of_Jobs_2020.pdf

Nasir, I. (2024, Dec. 17). The crucial role emotions play in productivity. *Time*. https://time.com/7201189/productivity-managing-emotions-essay

Saunders, T. (2024, Nov. 29). 'Bossware' computer racking devices harm workers' wellbeing, says report. *The Times*. https://www.thetimes.com/article/bossware-computer-tracking-devices-harm-workers-wellbeing-says-report-m37krsdr

HBR. (2019, Aug. 12). The EI advantage: Driving innovation and business success through the power of emotional intelligence. *Harvard Business Review*. https://hbr.org/sponsored/2019/08/the-ei-advantage-driving-innovation-and-business-success-through-the-power-of-emotional-intelligence

Cook, K. (2021, Mar. 23). The ROI of emotional intelligence at work. *Psychology Today*. https://www.psychologytoday.com/us/blog/emotional-intelligence/202103/the-roi-of-emotional-intelligence-at-work

Miller, M. (2023, June 13). How much is low emotional intelligence costing your organization? *Six Seconds*. https://www.6seconds.org/2023/06/09/cost-of-low-emotional-intelligence/

Carucci, R. (2024, July 2). In the age of AI, critical thinking is more needed than ever. *Forbes*. https://www.forbes.com/sites/roncarucci/2024/02/06/in-the-age-of-ai-critical-thinking-is-more-needed-than-ever

Glaser, E.M. (1941). An experiment in the development of critical thinking. *Teacher's College, Columbia University*. https://www.criticalthinking.org/pages/defining-critical-thinking/766.

The University of Louisville. (n.d). *What is critical thinking?* https://louisville.edu/ideastoaction/about/criticalthinking/what

Bookfield, S. (2012). *Teaching for critical thinking: Tools and techniques to help students questions their assumptions*. San Francisco, CA: Jossey-Bass.

Critical thinking (n.d.). In *Wikipedia*. https://en.wikipedia.org/wiki/Critical_thinking

Ratner, P. (2022, Mar. 13). How to think effectively: Six stages of critical thinking. *Big Think*. https://bigthink.com/neuropsych/how-to-think-effectively-6-stages-of-critical-thinking/

VI: DESIGNING + LEADING CHANGE: STRATEGIES FOR EXECUTIVES

Jack Welch Quotes. (n.d.). *BrainyQuote.com*. https://www.brainyquote.com/quotes/jack_welch_173305

Chapter 23

Andreatta, B. (2025). *Change Quest®* training program. Santa Barbara, CA: 7th Mind, Inc.

McKinsey & Co. (2021, Dec. 7). *Losing from day one: Why even successful transformations fall short*. https://www.mckinsey.com/capabilities/people-and-organizational-performance/our-insights/successful-transformations

Young, S., & Mhatre, A. (2022). *WTW Whitepaper: Employee experience in the age of disruption*. https://www.wtwco.com/en-us/insights/campaigns/employee-experience-in-an-age-of-disruption

Senge, P. (2006). *The fifth discipline: The art and practice of the learning organization*. New York, NY: Knopf Doubleday.

Globoforce (2016). *Employee recognition report*. WorkHuman.com.

Keller, S., & Schaninger, B. (2020, May 5). How do we manage the change journey? *McKinsey & Company*. https://www.mckinsey.com/capabilities/people-and-organizational-performance/our-insights/how-do-we-manage-the-change-journey

Chapter 24

Roloff, E. (2025, Mar. 19). Southwest Airlines change management flop. *TikTok*. https://www.tiktok.com/t/ZP82Qdgy9/

Southwest Airlines. (2025, Jan. 30). Southwest Airlines reports fourth quarter and full year 2024 results. *Southwest Airlines Investor Relations*. https://www.southwestairlinesinvestorrelations.com/news-and-events/news-releases/2025/01-30-2025-114608869

Kiddon, J. (2025, Mar. 10). Southwest Airlines makes marketing's biggest mistake. Branding Strategy Insider. https://brandingstrategyinsider.com/southwest-airlines-makes-marketings-biggest-mistake/

Glab, J. (2025, Mar. 15). Southwest fans furious as airline makes major changes. SF Gate. https://www.sfgate.com/travel/article/did-southwest-airlines-make-huge-mistake-20219664.php

Sass, J. (2013, Nov. 28). Scientific evidence to support "seven generations" future thinking. NRDC. https://www.nrdc.org/bio/jennifer-sass/scientific-evidence-support-seven-generations-future-thinking-our-toxic-chemical

Chapter 25

Ouedraogo, N. and Ouakouak, M.L. (2021). Antecedents and outcomes of employee change fatigue and change cynicism. *Journal of Organizational Change Management, 34*(1), 158-179. https://doi.org/10.1108/JOCM-05-2019-0141

Geddes, L. (2024, May 25). What are PFAS? Everything you need to know about the "forever chemicals" surrounding us every day. *The Guardian*. https://www.theguardian.com/environment/article/2024/may/25/what-are-pfas-everything-you-need-to-know-about-the-forever-chemicals-surrounding-us-every-day

Visual Paradigm Online. (n.d.). *What is a futures wheel?* https://online.visual-paradigm.com/knowledge/decision-analysis/what-is-futures-wheel/

Evanish, J. (2024, May 1). Developing leaders: 6 keys to identify & develop new leaders. *Lighthouse Blog*. https://getlighthouse.com/blog/developing-leaders-team-grows-big/

Swift, P. (2024, Nov. 7). 10 change communications best practices for internal transformation. *Cerkl Broadcast*. https://cerkl.com/blog/change-communications-best-practices/

Chapter 26

Brown, T. (2019). *Change by design: How design thinking transforms organizations and inspires innovation* (2e). New York, NY: Harper Business.

Miller, K. (2020, Mar. 19). 5 steps in the change management process. *Harvard Business School*. https://online.hbs.edu/blog/post/change-management-process

Guthrie, G. (2022, Oct. 21). How to create a change management plan (and get it right!). *Nulab*. https://nulab.com/learn/project-management/how-to-create-a-change-management-plan/

Chapter 27

Andreatta, B. (2025). *Brain Aware Executive®* training program. Santa Barbara, CA: 7th Mind, Inc.

Duke, A. (2022). *Quit: The power of knowing when to walk away*. New York, NY: Penguin.

Kahneman, D. (2011). *Thinking, fast and slow*. New York, NY: Farrar, Straus and Giroux.

Kahneman, D., Slovic, P., and Sunstein, C. (2021). *Noise: A flaw in human judgement*. New York, NY: Little Brown.
Burman, T. (2025, Feb. 6). California high speed rail update on 2030 target. *Newsweek*. https://www.newsweek.com/california-high-speed-rail-2030-target-update-2027130
Shalby, C. (2024, Mar. 21). Despite some progress, state's high-speed rail is $100 billion short and many years from reality. *Los Angeles Times*. https://www.latimes.com/california/story/2024-03-21/high-speed-rail
Staw, B. M. (1976). Knee-deep in the Big Muddy: A study of escalating commitment to a chosen course of action. *Organizational Behavior & Human Performance, 16*(1), 27–44. https://doi.org/10.1016/0030-5073(76)90005-2
Teller, A. (2016, Dec. 7). Tackle the monkey first. *X Moonshot Factory*. https://blog.x.company/tackle-the-monkey-first-90fd6223e04d
Barker, B. (2023, June 8). Which comes first? the monkey or the pedestal? *Deloitte*. https://action.deloitte.com/insight/3380/which-comes-first-the-monkey-or-the-pedestal
California High Speed Rail Authority. (2024, Mar. 19). *News release: Jobs first: California high speed rail achieves milestone of 13,000 construction jobs.* https://hsr.ca.gov/ja/2024/03/19/putting-jobs-first-california-high-speed-rail-crosses-13000-construction-jobs-milestone/
Heath, B. & Reid, T. (2025, Mar. 4). DOGE website offers error-filled window into Musk's government overhaul. *Reuters.* https://www.reuters.com/world/us/doge-website-offers-error-filled-window-into-musks-government-overhaul-2025-03-04/

Chapter 28

IMAA. (2025, Jan. 21). *2024 top global M&A deals*. https://imaa-institute.org/blog/2024-top-global-m-and-a-deals/
Sheynin, N. (2025, February 7). 9 major mergers and acquisitions of 2024. *AlphaSense*. https://www.alpha-sense.com/blog/trends/mergers-and-acquisitions-2024/
Levy, B. (2025, Jan. 28). 2025 outlook: Global M&A industry trends. *PwC Global.* https://www.pwc.com/gx/en/services/deals/trends.html
Volivach, K. (2025, March 18). Failed M&A deals (2023–2025): Data-driven insights on collapsed mega-mergers. *Medium*. https://medium.com/@katerinav0302/failed-m-a-deals-2023-2025-data-driven-insights-on-collapsed-mega-mergers-d151cd3a20ae
M&A Community. (n.d.). *The largest mergers and acquisitions in history*. https://mnacommunity.com/insights/the-largest-mergers-and-acquisitions-in-history/
M&A Equilibrium. (n.d.). Largest M&A deals in last 10 years. https://mandaequilibrium.com/largest-ma-deals-in-last-10-years/
Profitor. (n.d.). *The 10 biggest business mergers and acquisitions in history*. https://www.profitor.com/s/biggest-business-mergers-acquisitions-history
Loki Group. (2023, July 7). Why 90% of mergers and acquisitions fail - and how to beat the odds. *AccessWire Newsroom.* https://www.accessnewswire.com/newsroom/en/publishing-and-media/why-90-of-mergers-and-acquisitions-fail-and-how-to-beat-the-odds-766188
LLP, G. T. (2018, May 3). Survey: Most M&A deals fail to exceed expectations, lack of cultural alignment to blame. *PR Newswire*. https://www.prnewswire.com/news-releases/survey-most-ma-deals-fail-to-exceed-expectations-lack-of-cultural-alignment-to-blame-300642208.html
Private Equity Bro. (2024, Oct. 30). Top 10 global M&A deals of 2023. *Private Equity Bro*. https://privateequitybro.com/top-10-global-deals-of-2023
Staff. (2024, Nov. 26). Motives for mergers. *Corporate Finance Institute*. https://corporatefinanceinstitute.com/resources/valuation/motives-for-mergers
Dumont, M. (n.d.). 4 biggest merger and acquisition disasters. *Investopedia*. https://www.investopedia.com/articles/financial-theory/08/merger-acquisition-disasters.asp
Cisco. (n.d.). Cisco acquisitions. *Cisco Systems, Inc.* https://www.cisco.com/c/en/us/about/corporate-strategy-office/acquisitions.html
Kison, K. (2022, Oct. 24). Evolving to agile M&A at scale. *M&A Science*. https://www.mascience.com/podcast/evolving-to-agile-m-a-at-scale
Kacik, A. (2021, Dec. 6). J&J becomes more aggressive with M&A in medical devices. *MedTech Dive*. https://www.medtechdive.com/news/JnJ-mergers-acquisitions-medical-devices/619073/
Kansteiner, F. (2023, Jan 26). J&J CEO says M&A strategy will continue after medtech megadeals. *Fierce Biotech*. https://www.fiercebiotech.com/medtech/jj-ceo-says-ma-strategy-will-continue-after-medtech-megadeals
Danaher Corporation. (n.d.). *Danaher Business System*. https://www.danaher.com/how-we-work/danaher-business-system
Danaher Corporation. (n.d.). *Acquisitions*. https://www.danaher.com/how-we-work/acquisitions

VII: THE PATH AHEAD: FINAL THOUGHTS

Hoffer, E. (n.d.) *BrainyQuote.com*. https://www.brainyquote.com/quotes/eric_hoffer_109153

Chapter 29

Andreatta, B. (2025). *Change Quest®* training program. Santa Barbara, CA: 7th Mind, Inc.
Mead, M. (n.d.). *BrainyQuote.com*. https://www.brainyquote.com/quotes/margaret_mead_100502

05.08.25

ACKNOWLEDGMENTS: PRACTICING GRATITUDE

I cannot imagine a more perfect time to update this book than during this period of incredible upheaval and uncertainty. While the core principles from the first edition have stood the test of time, the world is more complex than before and moving faster than ever. I am grateful to have a career where I get to satisfy my deep curiosity while also sharing what I learn with others.

I could not have written this book without the help of many others and I'm grateful for every single person who played a part. First, thank you to the neuroscientists and researchers who shared their work with me. I'd also like to thank the executives I interviewed: Jim Conti, Erin Earle, Forest Key, Kelly McGill, and Brian Winterstein. I'm so grateful for the generosity of your time and expertise. And this book comes alive with the wonderful stories that so many shared of their change journeys.

Gratitude to Jenefer Angell (PassionfruitProjects.com) who brought her amazing editing skills to polish my words. This is our sixth book together and I always appreciate the funny commentary she adds to the margins. Claudia Arnett (BeTheMarkets.com) did a fabulous job coordinating the Change Stories, cover design poll, press releases, and posts. Claudia amplifies my voice through her marketing and social media expertise. Maya Nava did a great job with the hundreds of citations—never a fun task!

The book is better for the thoughtful input from my team at Brain Aware Training: Justin Reinert and Heloisa Vila. And to our partners who have translated this work into Spanish (Iñigo Sanchez-Cabezudo, Margarita Lozano-Job, and Alejandra Langarica) and Portuguese (Flora Alves and Tatiany Melecchi).

I'm grateful for my wonderful husband Chris and my daughter Kiana who support and love me all of the time, even when I am deep in "book mode." My kitties, Miso and Rosie, also lent their support by snuggling on my lap while I wrote. And of course, my family and friends who bring laughter, support, and love to my life.

Finally, to my tribe of leadership and learning professionals who work hard to bring out the best in their people and organizations through the power of learning: I am honored to share this important work with you and hope that it helps you support others in return.

May you all thrive on your change journeys!

ABOUT THE AUTHOR

Dr. Britt Andreatta is an internationally recognized thought leader who creates science–based solutions for today's challenges. As CEO of Brain Aware Training, Britt Andreatta draws on her unique background in leadership, neuroscience, psychology, and learning to unlock the best in people and organizations.

In 2024, the Association for Talent Development named Britt the Thought Leader of the Year "in recognition of her exceptional contributions of thought leadership to the profession of talent development, which has had sustained impact over a number of years."

In 2022, she was named a Top 10 Influencer in Learning, and in 2021, she was a Top 20 Learning Influencer and a Top 20 HR Influencer for Leadership Development. Britt's industry accolades include the Global Leadership Award from the World Training & Development Congress, and the Gold Medal for *Chief Learning Officer* magazine's Trailblazer Award. *Talent Development* magazine calls her as an "outstanding thought leader and pioneer."

Britt's other titles include *Wired to Become: The Brain Science of Finding Your Purpose, Creating Meaningful Work, and Achieving Your Potential; Wired to Connect: The Brain Science of Teams and a New Model for Creating Collaboration and Inclusion*; and *Wired to Grow: Harness the Power of Brain Science to Master Any Skill.*

She is a regular contributor to *Entrepreneur, Training Industry, Chief Learning Officer,* and *Talent Management* magazines.

As the former Chief Learning Officer for Lynda.com (now LinkedIn Learning), Britt is a seasoned professional with more than 25 years' experience. She regularly consults with businesses, universities, and nonprofit organizations on leadership development and learning strategy. Corporate clients include Fortune 100 companies like Comcast and Apple, and also Ernst & Young, John Deere, Microsoft, LinkedIn, Marriott, Splunk, Domino's, Franklin Covey, EvergreenHealth, DPR Construction, Rust-Oleum, Zillow, Pacific Life, SHI, Dell, and Sempra Energy.

Dr. Andreatta has worked with major educational institutions like the University of California, Dartmouth University, and the University of New Mexico, and nonprofit organizations like the YMCA and Prison Fellowship's Warden Exchange Program. She has served as professor and dean at the University of California, Antioch University, and several graduate schools.

Her courses on LinkedIn Learning, Skillsoft, and Cornerstone On Demand have received over 10 million views worldwide. Titles include *Leading with Emotional Intelligence, Advice for Leaders During a Crisis, Increasing Collaboration on Your Team, Creating Winning Teams, Organizational L&D,* and *20 Questions to Improve Learning at Your Organization.*

A highly sought-after and engaging speaker, Britt delivered a TEDx talk called "How Your Past Hijacks Your Future." She regularly speaks at corporate events and international conferences, receiving rave reviews and awards for "best session of conference."

Due to popular demand, Dr. Andreatta now offers certifications in her brain-based training programs. These award-winning programs drive sustained behavior change at organizations across a wide range of industries like technology, healthcare, finance, food, media, and manufacturing. Learn more at BrainAwareTraining.com.

Dr. Andreatta regularly consults with executives and organizations on how to maximize their full potential. To learn more, visit her website and social channels:

Website: BrittAndreatta.com

Instagram: Instagram.com/brittandreatta/

LinkedIn: Linkedin.com/in/brittandreatta/

Bluesky: @BrittAndreatta

Youtube: Youtube.com/c/BrittAndreattaTraining

LEARN MORE ABOUT TRAINING

Dr. Andreatta's robust, science-based training solutions feature her groundbreaking research, trademarked models, and uniquely effective learning design that drives real behavior change. Signature products include:

Brain Aware® Leader

This award-winning program gives leaders the critical skills they need to drive success. Discover the neuroscience of what brings out the best in others. In every engaging session, leaders actively apply content and concepts to their current teams and projects. There are six interconnected sessions as well as industry-specific versions for Sales, Healthcare, and Technology/Engineering.

Managing People

Coaching For Impact

Increasing Emotional Intelligence

Creating Peak Performing Teams

Leading Effective Change

Driving Execution + Accountability

Brain Aware® Executive

This program gives executives the sophisticated skills they need to drive successful strategy, vision, and innovation in their organizations for years to come.

Change Quest®

Why do 50 to 70 percent of change initiatives fail? Typical approaches don't take into account human biology and that we are wired to resist change. But once you understand the brain structures activated by change, you can mitigate their effects, increasing adaptability and resilience. With content for senior leaders, managers, and the recipients of change (i.e., employees, customers, etc.), participants gain new strategies they can use immediately.

Four Gates to Peak Team Performance®

Teams power more and more of today's work. Recent discoveries in neuroscience illuminate what differentiates high-performing teams from the rest. Learn how safety, inclusion, purpose, and belonging create the necessary conditions for true collaboration and team excellence. With sessions specifically for team leaders, team members, and senior executives, participants will gain effective strategies to consistently create peak-performing teams.

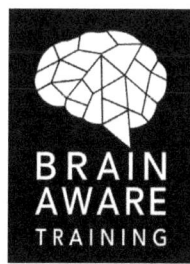

To get certified, contact us at:

Info@BA-Train.com

(805) 883-6616

BrainAwareTraining.com

PRAISE

Speaking

"You were not only the best keynote we have had for this annual conference, you were the best keynote I have seen, EVER."

Mark Walker, Board Member at Technology Affinity Group

"The top two sessions were Britt Andreatta and President Barack Obama" + "Your research/presentations are THE BEST! Thank you for pouring your passion and curiosity into your work and sharing it with us."

Attendees, Association for Talent Development's (ATD) International Conference and Expo 2024

"Britt, sending a ton of thanks for your support of the Leader meeting last week—a TERRIFIC experience. The talk you gave spirited people in such a positive way AND your delivery was flawless. Thank you for helping us to get our leaders into the "think differently" space. Loved it!"

Martha Soehren, Chief Talent Officer at Comcast

Training

"When a company has a major culture shift, you can rarely look to one person. Britt was an exception to this. What looked like company-wide management training became the foundation for the conversations, relationships, and plans to positively impact the culture. She was the rock star in the organization making sure the culture was solid."

Hilary Miller Headlee, EVP of Global Sales & Customer Success, Insight Partners (formerly Altryx and Zoom)

"You have powerful influence in our field and a whole generation of Learning & Development professionals is hungry for your message. People are better because of what you do."

Cory Kreeck, Executive Director for Training and Development, Beachbody

Executive Coaching

"I absolutely credit Britt's executive training and coaching for helping us to change our culture. As a result of working with her, we were able to have critical conversations, build better trust, and become a peak-performing team."

Tim Tully, Chief Technology Officer at Splunk

"I have partnered with Britt on several major initiatives. She rapidly assesses a business situation and is able to apply the perfect concepts and craft a learning journey that enhances participants' capability to achieve their goals. I can't imagine taking a company through rapid growth or major change without her."

Dr. Kelly McGill, Chief People Officer at Lighthouse (formerly Amazon, Avvo, and LinkedIn)

www.ingramcontent.com/pod-product-compliance
Lightning Source LLC
LaVergne TN
LVHW021951220725
816803LV00018B/918